Rooted in America

# Rooted in America
## FOODLORE OF POPULAR FRUITS AND VEGETABLES

Edited by

**David Scofield Wilson
and Angus Kress Gillespie**

The University of Tennessee Press / Knoxville

Cloth: 1st printing, 1999.
Paper: 1st printing, 1999; 2nd printing, 2000.

The paper used in this book meets the minimum requirements of
ANSI/NISO Z39.48-1992 (R 1997) (Permanence of Paper). The binding materials
have been chosen for strength and durability.
Printed on recycled paper.

Library of Congress Cataloging-in-Publication Data

Rooted in America : foodlore of popular fruits and vegetables /
edited by David Scofield Wilson and Angus Kress Gillespie. — 1st ed.
p. cm.
Includes index.

ISBN 1-57233-052-X (cl.: alk. paper)
ISBN 1-57233-053-8 (pbk.: alk. paper)
1. Fruit—United States—Folklore. 2. Vegetables—United
States—Folklore. 3. Food—Symbolic aspects—United States. 4. Food
habits—United States. 5. United States—Social life and customs.
I. Wilson, David Scofield. II. Gillespie, Angus K., 1942–
GR105 .R66 1999
398'.355—dc21
98-58096

For Sarah Emily Newton

—D. S. W.

In honor of
Mary Miller Kress Gillespie
and
in memory of Harold Edwin Gillespie

—A. K. G.

# Contents

# *Illustrations*

# Preface

## David Scofield Wilson

The essays collected here take as their subjects ten fruits and vegetables: apples, bananas, corn, cranberries, hot peppers, oranges, pumpkins, tobacco, tomatoes, and watermelons. Some are native, like tobacco; some are naturalized, like the apple; and some are exotic, like the banana. But all of them have been adopted as important to our everyday life, our cookery, our decorative arts, our gardening, and our festivities. They have slipped into our minds and hearts as symbols of what we value about ourselves and about the places we live, whether in Texas or New England, Virginia or California.

An earlier anthology, *American Wildlife in Symbol and Story* (University of Tennessee Press, 1987), explored the meanings attributed to particular wild animals—alligators, armadillos, bears, coyotes, foxes, rattlesnakes, and turkeys. These creatures roared and snapped and snaked their way into our hearts or nightmares. They animate American folklore, legends, tall tales, frontier art, book illustrations, history, and literature. The contributors to this volume have discovered that certain fruits and vegetables equally enter into the symbolic as well as practical life of Americans. From apples in pies to watermelons on paper plates, they have been made symbols of everyday health and happiness and of American abundance. At rural fairs the biggest or fairest or oddest of these fruits and vegetables win ribbons. They have come to play key roles in the gardening and cooking and eating habits of Americans over the years. And they have also slipped from the garden and kitchen and entered popular culture, whether as a cigarette on the lip of Humphrey Bogart in a movie or as virtual monsters, as in the mock horror-musical cult film, *The Attack of the Killer Tomatoes*.

In the early stages of our work on *Rooted in America*, we thought of the project as "Son of Wildlife," thinking of it as a natural complement to the earlier volume; five of the authors involved here contributed to that one.[1] But there is an immense difference between the fruits and vegetables that are the subjects of this volume and live wild animals. Animals, like us, initiate encounters, react to one another and to humans, and seem similar enough to us that we infer from them affect and intent, even understanding. We may mistake a bear's intention or malign a rattlesnake's by presuming its malice, but pumpkins or tomatoes hardly invite similar empathy. Fruits and vegetables do, however, "get in our face" in another and symbolically urgent way. We eat them, smoke them, and drink them. They cross a crucial boundary between self and other, and we are opened to their poison or spirit or virtue as surely as any shaman is to a spirit in animal or vegetable form. In this regard, some fruits and vegetables assume a presence not to be dismissed.

But they are also mere objects, inanimate things we have made meaningful by manipulation and interpretation. As products of society they "speak" of our values and meanings, as do other material culture constructs.[2] Their meanings derive from the contexts, from the stories told about them. Thus a particular fruit, say the cranberry, fits into a biological story of taxonomy and organic responsiveness to environmental conditions. And this story is different from the meaning made by inserting it in a festive, gustatory context, Thanksgiving. And different from the meaning of cranberries to an Ocean Spray grower. Similarly, regional stories may differently enfold the cranberry; Oregon coastal farms and Wisconsin cranberry bogs enjoy quite different weather conditions from those in New Jersey. Mass marketing and advertising form an additional and sometimes hugely biasing medium of meanings, as do the genres of folklore and folklife: recipes, superstitions, jokes, cures, cautions, urban legends, and more.

The more contexts, the more stories, the richer the narrative. But all this is only abstract here. The more particular and richly embellished stories of the apples, bananas, corn, cranberries, hot peppers, oranges, pumpkins, tobacco, tomatoes, and watermelons are best enjoyed when reading what each author herein has come up with about them. We all practice a version of the multivalent interpretation sketched above, but we speak in different voices and from diverse disciplinary backgrounds and scholarly preoccupations. And we present here for your inspection "imaginary gardens" with real apples or oranges or berries in them.[3]

Bon appetit!

## Notes

1. The five authors contributing essays to *Rooted in America* who had written on animals for *American Wildlife* include Angus Gillespie, who wrote on the armadillo; Jay Mechling, on the alligator; Theresa Meléndez, on

the coyote; David Scofield Wilson, on the rattlesnake; and Tad Tuleja, on the turkey.

2. In the sociology of knowledge subdiscipline of sociology, "social construction" is a phrase that carries a precise analysis of the ways we humans construct meanings and values and then impose them on the world and ourselves. We humans understand objects and ourselves and nature, in other words, in certain patterned ways strongly influenced by the ways we name things, institutionalize them, and legitimize them. See, for example, Peter Berger and Thomas Luckmann, *The Social Construction of Reality* (Garden City, N.Y.: Doubleday, 1966). But that analysis in no way denies the actuality of objects and others in our experience, only our understanding of them. While so-called postmodern deconstruction has adopted the insight that reality is constructed and made new uses of it, the view stretches at least a century back into scholarship that understands that all values and meanings are relative to the conditions and the contexts within which they are appreciated. Such constructionism has assumed a particular valence where Old World culture has encountered New World geography, flora, fauna, and peoples. In such cases older ideas may distort, or at least bias, understanding of newly encountered flora and fauna.

3. Marianne Moore's demanded of poetry that it "present for inspection, 'imaginary gardens with real toads in them,'" nicely prefigures a way in which abstract cultural contextualizations may mesh gracefully with the particular givens of the real fruits and vegetables that are the subjects of these essays. See Moore's 1921 poem, "Poetry," in *American Poetry*, ed. G. W. Allen, W. B. Rideout, and J. K. Robinson (New York: Harper and Row, 1965), 804–5.

# Apples

## Boria Sax

It was Halloween, and I, as a goblin, went trick or treating in Chicago with a few other kids. This was a far less dangerous activity at the time than it is today, even in comparatively rough neighborhoods like mine. We stood in a neighbor's doorway, chanted "Trick or treat," and held out our bags for candy. The people in many homes obliged, but a number of adults gave us apples instead.

When I finally got home, I had a great many pieces of candy and only a few apples, but the apples took up a disproportionate amount of room in my bag. From a grown-up's perspective, the sack was, no doubt, full of candy, but not from mine. I thought it was full of apples.

The apples were intended as a way to spare the teeth of children, as well as to foster more refined sorts of enjoyment. These thoughtful adults may have made a little headway toward the first goal, but they failed miserably in the second. The piles of candy were eaten in a few days, while the apples were sometimes left to shrivel and rot. I considered them a deception. One Halloween, however, I did find a use for them: carving sinister faces like jack-o'-lanterns on the skin.

At the age of six or seven, this conflict seemed to epitomize the difference between kids and adults. It may well have reflected a gap between generations as well as ages, but both the act of the thoughtful adults and my emotional response had a basis in traditions going back to the original Eden. For the adults who gave me apples, the fruit represented wholesome, healthy pleasures. By contrast, the candy represented greed and indulgence. For kids like me, on the other hand, the apple was a sort of trick, the candy, a treat.

Now, as a grown-up, I dispense treats to the very few children who still come around, usually accompanied by their parents, on Halloween. To spare the children's teeth, I can give them coins or small charms. There are times when I have, despite my childhood experience, wanted to give the children apples, but today I would not dare. Unless inspection proved otherwise, the apples would be presumed to contain strange chemicals or razor blades.

Apple blossoms in the spring, a bite of apple in summer, a cobbler in autumn, mulled cider in winter—all retain their power to evoke associations and stir feelings that stretch back into childhood and beyond. These fruits are easy to hold, to swipe, to eat raw, and to bob for. And yet firm and solid as they feel in hand, apples have a vast and perplexing range of meanings. These symbols of natural health ("an apple a day keeps the doctor away") can also be omens of death (Snow White's poisoned apple). They are emblems of both innocence ("apple-cheeked" young girls) and sin (in Eden).

Yet the story of the apple in America is not simply one of accumulated associations or horticultural innovations. Certain consistent themes run through this tale, with implications that extend far beyond the apple's role as a food or decoration. In every apple purchased at a local stand, nature still struggles with civilization, dreams with reality, individual personality with social norms. Above all, however, the story of the apple is about innocence and guilt. Perhaps this is also the major theme of American history, which is driven largely by the desire to cast aside the burdens of tradition and begin anew. This essay tells, through the changing forms and meanings of the apple, the story of America.

## In the Beginning

Long before being taken to America, European apples already were laden with cultural significance, stretching back into prehistoric times. The first apple orchards were probably somewhere in Asia Minor, but domestic use of apples had already spread to Europe by the Neolithic era. Remains of apples that were cut and dried for storage have been found in the homes of the Neolithic people known as Lake Dwellers in Lombardy, Savoy, and parts of Switzerland, dating between 3,000 and 2,000 B.C.[1] The symbolism of the apple, now integrated into our everyday lives, is built on ancient and medieval lore.

The Biblical Tree of Knowledge has almost invariably been identified in the West as an apple tree. In fact, its identity is not specified in the Bible. Since apples were not indigenous to ancient Mesopotamia, many scholars believe it was more likely a fig, an apricot, or citron. In speculating about the fruit, however, we should remember that our taxonomies are not universal, and our botanical concept of an apple might not even have been recognized in Biblical times. And, furthermore, erroneous though this popular idea may be, equating the forbidden fruit with the apple is symbolically appropriate. The prehistoric cultivation of apples in central Asia and Europe marks the transition from a hunter-gatherer life to an agricultural one. And such, in part, is how the Fall of Adam and Eve is presented in Genesis 3–4: "Cursed is the ground because of you; through painful toil you will eat of it all the days of your life."

Much of the symbolism associated with the apple recalls, however indirectly, the Biblical story of Adam and Eve. In European iconography of the Middle Ages, the apple is always associated with the fall from grace. Like so many other medieval symbols, however, it acquired an ambivalent meaning. Christ was often understood as "the second Adam," so when held by Christ or Mary the apple became a symbol of redemption.[2] Medieval painters sometimes showed Christ crucified upon an apple tree.[3] This symbolism is secularized as the apple migrates to America, but the essential meanings persist.

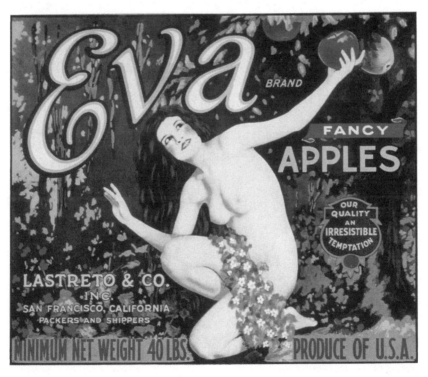

*Fig. 1.1. "Eva Brand Fancy Apples" logo. Note the absence of any snake in this Eden. Reproduced by West Publishing, Sacramento, California, used by permission.*

The apple still mediates between human society and nature. The continuous popularity of this fruit, under an enormous range of social and climactic conditions, is due largely to its variability, in both form and meaning. There are certainly several thousand cultivars in existence, though it is impossible to give an exact number.[4] And new ones are created as old ones lose their popularity. The size, shape, color, and taste of the apple, as well as its symbolism, have evolved over the ages, but the fruit itself has remained useful and popular.

This variability, in large part, is due to an odd feature that apples share with human beings. These fruits, like men and women, have a sort of taboo against incest. To put it in more botanical terms, the male and female organs of an apple tree reach maturity at different times of year. This means that apple trees can only reproduce by pollination with other varieties. All apples, therefore, are hybrids, to an extent. Their growth is unpredictable, and uniformity may only be obtained by grafting. Without this discipline, they are as quirky as boys and girls.

Thoreau called the apple "the most civilized of trees."[5] Like human beings, the apple must be raised with a great deal of care in order to contribute to human society. The hybrid nature of apples makes them an especially appropriate emblem of the American people. We, too, represent a mixture of races and cultures. Early in our history the apple acquired an economic value as produce and a symbolic value as a sign of progress, of agricultural improvement. Later, in the form of hard cider, it came to represent a humble, no-nonsense, republican ethos. Following the Civil War, nostalgia for a supposed simpler and purer past fixed on the apple and its champion, Johnny Appleseed. And recently with the Alar scare and Beechnut scandal, the apple may have begun to symbolize a decay of American values, somewhat in the manner of the "square tomato" (the square tomato is discussed in chapter 9). The protean pome takes on symbolic values appropriate to its day and useful to those who employ it in their rhetoric, from colonial sermons to contemporary street slang.

## Pyrus malus in the New Eden

Early settlers of the northeastern United States found a crab-apple now known as *Malus coronaria*. An additional type of crab-apple common in the United States is *Malus ioensis*, found primarily in the western prairies. In the early twentieth century it gained popularity as an ornamental tree. Commercial apples are all varieties of the species *Pyrus malus* (from *pyrus*, "pear," and *malus*, "apple"). The native apple trees were not altered through cultivation, and, apart from the making of jellies,[6] the settlers had little use for their fruit. Since, however, seedlings of the cultivars of *Pyrus malus* brought from the Old World often had difficulty surviving the New England winters, the colonists sometimes grafted new varieties on the roots of native apples.[7]

By 1638 William Blaxton of the Massachusetts Bay Colony had established the first American apple orchard.[8] Apples became so central to the lives of early colonists that they were sometimes used as a currency and as a measure of wealth. By 1800 Americans had already produced about 100 new varieties of apple, including such favorites as Jonathans, Winesaps, and Baldwins.[9]

To understand the symbolism of the apple in the early American colonies, we must remember that the relationship of the colonists to nature, particularly as represented by trees, was exploitative, even adversarial. Colonists confronted what William Bradford, the first governor of Plymouth, called "a hideous and desolate wilderness, full of wild beasts and wild men."[10] The process of claiming the wilderness for habitation by Europeans consisted first and foremost in the cutting down of trees. By 1700 more than half a million acres of woodlands in New England had been cleared. By the start of the nineteenth century, only a few isolated pockets of the original forest cover remained.[11] The planting of apple trees meant that the work of destruction was at an end. The settlers could make their peace with the natural world. As early as 1641, representatives of the king of England decreed that anyone receiving one hundred acres must plant apple trees.[12] Around the end of the eighteenth century, in parts of Ohio, planting of fifty apple trees or twenty peach trees within three years of settlement was a legal requirement to claim a piece of land.[13]

In the definitive work on orchards for mid-nineteenth-century America, A. J. Downing stated: "He who owns a rood of proper land in this country, and, in the face of the pomonal riches of the day, only raises crabs and choke-pears, deserves to lose the respect of all sensible men. The classical antiquarian must pardon one for doubting if amid all the wonderful beauty of the golden age, there was anything to equal our delicious modern fruits—our honied Seckels, and Beurres, our melting Rareripes."[14] By preferring the cultivated fruits to their wild prototypes, Downing affirms the ideals of progress and civilization. At the same time, he looks back to a vaguely identified period in the remote past, a putative "golden age," as his ideal. These apparently contradictory notions are partially reconciled in Downing's celebration of America. The New World becomes, in his view, a re-creation of an ancient paradise. Nostalgia and modernity blend, until they become almost indistinguishable, in this botanic version of the American Dream.

The powerful symbolism initially associated with apple trees made their propagation an almost religious act, a sort of consecration of the land. It should, therefore, not be terribly surprising that the person most intimately associated with the apple in America should be a highly religious figure. I refer of course to John Chapman, better known as Johnny Appleseed, who lived from 1774 to 1845.

American folk heroes, like Davy Crockett or Mike Fink, have often been unabashed braggarts, egotists, and men of violence. The Johnny Appleseed of legend, by contrast, practiced Christian humility, wandering about the frontier in rags or, in his later years, in a coffee sack. He went barefoot in summer

*Fig. 1.2. Earliest surviving picture of Johnny Appleseed. From H. S. Knapp,* History of the Pioneer and Modern Times in Ashland County, Ohio *(Philadelphia, 1863).*

and used only foot rags in winter. He made it his mission to prepare the way for future settlers by planting apple seeds in remote areas. A follower of Swedenborg, he also distributed religious pamphlets to anyone who would take them. Like several holy hermits of medieval lore, he had, according to tradition, a special relationship with animals. Wild beasts would never harm him, and Johnny Appleseed would not even kill hornets.[15]

Chapman was, according to all records, a devoted missionary. By 1817 reports of his activities had filtered back to the followers of Emanuel Swedenborg in England. At one point, he even attempted to exchange land for books in order to propagate the faith better. Many of the statements attributed to Appleseed remind one of the extravagant imagery in Swedenborg's visionary writings. Robert Price, the biographer of John Chapman, has shown how some of the eccentricity attributed to the orchardist resulted from misunderstanding of his Swedenborgian religion.[16]

Swedenborg was a distinguished scientist and engineer in eighteenth-century Sweden who, in middle age, abandoned his more pragmatic studies for religious works. No brief summary can do justice to the grandeur of his elaborate cosmology. He regarded all things as basically symbolic. As Emerson put it in an admiring essay, Swedenborg believed that "every sensible object—animal, rock, river, air—nay, space and time, subsists not for itself, nor finally for any material end, but as a picture-language to tell another story of beings and duties. . . ."[17]

Plants and animals, according to Swedenborg, are embodied "affections" or passions. In consequence, the gentler and more admirable of them will be found in heaven, while the more savage are in hell.[18] Viewed in the perspective of a theology that aligns physical with symbolic or spiritual reality, the significance of planting apples is apparent. It was to re-create the Garden of Eden in the New World.

The work that originally popularized the story of the itinerant orchardist is an article by W. D. Haley entitled "Johnny Appleseed: A Pioneer Hero," published anonymously in the November 1871 issue of *Harper's New Monthly Magazine*. Haley explained how the patron saint of apples felt about modern agriculture: "He [Johnny Appleseed] would describe the growing and ripening fruit as such a rare and beautiful gift of the Almighty with words that became pictures, until his hearers could almost see its manifold forms of beauty present before them. . . . But he denounced as absolute wickedness all devices of pruning and grafting, and would speak of the act of cutting a tree as if it were cruelty inflicted on a sentient being."[19] Nevertheless, nearly all of the trees in orchards of the more settled parts of America were pruned and grafted. This passage shows, once again, an ambivalence toward the ideal of settlement. Haley's Johnny Appleseed simultaneously prepares the way for settlement by planting apples and rejects everything the settlers will do. Many

writers and artists of the nineteenth century—Walt Whitman, for example—
manifest a similar ambivalence, simultaneously celebrating nature and ap-
plauding its conquest.

The popular image of Johnny Appleseed as a cheerful eccentric with a tin
pan on his head comes largely from an animated film about him entitled
*Melody Time,* produced by Disney Studios in 1936. This image is constantly
invoked in advertising by the apple industry. Richard Dorson has complained
that the lore of Johnny Appleseed owes less to genuine oral traditions than
to what he calls "fakelore," or journalistic fabrications.[20]

Except perhaps for some tales of Native Americans, almost no major folkloric traditions of the United States are untouched by commercialism, so it
may be that Dorson is unrealistic in his demand for purity. Just as the folklore of Europe so often reflected medieval society, that of America inevitably
reflected an optimistic faith in capitalism. Stories of heroes like Paul Bunyan
and Pecos Bill may be full of colorful exuberance, yet they do little to help us
confront mortality. Like the gods of Greece and the stars of Hollywood, these
figures do not seem to be challenged by human frailty. Tragic heroes, like John
Henry, are very rare in American folklore.

But Johnny Appleseed, like saints of European lore, sometimes appears to
transcend even death. Planting trees may alter our perception of time. The
propagation of trees involves a perspective in which many everyday concerns
and the frenetic pace of modern life are no longer troubling. Mark Phillips
has recently written, "I believe that my father, who insisted on planting 500
trees that he had no chance of seeing grow to more than a few feet high, pos-
sessed a touch of Chapman's saintliness."[21]

The American continents, in the time of the early settlements, were often
referred to as "the New Eden."[22] The early colonists tended to interpret their
experience in terms of Biblical paradigms,[23] and imagery drawn from the Book
of Genesis helped to shape American culture. In the second of the two creation stories in Genesis, Adam is made before Eve. The myth of "Adamic man"
involves an unattached male figure who confronts the New World alone,
unencumbered by the past, facing unlimited possibilities. There are variations
of Adamic man in major works of American literature, including Cooper's
Leatherstocking series, Thoreau's *Walden,* Whitman's "Song of Myself," and
many subsequent books.[24] The Johnny Appleseed of legend also exemplifies
Adamic man, in that he works entirely alone. But, unlike those pragmatic
Yankees, Johnny, for all his eccentricity, seems too intimately identified with
nature to come across as an individual personality.

The story of Johnny Appleseed addresses a naive curiosity about the formation of our world. Like a natural force, Johnny acts anonymously, preparing the
land to receive people. The Appleseed story stands as an American creation myth.
He functions as a sort of nature deity. I can still remember looking, as a child, at

a gnarled apple tree in an abandoned field and wondering whether Johnny Appleseed might have planted it.

## The Profane *Pyrus* and American Culture

The apple served early Americans in a number of ways, practical as well as festive. Apple pie has been an American favorite since the 1760s. Apple sauce and apple butter became popular in the next decade.[25] Apple cider, generally fermented, was drunk by Americans of all ages with every meal from early colonial times through the first half of the nineteenth century. Horace Greeley recalled that "a barrel of cider per family per week was the average allotment for upstate Vermont. . . . The pious probably drank more discreetly than the ungodly; but they all drank to their own satisfaction."[26]

Fermented cider clearly ranked as one of the benefits of New World abundance. It was a home-made brew made "wherever the apple tree grew."[27] In colonial and federal America, wine, ale, beer, and cider were a common supplement to meals. So was rum in New England, whisky on the frontier, and brandy in the South. In an age when many people made their own medicines, spirits held a place in most medical cabinets as well as on many sideboards. In the early decades of the nineteenth century, reformers such as Dr. Benjamin Rush promoted abstinence from alcohol on grounds of health and social betterment. Many of them, however, still drew a distinction between distilled ("hard") spirits and the more natural alcoholic drinks, such as wine, beer, ale, and cider: "Spiritous liquors were condemned as misused and harmful, but beverages of smaller alcoholic content were tolerated and, indeed, were recommended as substitutes."[28] The homely and republican reputation of cider derives partly from this distinction.

This began to change as the temperance movement became a passionate crusade. Some opponents of alcoholic beverages not only called on people to take a pledge of total abstinence but also to withdraw support from all those engaged in the production of such drinks. A pamphlet published by the New York State Temperance Society in 1839 proclaimed, "The time is not far distant when it will be as disreputable to manufacture or sell alcoholic liquor for a beverage, as to cast poison into a neighbor's well." Cider was the mildest of all alcoholic beverages, but it was also by far the most common. Crusaders against alcohol occasionally went so far as to advocate cutting down the apple trees on farms where cider was produced.[29]

With respect to both virtues and vices, the apple became thoroughly domesticated. While John Chapman prepared the way for civilization, Henry David Thoreau, about a generation later, tried intermittently to escape it. Thoreau wrote of the apple in highly anthropomorphic terms, comparing the cultivars to immigrants and the native crab apples to Indians. One might expect that his habitual sympathy for Indians and wild nature would have made Thoreau prefer the crab apples. While he did express some characteristic scorn for rows of grafted trees,[30] he identified not so much with the crab apples as with cultivars that had escaped from the orchard and taken root in the wild. He praises these in the following passage from his essay "Wild Apples": "But though these [crab apples] are indigenous, like the Indians, I doubt whether they are any hardier than those backwoodsmen among apple trees, which, though descended from cultivated stocks, plant themselves in distant fields and forests, where the soil is favorable to them. I know no trees which have more difficulties to contend with, and which more sturdily resist their foes. These are the ones whose story we have to tell."[31] Like many other writers of his time, Thoreau attempts to balance the claims of nature and civilization. The solution here is to celebrate an apple that, he maintains, combines the refinement of cultivated society with the ruggedness of the wild.

The extreme genetic variability of the apple enables single trees to thrive in comparative isolation. It also prevents apples in the wild from taking over entire fields. Only human intervention can bring these botanic individualists, celebrated by Thoreau, into a society of peers. For the most part, however, the apple is far more associated with love and marriage than with austere isolation.

From very early times, fruits with many seeds—including the apple, fig, and pomegranate—have been associated with fertility.[32] In Greek mythology the apple was often associated with Aphrodite, the goddess of love. The prince Paris chose Aphrodite over Hera and Aphrodite to receive a golden apple[33] with the words "for the fairest." The apple has since continued to be closely associated with erotic themes. During the High Middle Ages, these ancient symbols of fertility had been linked with romantic love. Viewed from the side, especially when cut vertically, the apple has the shape of a heart. The stylized heart of playing cards and valentines may, in fact, be modeled more on the apple than on the human organ.

That "signature" on the fruit may have fed popular beliefs about its virtues and significance. A great many American divination charms designed to secure or identify a sweetheart involve the use of apples or apple seeds. In parts of the United States, bobbing for apples, an ancient Celtic means of divination,[34] has been used to select a spouse.[35] In Kentucky people said an apple seed shot upwards would go in the direction of a future sweetheart's home.[36]

The use of the apple in modern, mass-media advertising has often been simply sexual. Typical is an ad for Eva apples produced during the 1920s, depicting a naked woman picking an apple, with the slogan "Our quality: an Irresistible Temptation." At times apples are identified with the breasts of women. A radio commercial once promised that, if a man used a certain aftershave, the secretaries would start offering him a "bite of their apple turnovers"!

This exploitation of women's bodies and Biblical iconography risked public revulsion as well as amused attention. Obviously, the companies believed that the appeal of the advertisements warranted taking the chance. Perhaps they thought that few would be offended while many would be tempted, albeit vicariously. In an increasingly secular society, such use of Biblical imagery may no longer be perceived as blasphemous. But as we will see later, the appeal of the apple has always depended on a delicate tension between conflicting values, a balance that is becoming increasingly precarious.

## Apple Cider's Last Hurrah

An example of skillful, though cynical, manipulation of apple symbolism may be found back in the 1840 presidential campaign of William Henry Harrison. Assuming the name of "Tippecanoe," after a battle he had won over the Indians, Harrison had himself represented as the embodiment of rugged, simple frontier life. Though he was the scion of a prominent aristocratic family, campaign literature constantly described Harrison as born in a log cabin.

Harrison fostered an image of himself as a drinker of cider, in contrast to the effete supporters of incumbent President Martin Van Buren, who allegedly drank champagne. A typical verse from a campaign song used by Harrison and published in the *Harrison Almanac* of 1841 is the following:

> No ruffled shirt, no silken hose,
>   No *airs* does Tip display;
> But like "the pith of worth," he goes
>   In homespun "hoddin-grey."
> Upon his board there ne'er appear'd
>   The costly "sparkling wine,"
> But plain *"Hard-cider!"* such as cheered
>   In days of old lang syne.

At campaign rallies, Harrison always had a pitcher of cider on the podium, and cider was distributed free in large quantities at rallies.[37] Even after his election, a newspaper devoted to Harrison, called *The Log Cabin,* was published weekly, each issue of which contained a jingle like the one just quoted.

The use of cider as a symbol in the Harrison campaign was far too systematic to have been accidental. Cider was homemade, plain fare, and the Harrison campaign was bent on adopting the associations with plain folks and simple living that Andrew Jackson had so exploited. Campaign literature often portrayed Harrison striking some theatrical pose before a log cabin with a large barrel marked "hard cider" nearby.

The symbolism of the Harrison campaign drew upon three conditions we can only touch on here: the depression, the contest between the Whigs and Democrats, and Jackson's image. In 1840 the Whigs co-opted the Democrats' symbolism and cast their man as a log-cabin candidate. In the words of John

Fig. 1.3. Hard Cider and the William Henry Harrison Campaign.
From The Harrison Almanac 1841 (New York, 1841).

William Ward: "The log cabin, with its evocation of the frontier, the simple life, closeness to nature, and distinctive Americanism, was placed at Harrison's disposal. The accumulated sentiment embodied in the single image of the pioneer's cabin was enough to convince an electorate suffering a depression that William Henry Harrison stood for, and Martin Van Buren perverted, all the virtues Andrew Jackson had represented."[38]

The "hard cider" played to that image. The word "cider" was, at the time, used to designate a drink that was assumed to be alcoholic. The Harrison campaign, nevertheless, preferred to add the adjective "hard," unequivocally emphasizing the alcoholic content of the beverage. A piquant suggestion of menace may have helped to balance the otherwise absurdly sanctimonious impression that Harrison cultivated. The candidate's close association with hard cider may also have comforted those who were frightened by the temperance movement. Advocates of abstinence, on the other hand, were not very likely to take offense, since Van Buren was stigmatized as the purveyor of an even more potent beverage. But even in Harrison's day, cider evoked nostalgic associations. These were to grow over the next few decades. The urban migration following the Civil War left many farms, with their apple orchards, abandoned. Today an apple tree in the middle of a forested area is understood by archaeologists and local historians as an indication of previous habitation. It is these "good old days" that much apple lore and, especially, Johnny Appleseed call us to honor.

As the nineteenth century progressed, cider gave way to a great variety of more popular "soft" drinks as well as "hard" ones. Today hard cider continues to be drunk regularly in parts of England, but it can hardly be found in the United States, apart from roadside stands in rural areas. Beer has taken over the symbolic role of cider. Beer is now viewed as the drink of rugged but unpretentious people, usually males, often working class. Were he running for president today, Harrison might choose to be photographed drinking beer in a bar frequented by construction workers.

## The Flawless Apple

In the latter part of the nineteenth century, the popular naturalist John Burroughs wrote: "Nearly every farmhouse in the Eastern and Northern states has its setting or its background of apple-trees, which generally date back to the first settlement of the farm. Indeed, the orchard, more than almost any other thing, tends to soften and humanize the county, and give the place of which it is an adjunct a settled, domestic look."[39]

This tone of devotion, adopted in nineteenth-century writing about the apple in America, is sometimes so fervid that the modern reader may feel a bit perplexed by it. To an extent, the rhetoric reflected the intellectual tradition of "natural theology," which, particularly as it was articulated in countless popular books on natural science, regarded the entire world as created for the benefit of people. In this anthropocentric perspective, the degree of usefulness of animals and plants for human beings was equated with moral virtue. This placed the apple at or near the top of the botanical hierarchy. But natural theology, originally proclaimed by religious thinkers such as William Paley, was sometimes given a secular and very American twist. Henry Ward Beecher wrote in 1874: "Of fruits, I think [the apple], above all others, may be called the true democratic fruit. There is some democracy that I think must have sprung from the first apple. Of all fruits, no other can pretend to vie with the apple as the fruit of the common people. This arises from the nature of the tree and the nature of the fruit." Beecher then goes on to describe the apple tree as "homely" but "tough" and "hardy."[40] The apple becomes, for Beecher, a sort of sacramental object in the new religion of democracy.

The association of the apple with domestic harmony and order surfaces in many popular sayings. The expression "upsetting the apple cart" dates from at least 1796, "in apple-pie order" from 1813. Healthy young girls have been referred to as "apple-cheeked" since the 1850s.[41] Today the popular phrase "American as apple pie" still designates something wholesome and enjoyable.

At the beginning of the nineteenth century, the vast majority of apples in the United States were grown and consumed locally. Smaller farms would supply single families, while apples from larger farms would be sold in neighboring villages. Improvements in packaging and transportation slowly led to more centralized marketing. Early in the reign of Queen Victoria, large quantities of American apples began to be exported to England. The traditions of local production, however, remained fairly strong into the twentieth century. Largely because of this, at the end of the 1900s, about one thousand varieties of apple were being grown in the United States,[42] appreciably more than today, though numerous varieties still compete for the gardener's and orchardist's favor. To take just one regional example: the *Sunset Western Garden Book* lists fifty-four varieties: Akane, Anna, Apple Babe, Arkansas Black, Bellflower, Beverly Hills, Chehalis, Cox Orange Pippin, Cortland, Criterion, Delicious, Dorsett Golden, Early Crimson, Erin Shemer, Empire, Fuji, Gala, Garden Delicious, Golden Delicious, Gordon, Granny Smith, Gravenstein, Holland, Idared, Jonagold, Jonathan, King, Liberty, Lodi, Macoun, McIntosh, Melrose, Moliere's Delicious, Mutsu, Newtown Pippin, Northern Spy, Paulared, Pettingill, Red Fireside, Red Free, Red Gold, Red Melba, Rome Beauty, Sierra Beauty, Spartan, Spitzenberg, Stayman Winesap, Summerred, Tydeman's Red, Valmore, Wealthy, Winter Banana, Winter Pearmain, and Yellow Transparent. Cryptic geography, biography, food ways, and popular belief have contributed enough to these resonant names for a separate essay.

Around the start of the twentieth century, dramatic changes took place in the growing of apples. As the Industrial Revolution of the nineteenth century progressed, the standards for manufactured items came to be applied to agriculture. Apples, especially, were increasingly expected to be uniform and flawless. This meant careful sorting of apples into grades, as well as increased regulation of the conditions under which they were grown.

The prevailing ideal required that an apple be large, symmetrical, and bright red, even at the cost of a certain blandness in taste.[43] These are, of course, the qualities of the Red Delicious variety, which was first developed in Iowa around 1881. This apple enabled the Northwest to become the dominant region in the apple industry. Today it is by far the most popular variety in the United States.

As in other commercial hybridizing enterprises, the living apples must have been "edited" partly to conform to stylized representations by visual artists. The symmetrical shape and the pure red color are, of course, the sort of simplifications that illustrators have always employed. The increased size of the apple reflects the convention of magnifying important items in a picture. Sight, a sense considered relatively objective, was being preferred over more intangible culinary qualities, as the apple was modified to conform to an ideal.

Since the West had been settled later, farms there tended to be larger and more mechanized. This region, particularly the state of Washington, became known as the "land of the big red apple." Agriculturalists around the turn of the century constantly urged landowners in the Northeast to abandon the tradition of the "gentleman farmer" in favor of greater specialization, so as to compete economically.

The demand for uniform quality meant reduced tolerance for insect pests. Although the new requirements for apples followed the same basic pattern as other commercial products, they had a special basis in tradition. Flaws in fruit may, if necessary, be either tolerated or cut out. Since, however, the apple was a symbol of wholesomeness, the defects suggested corruption. On the inside where an apple is white, the color of purity, bruises show up as brown, "dirty" blemishes—pollution. Holes of larvae are worse, suggesting invasion, violation of the skin. The English word "worm" originally meant "snake," and any worm at the heart of the apple can still call to mind Eden's serpent.

These insects tended to inspire the same sort of revulsion as snakes. Oliver Goldsmith had written in *The History of Animated Nature*, the most popular book on natural history in America during the late eighteenth and early nineteenth centuries, "Many persons, of which number I am one, have an invincible aversion to caterpillars and worms of every species: there is something disagreeable in their slow and crawling motion, for which the variety of their color can never compensate."[44] One religious tract from Philadelphia around the start of the twentieth century showed the apple as the human heart, while various vices bored through it like insect pests. In any case, there existed compelling aesthetic, symbolic, and commercial reasons to rid apple orchards and apples of unwelcome pests.

Early in the twentieth century, agriculture was revolutionized by chemical sprays. With these powerful new weapons at their disposal, emerging agribusiness could welcome any challenge. One agriculturalist writing in 1912 observed that the number of fruit trees around private homes or grown as a sideline in Massachusetts was still five times that grown by commercial orchards.[45] Faced with the invasion of a new, and particularly injurious, insect known as the San Jose Scale, he wrote, "A fruit raiser who understands the proper methods of treatment has no fear of this pest; and to him . . . it is on the whole a blessing in disguise, for it means that this pest will destroy so many fruit trees which are not given proper care as to greatly increase his markets and improve his prices."[46] Until the latter part of this century, there was virtually no awareness of the ecological consequences of heavy spraying. The traditional grower had virtually no intellectual means of defense against it beyond romantic appeals to sentiment.

The original spraying devices were actually comparatively ineffective and innocuous, consisting simply of a hose transported by means of a tractor or cart. In 1921, however, the technology developed during the First World War was applied in the war on pests, as the army began dusting crops from planes in the fields of Ohio. From that point, it became increasingly difficult for the small grower to compete effectively, and apples became, for the most part, a province of big business.

## The Deceptive Apple

Unanticipated ecological side effects of widespread spraying were one cost of the search for the flawless apple. But beyond that there is always something suspicious about putative flawlessness, something that just doesn't seem right. We think, "It can't be natural; there must be a trick." This is reflected in the popular distrust of those (usually ingratiating) students who since the Great Depression have been called "apple polishers." Stolen apples, which are not commercialized, acquire a special romance. This symbolism, so complex and ambiguous, is explored by Sherwood Anderson in a famous passage from *Winesburg, Ohio:*

> In the fall one walks in the orchards and the ground is hard with frost underfoot. The apples have been taken from the trees by the pickers. They have been put in barrels and shipped to the cities where they will be eaten in apartments that are filled with books, magazines, furniture, and people. On the trees are only a few gnarled apples that the pickers have rejected. . . . Into a little round place at the side of the apple has been gathered all of its sweetness. One runs from tree to tree over the frosted ground picking the gnarled, twisted apples and filling his pockets with them. Only the few know the sweetness of the twisted apples.[47]

By stating that they were rejected, Anderson implicitly contrasts the twisted apples with commercially successful ones. He thereby attacks the superficiality, the emphasis on appearance, that pervades mass culture. The irregular fruits are the antithesis of everything that is marketable. They may be had for nothing, but only by the small number of people who preserve independence of judgment.

In the animated film *Snow White and the Seven Dwarfs,* made in 1938 after a story from the Grimm brothers, Disney Studios firmly impressed on the public imagination the idea that the enticing appearance of an apple is not to be trusted. The poisoned apple that the wicked queen gives Snow White has become perhaps the most famous fruit since the original Eden. It is completely round, large, and almost unnaturally red.[48]

The Disney film can be viewed as a retelling of Genesis with a happy ending. The serpent, traditionally represented as female, is replaced by the wicked queen. Once again, Eve succumbs to temptation, but this time she and Adam can still live in Paradise forever. Borrowing a motif found in most popular versions of the tale "Sleeping Beauty" (though not in that of Charles Perrault), Disney has the prince wake Snow White with a kiss. The apparently bland little cartoon contains some fairly complicated messages. The apple, though used by the wicked, ultimately proves an instrument of good. Only because Snow White has eaten of the apple and fallen into a trance is the prince able to find and rescue her. And the wicked queen, after poisoning Snow White, is caught in a storm and falls off a cliff to her death. Opening during the Great Depression, the film helped reassure people that modern technologies, even if they sometimes caused disruptions in our lives, were ultimately a source of progress. In a difficult period, it affirmed the traditional optimism of Americans.

During the same era, the city of New York became known as "the Big Apple," because of the people who were enticed there by the hope of work.[49] Once again, the appearance of the apple proved deceptive. The designation must have been at least partly ironic, since the actual opportunities for employment in New York were extremely limited. Finding nothing else, many people revived a traditional occupation of the poor by selling apples on a street corner for a nickel each.

Gradually, the apple lost more of its association with purity and innocence. In the fall of 1988, the Beechnut company was found to be marketing apple juice that, while not harmful at all, was almost entirely synthetic. Since the product is always marketed in such a highly processed form, it was possible for Beechnut to conceal the deception for five years. It is not entirely clear to what extent even the company executives were aware that there was no apple in their "apple juice." At the very least, they refrained from scrutinizing an inexpensive but dubious supplier. According to the Consumers Union, apple juice is "best understood as a manufactured product": It is easy to counterfeit because "by the time apple juice reaches the store, the typical juice has been screened, filtered, blended with apples from other orchards and perhaps dosed with a little ascorbic acid to help maintain its clarity. Then it has been concentrated, reconstituted with water, and pasteurized."[50] Beechnut eventually had to pay a fine, but the case raises many philosophical and legal questions that will not easily be resolved. At what point does an item like apple juice cease to be a natural product? Does it matter? And why?

The production and marketing of apples are now so elaborately controlled, one can even question whether the apples in the supermarket are more natural or manufactured. By now almost all commercial apples are not only grafted and grown on dwarf trees, but also cultivated using chemical sprays and highly sophisticated fertilizers. After picking, they are stored in carefully regulated atmospheric conditions. Furthermore, new developments in genetic engineering promise (or threaten) to bring apples even more into line with commercial values.

The prevailing distrust of commercial apples doubtless played a role in the Alar scandal of 1989. The television show *60 Minutes* aired a report that the chemical Alar, used on apples to regulate growth and purify color, contained a possible carcinogen. Apples were almost immediately removed from school cafeterias in major American cities.[51] In retrospect, it appears that the public reaction was excessive. Only a relatively small number of apple growers even used Alar. The dangers associated with the chemical were unproven.[52] In June of 1989 manufacturers were, nevertheless, forced to halt production of Alar. In popular perception, the chemical had come to symbolize all of the insidious poisons concealed by the attractive appearance of products on the shelves of our supermarkets.

Apples, as we have seen, have acquired a wide range of symbolic meanings in American culture. Several clusters of symbols, however, can be identified: the linkage of apples to health, to rural and domestic industry, to sin and sex, to purity and danger, and to all-American identity. Many of our attitudes toward apples appear to be flavored by the relative contributions of nature and human industry to the fruit we hold in hand, and by our feelings about these two respective forces. Since the 1950s, "silent springs," nuclear accidents, toxic dumps, acid rain, oil spills, global warming, and revelations of harm caused to women by contraceptive devices and to children by medicines prescribed by physicians have made citizens increasingly wary of human intervention into natural processes such as eating, sleeping, reproducing, dying. This discomfort is reflected in the rumors of razor blades placed in apples and given to children on Halloween, a "fact" that, despite a complete lack of confirmation, continues to be reported in the press and by word of mouth.[53]

Still, modern horticulture presents technology in one of its least threatening aspects. Contemporary techniques can produce apples with dazzling range of sizes and colors.[54] These include apples that are more resistant to diseases and insects, partially eliminating the need for chemical sprays. Furthermore, many of the sophisticated hybrids look natural, as if they were produced without any human intervention. The apple is now sometimes used to suggest that products and institutions may be mechanized and artificial without loss of "humanity." A leading manufacturer of artificial intelligence calls itself "Apple Computers." They named their popular home computer "Macintosh," after a popular variety of apple grown primarily in the Northeast. One prominent financial institution in New York City is the "Apple Bank," and a project started by the Commonwealth Edison Company to encourage small businesses is known as "Project Appleseed."

Those who invoke the apple to make computers and companies appear "user friendly," in the lingo of the trade, might well beware. As the *Winesburg, Ohio* excerpt and the Snow White story suggest, a too perfect and too shiny apple may arouse suspicion. And appearances give no assurance of inner quality. That understanding lies behind the disdainful epithet, "apple," which some Native Americans apply to fellow "Indians" they believe may be "redskins" outside but really "white" to the core. Interestingly, "banana," applied to an Asian American, and "Oreo," to an African American, similarly ridicule ethnic sham by invoking popular foods. "We eat what we are," may be the message, "so take care."

While eating remains a symbolically resonant behavior, fashions in what Americans choose to eat change, and the apple has lost popularity in recent years. The industry is experiencing a minor crisis. After being the foremost American fruit since colonial days, the American apple has been far surpassed by the orange in popularity (see Jay Mechling's essay on oranges below). This may reflect recent demographic and cultural changes, as the heritage of northern Europe, which brought the apple to American, cedes some of its dominance to that of more tropical regions where citrus fruits are generally grown. But, if that is the case, the change is more cosmetic than substantial. The oranges of today, with their large size, rounded forms, and bright color, reflect an aesthetic that was developed in reference to apples.

And, however much we may cultivate the apple, this fruit is not dependent on human beings. Generally, it is only the toughest weeds that survive in the area among the railroad tracks on the Harlem line, moving northward from Manhattan through the Bronx. For the railroad workers, these dirty shrubs are not worth the trouble of killing. For the commuters, who pass with their eyes on newspapers or laptop computers, the plants are not worth looking at. But among these weeds, in this most desolate of places, is an apple tree, which explodes in a beautiful profusion of white blossoms every spring, and bears fruit every summer, just as it may have done when railroads were new.

## Notes

1. Edward Hyams, *Plants in the Service of Man: 10,000 Years of Domestication* (Philadelphia: J. B. Lippincott, 1971),119–23.
2. Gertrude Grace Sill, *A Handbook of Symbols in Christian Art* (New York: Collier Books, 1975), 53–54.
3. John Williamson, *The Oak King, the Holly King and the Unicorn: The*

*Myths and Symbolism of the Unicorn Tapestries* (New York: Harper and Row, 1983), 170–71.

4. Hyams, *Plants in the Service*, 123.

5. Henry David Thoreau, *The Natural History Essays* (Salt Lake City: Gibbs M. Smith, 1984), 180.

6. Fred Lape, *Apples and Man* (New York: Van Nostrand Reinhold, 1979), 110.

7. Eric Sloane, *A Reverence for Wood* (New York: Funk and Wagnalls, 1965), 39–41.

8. Vrest Orton, *The American Cider Book: The Story of America's National Beverage* (New York: Farrar, Straus and Giroux, 1973), 15.

9. Stuart Berg Flexner, *I Hear America Talking: An Illustrated Treasury of American Words and Phrases* (New York: Van Nostrand Reinhold, 1976), 10. For a detailed description of a great many of these varieties, complete with illustrations, see the two-volume work by S. A. Beach, *The Apples of New York* (Albany: New York Department of Agriculture, 1905). Many can also be found in A. J. Downing, *The Fruits and Fruit Trees of America* (New York: Wiley and Putnam, 1847), 58–429.

10. James Oliver Robertson, *American Myth, American Reality* (New York: Hill and Wang, 1980), 45.

11. Donald Worster, *Nature's Economy: The Roots of Ecology* (New York: Anchor Press/Doubleday, 1974), 67.

12. Alice A. Martin, *All About Apples* (Boston: Houghton Mifflin, 1976), 73.

13. Robert Price, *Johnny Appleseed: Man and Myth* (Gloucester, Mass.: Peter Smith, 1966), 40.

14. Downing, *Fruits and Fruit Trees*, iii.

15. B. A. Botkin, ed., *A Treasury of American Folklore: Stories, Ballads, and Traditions of the People* (New York: Crown, 1944), 261–70.

16. Price, *Johnny Appleseed*, 119–43.

17. Ralph Waldo Emerson, "Swedenborg; or, the Mystic," *The Complete Works of Ralph Waldo Emerson*, ed. with notes by Edward Waldo Emerson (Boston: Houghton, Mifflin, 1903), 14: 118.

18. Emmanuel Swedenborg, *God, Providence, Creation*, trans. from the Latin by the Swedenborg Society (London: The Swedenborg Society, 1976), 163–64.

19. W. D. Haley, "Johnny Appleseed: A Pioneer Hero," *Harper's New Monthly Magazine* (Dec. 1871): 834.

20. Richard M. Dorson, *Folklore and Fakelore* (Chicago: Univ. of Chicago Press, 1962), 232–36.

21. Mark Phillips, "Growing Pains," *New York Times Magazine*, Sept. 23, 1989, 45.

22. I am indebted to Prof. Susan Gannon of the English Department of Pace University in Pleasantville for calling my attention to the significance of

this designation. Furthermore, a review of commercial road maps reveals twenty-three towns in the United States (none in Canada) named for Eden: fifteen are specifically named Eden (those in Alabama, Georgia, Indiana, Illinois, Minnesota, New York, North Carolina, Pennsylvania, Texas, Utah, Washington, West Virginia, Wisconsin, Wyoming); there is one Eden Junction (in Michigan); one Eden Park (in Ohio); one Eden Prairie (in Minnesota); one Eden Valley (in Minnesota); one Edensburg (in Pennsylvania); two named Edenton (in North Carolina and Ohio); and one Edenville (in New Jersey).

23. Giles Gunn, "The Myth of the American Adam," in *Handbook of American Folklore*, ed. Richard M. Dorson (Bloomington: Indiana Univ. Press, 1983), 79–80.
24. Ibid., 80–84.
25. Flexner, *I Hear America Talking*, 11.
26. Alice Felt Tyler, *Freedom's Ferment* (New York: Harper and Row, 1962), 310.
27. Tyler, *Freedom's Ferment*, 310.
28. Ibid., 316.
29. Martin, *All About Apples*, 55.
30. Thoreau, *Natural History Essays*, 198.
31. Ibid., 190–91.
32. Eugene Stock McCartney, "How the Apple Became a Symbol of Love," *Transactions and Proceedings of the American Philological Association* 56 (1925): 74–78.
33. Tradition now identified many fruits of classical mythology, like that of the Biblical Tree of Knowledge, with the apple, but this is not necessarily what was originally intended. The fruit given by Paris to Aphrodite might, for example, have originally been a pomegranate. For a discussion of this question, see ibid.
34. Hennig Cohen and Tristan Potter Coffin, eds., *The Folklore of American Holidays* (Detroit: Gale Research, 1987), 310.
35. Daniel Linsey Thomas and Lucy Blayney Thomas, *Kentucky Superstitions* (Princeton: Princeton Univ. Press, 1920), 41.
36. Ibid., 25–26.
37. Martin, *All About Apples*, 53.
38. John William Ward, *Andrew Jackson, Symbol for an Age* (New York: Oxford Univ. Press, 1962), 92–93.
39. John Burroughs, "The Apple," in *Readings in Nature's Book*, ed. William and George R. Cathcard (New York: D. Appleton, 1882), 64–69.
40. Henry Ward Beecher, *Pleasant Talk About Fruits, Flowers and Farming* (New York: J. B. Ford and Company, 1874), 4–5.
41. Flexner, *I Hear America Talking*, 10.
42. Martin, *All About Apples*, 34–35. For a detailed description of a great

many of these varieties, complete with illustrations, see Beach, *Apples of New York*. See also Downing, *Fruits and Fruit Trees*, 58–429.

43. Lape, *Apples and Man*, 45–52.
44. Oliver Goldsmith, *The History of Animated Nature* (Cheapside: T. Tegg, 1838), 4: 374.
45. T. H. Fernald, "Massachusetts Fruit Trees and their Insect Foes," in *Apple Growing*, ed. Massachusetts State Board of Agriculture (Boston: Wright and Potter, May 1912), 124–25.
46. Ibid., 129.
47. Sherwood Anderson, *Winesburg, Ohio* (New York: Viking Press, 1966), 36.
48. I wrote to the Disney Company requesting permission to reproduce a picture from the cartoon. In a reply dated October 18, 1989, the company informed me that "our established policy prevents our granting you the right to use any of our characters, or our name, in connection with ac- tivities, projects or services unconnected with us." Obviously, Disney takes symbolic implications very seriously.
49. The precise origin of the term "Big Apple" has long been a subject of debate. According to one theory, it was first used by Alain Locke, a phi- losophy professor, to describe Harlem in the 1920s when it attracted many African American entertainers, jazz musicians, and intellectuals. See Geraldine L. Daniels, "Harlem Renaissance Gave Us 'Big Apple'" (letter to the editor) *New York Times*, Aug. 26, 1990. The term does have a jazzy ring to it.
50. Consumers Union, "Alar in Apples: Facts and Fantasies," *Consumer Re- ports* (May 1989): 291.
51. Margaret Carlson, "Do You Dare to Eat a Peach?" *Time*, Mar. 27, 1989, 24–27.
52. Consumers Union, "Alar in Apples," 291.
53. Jan Harold Brunvand, *Curses! Broiled Again! The Hottest Urban Leg- ends Going* (New York: W. W. Norton, 1989), 53.
54. For an attractive catalogue containing several new varieties, as well as some antique apples, the reader may write to Miller Nurseries/West Lake Road/Canandaigua Lake, NY, 14424. For information about the apple industry in general, the reader may write to International Apple Insti- tute/6707 Old Dominion Drive, Suite 210/P.O. Box 1137/McLean, VA 22101. I wish to thank the International Apple Institute for helping to supply some of the information for this essay.

# Virginia S. Jenkins

I began to think about bananas after reading the first *Boy Scout Handbook*, published in 1915. Included in the list of good deeds one might do each day are chopping fire wood for Mother, helping an old lady across the street, and picking up banana peels from the sidewalk. How many banana peels were there on the sidewalk? Were bananas so popular and litter so prevalent that this was a real hazard to be guarded against? These questions led me to look at the place of the banana in American culture.

## Bananas as Exotic Fruit

Bananas do not grow on trees. They grow on huge herbaceous plants fifteen to thirty feet tall. When the bunch of bananas is cut, the entire plant is cut down. New plants grow again from the roots. The roots, or rhizomes, have buds or "eyes" like a potato, which can be cut up and transplanted to establish new plants. The Latin name for the banana is *Musa sapientum,* or "fruit of the wise men," so named by the Swedish botanist Linnaeus from Pliny's account of wise men in India who lived on this fruit. Linnaeus named the related plantain *Musa paradisiaca,* or "heavenly fruit," for a legend that it was the forbidden fruit of the Garden of Eden.[1]

Bananas were introduced into the Western Hemisphere from the Canary Islands by Friar Tomas de Berlanga in 1516. He first planted banana rhizomes on the island of Hispaniola and then took some with him to the mainland when he was made Bishop of Panama.[2] The Spanish also introduced bananas to Florida, where they were grown as dooryard plants for family consumption. Bananas grew well in the jungle regions of the Caribbean and were used for human consumption and to fatten pigs. Banana plants were also used on coffee plantations to shade the young trees and shelter the coffee berries from wind. Commercial production of bananas in the Caribbean officially began in 1883, although an American named Minor Keith grew bananas as a commercial crop in Costa Rica in 1871.[3]

In 1876 the largest banana plantation in the United States, located near Silver Lake, Florida, contained ten thousand plants. At the time, commentators predicted that the unlimited capacity of Florida and the West India Islands would always be able to supply bananas equal to any possible demand.[4] By the early twentieth century, American-owned banana plantations had spread to Central America in response to the growing demand for bananas, and Costa Rica, Honduras, Guatemala, and Nicaragua became much more important than the Caribbean Islands. Florida never had a chance. Commercial production of bananas in North America was not successful, despite concerted efforts of the Florida Banana Growers Association during the Florida real estate boom of the early 1920s. A publication of the Florida Department of Agriculture in 1952 encouraged commercial banana production in competition with imported fruit but had to admit that "the one great difficulty in growing bananas in Florida is the rather general unsuitability of our climatic conditions to most varieties of bananas."[5]

American fruit companies taught Americans to eat bananas in quantity at the same time as they taught the people of the Caribbean basin to grow bananas commercially. Banana consumption has steadily increased in the United States, except for the years 1942 and 1943 during World War II when bananas became virtually unavailable due to a submarine blockade.[6] In 1995 Americans consumed over twenty-seven pounds of imported tropical bananas per capita, nine pounds more than the annual per capita consumption of apples, the next most popular fruit. That was a banana a week for every person in the United States.[7] Bananas are the cheapest fruit in the grocery store, less expensive than apples, peaches, or pears grown in the same state.

Americans' love of bananas began after the Civil War when steamships and refrigerated ships and railroad cars made it possible to transport bananas to the North American market before they ripened and rotted. The Boston Fruit Company (it became the United Fruit Company in 1899) made a deliberate decision to keep the price low and to import in quantity. Banana consumption was described in 1916 as follows: "Forty years ago it was a rarity; thirty years ago a luxury; ten years ago a commodity. Today it is a food eaten by the humblest and the highest."[8] By 1927 the banana had claimed an important place in the "laborer's dinner-pail, the children's lunch-box, the school and factory cafeteria, and the picnic-hamper."[9]

Up until the 1890s bananas were a luxury or novelty item sporadically available at East Coast ports. Most Americans had never seen or tasted a banana. Many visitors to the Centennial Exposition in Philadelphia in 1876 ate their first bananas sold wrapped in tin foil for ten cents apiece. One of the leading attractions in the horticultural department was a banana plant with a bunch of bananas growing on it that had to be guarded by an attendant so that curious visitors did not pick it apart for souvenirs.[10]

Bananas picked green in the Caribbean ripen in transit, in the warehouse, in the grocery store and in the home. For many years, bananas were shipped as they grew with twelve to eighteen bunches to a stem. These stems were hung upside-down on hooks or suspended by rope in store windows or other places where they would be readily seen, and merchants and consumers were instructed to use a specially designed banana knife to slice off the "hands" so as to not split the skins of the individual banana "fingers." In the winter, merchants took care to protect the fruit from draughts of cold air and to cover the bunches with paper bags or wrappings at night.[11]

Banana stalks harbored snakes, spiders, and other jungle creatures, and the bunches were handled very gingerly at the wharf. Venomous tarantulas and scorpions were mentioned in an article on the banana trade in *Popular Sci-*

*Fig. 2.1. Banana Vendor. From United Fruit, U. F. Report, no. 1, Apr. 1951.*

*ence* in 1894.[12] Forty years later readers of *Newsweek* were told that tarantulas stowed away in bananas and were put to sleep by the cold air of the refrigerated ships. The spiders revived when the bananas were unloaded and menaced banana handlers. However, readers were assured that the Central American tarantula was not as big as the hairy, Brazilian eight-legged monster, and that its bite was rarely fatal.[13] The discovery of a snake emptied a railroad car or ships' hold of workers, and "snake in this car" was chalked on

*Fig. 2.2. United Fruit Company school campaign to build interest in bananas, from* U. F. Report, *no. 2, 1954.*

the outside.[14] A popular story in my family was of the local veterinarian who adopted a baby boa constrictor found in a banana freighter in the New Haven harbor, only to lose it in his house. He and his wife looked everywhere, finding it some days later curled up in their bed springs. In the 1950s, fruit companies began to separate the hands of bananas where they were grown and ship them to North America in boxes. The hands were dipped in vats of antiseptic solutions to kill any insects, and fungicide was painted on the end of each stalk to prevent deterioration.[15] Handling and shipping of the hands proved to be much easier, eliminating some of the danger of bruising and all the danger of hitchhiking critters. In addition, fruit companies experimented with banding, "cello-trays" (cardboard boxes with transparent cellophane tops), and shrink-wrapping to encourage shoppers to buy a whole hand rather than break off a few bananas.[16] Despite all the handling that bananas receive before retail sales, many people still associate tarantulas with bananas.

In the 1870s, Americans were told that the banana, available in East Coast markets from March to October, "is brought to the table as dessert and proves universally acceptable. . . . [Bananas are] eaten raw, either alone or cut in slices with sugar and cream, or wine and orange juice. They are also roasted, fried or boiled, and are made into fritters, preserves, and marmalades."[17] A recipe for banana pudding was included with the menu for an elaborate christening collation in 1876.[18] A cookbook published in 1887 noted that the aim of the book was "to collect such rich, rare, and racy, as well as time-honored, recipes as have never been given to the public." The recipes included a cake with banana slices in the filling, banana float, and graham mush with bananas.[19]

## At Home in American Culture

By 1910, the place of the banana in the American diet had changed dramatically. In an article titled "The Banana in Cookery," Fannie Merritt Farmer (author of *The Fannie Farmer Boston Cooking School Cookbook*, first published in 1896) noted that "less than forty years ago this fruit was almost unknown in the United States, and now it ranks with the oranges in extent of consumption. In fact, during the winter months these two are the only fresh fruits obtainable in many remote country districts."[20] She provided recipes for baked bananas to be served at breakfast, sautéed bananas to be served with Tournedos of Beef á la St. Denis or Delmonico Chicken, bananas in fruit cocktail, banana ice cream, banana sponge, and banana cream. Sato salad, made from cubed bananas, canned peas, and French dressing, was to be served in banana-skins sliced vertically and placed star shape on a lettuce leaf.

Farmer and others recommended scraping bananas with a silver knife after peeling them as part of the preparation process.[21] An article in *Parents Magazine* instructed mothers that the banana "may be served raw. All its vitamins are surely retained if this is done. The stringy fiber on the outside of the peeled banana is scraped off with the blunt edge of a knife. Then the fruit which Nature so thoughtfully gave a sanitary protective covering, is ready for consumption."[22] It is not clear why this was an issue. Most bananas appear to have been eaten straight from the skin without scraping. Some cookbooks called for scraping bananas for some recipes and not in others. It may be that the Gros Michel (or Big Mike) commercial banana that dominated the American market until the 1950s had tough fibers that clung to the pulp. But scraping the banana with a knife seems a bit drastic.

The United Fruit Company published a pamphlet during World War I that provided consumers with a number of "Points About Bananas." The company recommended bananas as wholesome, cheap, nutritious, delicious, easily digested, always in season, available everywhere, no waste, convenient for the dinner pail, good food when cooked, good food when not cooked, the poor man's food, the children's delight, endorsed by physicians, put up and sealed by nature in a germ-proof package, and produced without drawing on the nation's resources.[23] The United Fruit Company promoted bananas as a breakfast food and claimed that they were "already adopted in a great majority of the homes throughout the country."[24] Readers were instructed to remove the skin from a ripe banana, scrape to remove coarse threads, slice around a dish of corn flakes or other cereal, serve with milk and sugar. An advertisement for Puffed Wheat and Puffed Rice, published in 1910, showed the cereal being spooned over a dish of sliced bananas for "A Morning Treat."[25] Cold cereal and bananas proved to be a popular and enduring combination, and manufacturers continue to advertise cereal in combination with fresh fruit, frequently bananas.[26]

In an attempt to increase the consumption of bananas, the United Fruit Company suggested that the banana could be eaten in a salad at lunch and fried with meat for dinner.[27] Despite the best efforts of banana promoters, cooked bananas have never been popular on the American dinner menu other than in dessert. Part of the problem is that they become mushy when cooked. Plantains, a close relative of the banana, are starchier and hold their texture when cooked. Plantains are popular main course items in Central American cooking but have not been widely adopted by most Americans.

The United Fruit Company also promoted bananas as between-meal snacks, both raw and in combination with ice cream and other soda fountain concoctions. The banana split (invented 1927) and later the banana boat (combinations of ice cream, sliced banana, various ice cream sauces, whipped cream, and a maraschino cherry) became popular treats enjoyed by teenagers.[28] Banana powder, developed through research sponsored by the United Fruit Company, was the main ingredient of Melzo, a home and soda fountain drink promoted in the 1930s. It contained banana powder, maltose-dextrin, skimmed milk, yeast, and vanilla and was advertised as a health food for children and old folks, as a corrective for certain indigestions, and as a revitalizer for all who are sluggish mentally or physically. Free samples were provided to soda jerkers and one-hundred-dollar cash prizes were offered for alluring combinations sold to the public.[29]

In addition to banana powder, other banana products, such as banana flour, banana chips, and banana vinegar, have been experimented with and marketed with greater or lesser success. Readers of *Scientific American* in 1900 learned that in Central America, "banana flour is prepared on a large scale, and sold under the name of Musarina."[30] This flour was said to be good for children, aged people, convalescents, nursing women, and those suffering from complaints of the stomach. Five years later, readers were told that numerous attempts had been made to produce banana flour on a commercial basis for use in cake and bread.[31] The banana flour idea persisted, and it was seen as a potential substitute for wheat and rye flour during World War I.[32] In 1917 the U.S. Department of Agriculture, in conjunction with the United Fruit Company, announced that, with proper facilities at Caribbean seaports, "it should be entirely feasible to manufacture into flour an enormous quantity of bananas that are ordinarily too ripe or otherwise unfit for shipment to the United States."[33]

Five years later, Americans were again notified that banana figs, banana chips, and banana flour might soon be common articles of commerce.[34] Dried, or dehydrated, banana "figs" would be cheaper to ship and less subject to spoilage. One author suggested that dried bananas ought to bring higher prices than fresh "owing to their fine flavor and the fact that they require no sweetening."[35] "Evaporated" bananas could be kept for years in any climate and safely and cheaply transported to any part of the earth. He also suggested that dried bananas would make an ideal ration for soldiers or travelers on long inland tours.

A number of patents were granted for banana products, beginning in 1911 with a "breakfast food or coffee substitute" from bananas. Methods for producing banana flour, preserved bananas, dried bananas, and breakfast flakes were all approved.[36] Banana cider and vinegar were produced by a researcher for the United Fruit Company in 1929. The work was undertaken to find ways to use spoiled bananas not readily marketable because of scarring or overripeness. The United Fruit Company did not produce or market these products commercially.[37] Banana powder, never widely available to the general public, was used in medically prescribed diets and infant formula. It is now used in baking and pudding mixes. United Brands developed the first commercial all-natural banana essence and began marketing it in 1982 to be used in desserts, toppings, juices, and drinks.[38] Dried banana chips are widely available in supermarkets and health food stores along with other preserved fruit and are included in "tropical" trail mixes of fruit and nuts.

Consumers were warned not to place bananas in the ice chest (and later the refrigerator) and to wait until the fruit was yellow flecked with dark "sugar spots" before eating it.[39] There was a great deal of concern about the digestibility of bananas and at what stage they should be eaten. According to one magazine author, "The chief reason for the unfavorable reputation attained by the banana, when eaten uncooked, appears to lie in the failure of most persons to understand what a ripe banana really is." The December 1921 *Scientific American* warned: "When eaten before thoroughly ripe or gulped down without mastication it is not surprising that it often causes discomfort. Mixing it with bread or cereal prevents it from forming a mucilaginous mass in the stomach and thus promotes its digestion, while baking it quickly in the skin until soft and juicy renders it perfectly harmless for most persons."[40] United Fruit Company promotional material assured potential customers that bananas required no preparation to be edible, digestible, and palatable.

The early twentieth century witnessed the discovery of germs, vitamins, and minerals, and banana advertising played to concerns about health and nutrition.[41] Nineteenth-century food writers, such as the author of *The Housewife's Library*, were able to claim that "fruits do not take an important place as nutrients. They belong rather among the luxuries, and yet, as an agreeable stimulant to digestion, they occupy a front rank."[42] By World War I, bananas were routinely promoted as being protected by a germ-proof covering and nutritious.[43] Bananas, if properly handled, were "uncontaminated by dirt and pathogenic germs even if purchased from the push-cart in our congested streets."[44] Bananas were publicized as important substitutes for cereal grains during World War I, and consumers were told that "the banana exceeds in real food value many foods of different classes which are in almost daily use, such as whole milk, boiled oatmeal, shellfish and other fish, and fresh vegetables."[45]

The United Fruit Company promoted bananas as useful in normal diets at all ages. In addition, bananas were suited to special diets for infants suffering from malnutrition and gastrointestinal disturbances, as well as for children and adults with nephritis, ulcers, colitis, tuberculosis, diabetes, scurvy, gout, and fertility problems. Bananas were also said to be helpful in diets for both the overweight and the underweight, and for both diarrhea and constipation.[46]

Celiac disease, a chronic intestinal malabsorption disorder caused by intolerance to gluten, was often fatal to babies before the cause of the disorder was diagnosed.[47] In 1924 Dr. Sidney V. Hass began advocating a banana diet for patients with celiac disease. According to Hass, celiac sufferers would be cured in one to three years.[48] Eight years later the American Medical Association announced that bananas in a child's diet would provide relief for the disease or even cure it,[49] and bananas quickly became a staple food for infants and young children.[50]

The banana shortage of 1942 caused panic among many mothers, particularly those with children with celiac disease. *Newsweek* reported that Mrs. Valentine Dreschal carried her twenty-one-month-old son into the office of the *New York Journal-American* to ask for help in obtaining bananas that the baby's life depended on. In another instance, Brooklyn police, after hours of searching, found twenty-four bananas and rushed them to the home of fifteen-month-old Helena Gottlieb. The United Fruit Company announced that physicians who needed bananas for their patients could write or wire the Fruit Dispatch Company for supplies, and another importing company, Villar & Osorio, announced that an adequate supply of banana flour was available to doctors.[51] *Science Newsletter* reported that other strained fruits could be used in infants' diets, apparently satisfactorily.[52]

## Movies, Jingles, Skits, Cartoons, Folklore, and Festivals

Carmen Miranda (known as the Brazilian Bombshell) starred in the Busby Berkeley film *The Gang's All Here* wearing a fruit-bowl hat containing bananas. The United Fruit Company created a figure named Chiquita Banana based upon Miranda for an advertising jingle with a calypso beat. The jingle, in a version recorded by Patty Clayton, reached the top of the hit parade in 1944, and GI's voted Chiquita "the girl we'd most like to share a foxhole with."[53] Even though the jingle has not been used in advertising since the 1950s, many Americans can still sing it.[54] In part this is because United Fruit Company distributed copies of the sheet music to public schools to "build interest in bananas among many millions of future food purchasers."[55] The image of Chiquita, a banana dressed in a many-layered skirt and fruit-bowl

*Fig. 2.3. Banded fruit in supermarket display. From* U. F. Report, *no. 3, Sept. 1951.*

hat, was used by the United Fruit Company for supermarket displays and on stickers on the fruit itself.

In addition to being good to eat, bananas are funny. Everyone smiles when bananas are mentioned. Bananas were used as props in Vaudeville acts: Annette Kellermann's act included eating a banana underwater while sitting in a large tank on the stage, and part of A. Robbins's performance consisted of taking a seemingly endless number of bananas from his pockets. According to *Billboard* in 1930, it was "a sure-fire act." George L. Rockwell, known as "Dr. Rockwell, Quack, Quack, Quack," gave a lecture on human anatomy using a banana stalk as a skeleton. This act was popular for thirty years until he retired in the early 1940s.[56] In burlesque, the most important or senior comedian was known as the top banana.[57] Phil Silvers starred in the film *Top Banana* in 1954, based on a Broadway play by the same name. The theme song's lyrics told the audience that "if you wanna be the top banana, you've got to start at the bottom of the bunch."

In the 1880s the comic pratfall was associated with any moist litter. Bananas had not yet claimed a place in the popular imagination. A joke published in 1885 went as follows: "'Sa-ay, Jonnie, wot'll you buy for yer lunch?' said a boot-black to another. 'N orange.' was the reply. 'High-toned, ain't yer?' said the first. 'No,' said the other, 'but the skins is good to make people fall down with.'"[58] As bananas became widely available in the United States, the notion of slipping on a banana peel has become deeply ingrained in our culture. When someone is in trouble they are said to have one foot in the grave and the other on a banana peel. Americans were taught that the gutter was the proper place for banana skins: "If you buy and eat bananas in the street, don't throw the skins under anybody's feet. The banana is a delightful fruit, but the skin becomes an engine of destruction if left where people can slip on it and stumble. If you find a banana rind on the sidewalk, where some thoughtless sinner has dropped it, be kind enough to kick it into the gutter."[59] Another writer noted, "We admire its texture and enjoy its flavor; but we rarely give it serious thought unless constrained to do so while yielding to the smooth invitation to tarry a while that its cast-off skin extends."[60] Several successful lawsuits were brought against railroad companies by passengers who claimed bodily injuries resulting from slipping on banana skins.[61] Bananas peels have even been included in epitaphs. One tombstone attributed to Enosburg, Vermont, reads:

> In Memory of Anna
> Here lies the body of our Anna
> Done to death by a banana.
> It wasn't the fruit that laid her low,
> But the skin of the thing that made her go.[62]

The banana pratfall was a favorite comic ingredient of silent films. An English film appeared in 1908 with the title *Banana Skins* and shows a banana vendor standing on a street corner with a stalk of bananas strapped across his front. A woman and boy stop to buy a bunch, and as they leave the vendor laughs uproariously. The rest of the film is spent showing the havoc that they wreak as they eat the bananas, dropping the skins as they go. The grand finale is a line of marching policemen who fall on the last two skins.[63] Buster Keaton's film *Sherlock Junior* has Keaton slipping on a banana peel meant for his rival.[64]

In 1923, "Yes! We Have No Bananas" was one of the top hit songs of the year. Written by Frank Silver and Irving Cohn, the song is still widely known. Silver traded on the popularity of the song to tour with a "Banana Band" whose musicians wore gold costumes and played on daises adorned with glittery banana cutouts.[65] It is reported that flappers and their partners carefully did the Charleston to tunes such as Silver's on banana peel–strewn dance floors.[66]

In more contemporary times, despite the fact that banana peels are seldom found on the sidewalk, cartoonists continue to use this convention.[67] A children's book published in 1991 included an illustration of a purse snatcher sprawled on the steps of the New York Subway having slipped on a banana peel.[68] The Sunday crossword puzzle in the *New York Times Magazine* section for September 22, 1991, was titled "Ooh, That Banana Peel!"

Bananas also have sexual connotations. Their shape is phallic and bananas have been used as sexual symbols in movies. Josephine Baker, a Black American dancer "astonished and delighted" audiences in Paris in 1925 when she appeared wearing only a girdle of shiny bananas and several ropes of pearls.[69] Today, bananas are used in sex education classes to demonstrate condom use.

For a few months in 1967 bananas made the headlines as the latest ingredient for a psychedelic trip. Underground newspapers in Berkeley, New York, and Los Angeles published instructions for drying the fiber from banana peels to be rolled in a joint or in a pipe and smoked. It was called Bananadine or Mellow Yellow. Scientists at the University of California at Los Angeles, at New York University, and at the National Institute of Mental Health analyzed banana fiber and the effects of banana smoking. They concluded that the effects were psychological rather than pharmacological. The Federal Drug Administration reported extensive testing that turned up no evidence of hallucinogens in banana smoke. Interviews with banana smokers revealed that hippies fabricated the story to bait the authorities. It certainly got a rise out of the scientific community. Even the United Fruit Company felt impelled to protest the innocence of its product. Congressman Frank Thompson (D-NJ) proposed a tongue-in-cheek banana labeling act to halt thrill seekers. According to Thompson, "It is a short but shocking step to other fruits. Today, the cry is 'burn, banana, burn.' Tomorrow, we may face strawberry smoking, dried apricot inhaling, or prune puffing."[70] The banana became a psychedelic symbol with sexual and comic connotations, carried at "be-ins." Chiquita Banana stickers were popular on school notebooks. British singer Donovan's popular song "Mellow Yellow" was about electrical bananas, and artist Andy Warhol provided a banana for the cover of an album for the Velvet Underground.

Bananas moved from psychedelic to camp in the 1970s. Chiquita Banana and Carmen Miranda joined the pink plastic flamingo as a symbol of outrageous taste. And they are still with us. In October 1991, the *New York Times* reported a "Carmen Miranda" party benefiting the Brooklyn Academy of Music to which several guests wore Carmen Miranda–style turbans decorated with plastic fruit. The dinner dance was decorated with banana plants and an enormous painting of bananas was hung against one wall.[71]

Fulton, Kentucky, and its neighbor South Fulton, Tennessee, are the unlikely home of an annual International Banana Festival begun in 1963. Fulton was the hub of the railroad banana business for about seventy years when boxcars of bananas shipped from New Orleans were checked, iced, or heated, as the weather dictated, and dispatched to various midwestern destinations. Until the mid-1960s, Fulton was the distribution point for 70 percent of all bananas brought to the United States.[72] The town claimed the title "Banana Crossroads of the United States" and "Banana Capital of the World." Bananas are no longer distributed in Fulton, but the lack of bananas has not stopped the annual celebration.

Unlike the hip be-ins and psychedelic iconography of the late 1960s, Fulton sponsors a very traditional, middle-American, hometown program. Competitions for the Banana Princess, Little Mr. & Miss Banana, and the Junior Banana Princess lead up to a week-long celebration in the middle of September. The schedule of events includes a Banana Olympics, a Banana Bonnet Contest, a Banana Bake-Off and auction, a Banana Split Eating Contest at the South Fulton Dairy Queen, and a Banana Derby. The festivities also include a community patriotic sing, gospel jubilee, daily carnival, a library book sale, quilt fair, football game, foot race, square dance, pistol shoot competition sponsored by the Fulton Police Department, and a car show. Fulton is proud of holding the record for the World's Largest Banana Pudding. The one-ton pudding, made each year with 3,000 bananas, 250 pounds of 'Nilla Wafers, and 950 pounds of Regency Banana Creme Pie Filling, rides in the grand parade on the final day of the festival and is served free to 10,000 people at the bandstand.

The original organizers of the festival emphasize that in earlier years an exchange program brought young Latin American students to Fulton to enhance understanding and good will on a person-to-person basis. The banana business was seen as a link between the people of Fulton and those of remote countries where bananas are grown. In addition, the festival was attended by distinguished national and state leaders, including officials from the U.S. State

Department, congressmen, senators, and governors. Latin American guests came from Ecuador, El Salvador, Guatemala, Honduras, Costa Rica, Peru, Columbia, Panama, Nicaragua, Mexico, Argentina, and Venezuela.[73] A 1974 description noted that the festival "brings together the peoples of the Americas and joins them in an atmosphere of friendship and understanding."[74] Dancing to the marimba band from Guatemala was listed as part of the festivities. These deliberate links with Central America have disappeared, and the festival has turned inward, perhaps because of national concern with illegal immigrants and imported drugs.

The era of exotic, romantic, tropical jungles and the United Fruit Company's Great White Fleet of ships has passed. Young men and women are no longer recruited in North America to live and work in company fruit towns in Central America.[75] We receive our bananas from a variety of companies and countries. But the image lives on. Woody Allen directed a film released in 1971 named *Bananas* about the adventures of a New Yorker during a revolution in a tropical "banana republic." A clothing chain named Banana Republic sells vacation clothes. Ornamental banana plants are popular in gardens as far north as Washington, D.C., and in California.[76] In the Washington, D.C., area, domestic banana plants and the growing variety of banana types available in the grocery stores may be attributed, in part, to the large Latin American population. But bananas have not lost their place in the American diet. Athletes and the elderly now eat bananas for potassium, fiber, and carbohydrates. Bananas are also touted as cholesterol-free.[77] Kelloggs and Nabisco breakfast cereals and 'Nilla Wafers offer coupons for "free" bananas. Americans continue to consume nearly thirty pounds of bananas apiece every year. That's over 15 billion banana peels thrown away.[78] But have you ever known anyone to slip on one?

## Notes

1. *Bananas* (Washington, D.C.: Pan American Union, 1956), 3; J. R. Magness, "Fruit of the Wise Men," *National Geographic* (Sept. 1951): 358.
2. "Bananas: Production in Latin America," *Americas* (May 1972, supplement): 21.
3. "Banana Production," *Science*, May 22, 1891, 289; and Floyd L. Darrow, "Fruit of the Wise Men," *St. Nicholas* (Aug. 1929): 822.
4. Charles F. Wingate, ed., *The Housekeeper: A Journal of Domestic Economy* (Aug. 1876): 133.
5. Scott U. Stambaugh, *Bananas in Florida* (Tallahassee: Dept. of Agriculture, 1952), 4.
6. *Tropical Agribusiness Structures and Adjustments—Bananas* (Boston: Arthur, Houck and Beckford, 1968), 184; Stacy May and Galo Plaza, *The United Fruit Company in Latin America*, seventh case study in an NPA

series on United States Business Performance Abroad, National Planning Association, 1958, 137.

7. "Facing Falling Consumption," *The Packer*, Dec. 2, 1996, 6A.
8. "The Epic of the Banana," *Current Opinion* (Dec. 1916): 424.
9. Philip Keep Reynolds, *The Banana: Its History, Cultivation and Place Among Staple Foods* (Boston: Houghton Mifflin Company, 1927), 133.
10. *Visitors' Guide to the Centennial Exhibition and Philadelphia, 1876* (Philadelphia: J. B. Lippincott & Co., 1875), 16, and *Frank Leslie's Illustrated Historical Register of the Centennial Exposition, 1876* (New York: Frank Leslie, 1876), vol. 1, no. 7, 219.
11. Frederick Upham Adams, *Conquest of the Tropics* (New York: Doubleday, Page and Company, 1914), 20.
12. James Ellis Humphrey, "Where Bananas Grow," *Popular Science* (Feb. 1894): 486.
13. "United Fruit: 50,000,000 Bunches boost 1935 Profits," *Newsweek*, Mar. 30, 1935, 35.
14. C. B. Hayward, "Culture and Transportation," *Scientific American*, Jan. 28, 1905, 80.
15. *Bananas*, 16; "Banana Stem Rot Can Be Prevented," *Science Newsletter*, Oct. 2, 1954, 213; and Hugh M. Smith, Wendell E. Clement, and William S. Hoofnagle, "Merchandising of Selected Food Items in Grocery Stores," Marketing Research Report No. 111, Agricultural Marketing Service, Washington, D.C., Feb. 1956, 2.
16. *Bananas*, 16; May and Plaza, *United Fruit Company*, 60; Paul Franklin Shaffer, "Produce Packaging at the Central Warehouse—Bananas," Agricultural Research Service, New Series ARS 52–7, Oct. 1965, 3.
17. Todd S. Goodholme, ed., *A Domestic Cyclopaedia of Practical Information* (New York: Henry Holt, 1878), 14.
18. Wingate, *The Housekeeper* (June 1876): 93.
19. *175 Choice Recipes Mainly Furnished by Members of the Chicago Women's Club* (Chicago: Charles H. Kerr, 1887), 4.
20. Fannie Merritt Farmer, "The Banana in Cookery," *Woman's Home Companion* (Mar. 1910): 60.
21. United Fruit Company, "Bananas, Wholesome, Nutritious, Cheap: A Few Appetizing and Inexpensive Recipes," Boston, c. 1917, 2–3.
22. Nichols, "Bananas for the Underweight," *Parents Magazine* (Oct. 1930): 38.
23. United Fruit Company, "Bananas, Wholesome," 4.
24. Ibid., 2.
25. *Woman's Home Companion* (Mar. 1910): 58.
26. Advertisement for Shredded Ralston, *American Magazine* (Nov. 1939): 143.
27. "From the Tropics to Your Table," New York: Fruit Dispatch Company, 1926, 26.

28. T. S. Elrod, "Banana Split," *Scribner's* (Dec. 1927): 677–85.
29. "United Fruit Bananas Converted into a New Drink and a Baby Food: Melzo," *BusinessWeek*, Oct. 7, 1933, 10.
30. "Banana Flour," *Scientific American Supplement*, Aug. 18, 1900, 20601.
31. Hayward, "Culture and Transportation," 80.
32. "Banana Flour, a New Substitute for Wheat and Rye Flour," *Scientific American*, July 3, 1915, 35.
33. "Banana Flour To Help Fortify America Against a Bread Famine," *Current Opinion* (Nov. 1917): 356.
34. "Possibilities of Dried Bananas," *Literary Digest*, Jan. 7, 1922, 21.
35. S. E. Worrell, "Dry Bananas," *Scientific American*, Apr. 16, 1904, 311.
36. J. A. LeClerc and V. A. Pease, "Banana Flour or Meal, and Other Commercial Food Products from the Banana: Selected References and Patents Covering Preparation, Uses, Properties," Agricultural Chemical Research Division, Bureau of Agricultural Chemistry and Engineering, Feb. 27, 1941, rev. by Harry W. von Loesecke, Aug. 27, 1942, 11–12.
37. "Cider and Vinegar from Bananas," *Literary Digest*, Mar. 16, 1929, 34.
38. R. H. Stover and N. W. Simmonds, *Bananas* (New York: Longman Scientific and Technical, 1987), 400.
39. Reynolds, *The Story of the Banana*, 29; Home Economics Department, *A Study of the Banana: Its Every-day Use and Food Value* (Teachers' Manual), New York: United Fruit Company, 1939, 13; Dorothy Kirk, "Banana Bonanza," *Woman's Home Companion* (Sept. 1947): 90; Lila M. Jones, "Bananas, a Vegetable, Too!" *Good Housekeeping* (Feb. 1948): 147; the Chiquita Banana Song 1944; and Anna May Wilson, "Forbidden Fruit?" *Todays Health* (May 1951): 51.
40. "Cook Your Bananas," *Literary Digest*, Feb. 16, 1918, 22; William A. Murrill, "The Banana and Its Uses: Getting Acquainted with This Tropical Fruit of Which There Are Over Seventy Varieties," *Scientific American* (Dec. 1921): 119.
41. Banana Growers Association advertisement, *The Parents' Magazine* (Oct. 1930): 61.
42. George A. Peltz, ed., *The Housewife's Library* (Philadelphia: Hubbard Bros., 1883), 201.
43. United Fruit Company, "Bananas, Wholesome," 3; Skinner, Sherman and Esselen, Inc., *The Food Value of the Banana* (Boston: W. M. Leonard, 1926), 8; Winifred Wichard, "Bananas, The Mainstay of the Menu," *Pictorial Review* (Apr. 1927): 39.
44. "Cook Your Bananas," 22; Samuel C. Prescott, "Banana: A Food of Exceptional Value," *Scientific Monthly* (Jan. 1918): 67.
45. Prescott, "Banana: A Food," 67.
46. Education Dept., *The Story of the Banana*, 5th ed. (Boston: United Fruit Company, 1929): 39; Lotta Jean Bogert, *Dietary Uses of the Banana in*

*Health and Disease* (New York: Research Dept., United Fruit Company, 1935), 5; Research Dept., *Nutritive and Therapeutic Values of the Banana: A Digest of Scientific Literature* (Boston: United Fruit Company, 1936).

47. Robert Berkow, M.D., editor-in-chief, *The Merck Manual of Diagnosis and Therapy* (Merck Sharpe and Dohme Research Laboratories, Rahway, N.J., 1982), 775.
48. Bogert, *Dietary Uses of the Banana*, 12; "Banana Priorities," *Newsweek*, Aug. 10, 1942, 57.
49. "Bananas Are Essential to Diet in Celiac Disease," *Hygeia: The Health Magazine*, American Medical Association (Sept. 1932): 854; "Banana—Cure for Childhood Disease," *Literary Digest*, June 25, 1932, 24.
50. Walter H. Eddy and Minerva Kellogg, "Place of the Banana in the Diet," *American Journal of Public Health* (Jan. 1927): 27–35; Ruth Washburn Jordan, "Bananas Up To Date," *Parents Magazine* (Feb. 1929): 40; Education Dept., *The Story of the Banana*, 39; Nichols, "Bananas for the Underweight," 38; Bogert, *Dietary Uses of the Banana*.
51. "Banana Priorities," *Newsweek*, Aug. 10, 1942, 57.
52. "Yes, We Have No Bananas, But Babies Need Not Suffer," *Science Newsletter*, Aug. 8, 1942, 87.
53. David Widner, "America's Going Bananas," *Readers Digest* (July 1986): 118; Alex Abella, *The Total Banana: The Illustrated Banana: Anecdotes, History, Recipes and More!* (New York: Harcourt, Brace, Jovanovich, 1979), 33.
54. "Yes, They Sell More Bananas," *BusinessWeek* (July 8, 1967): 92.
55. *U. F. Report*, no. 2, 1954, 3.
56. Anthony Slide, *The Vaudevillians: A Dictionary of Vaudeville Performers* (Westport, Conn.: Arlington House, 1981); Kellermann is mentioned on 83; Robbins on 123; Rockwell on 126.
57. Harold Wentworth and Stuart Berg Flexner, *The Pocket Dictionary of American Slang* (New York: Pocket Books, 1967), 12.
58. "The Cook: A Weekly Handbook of Domestic Culinary Art for All Housekeepers," 1 (9) (Aug. 3, 1885): 11.
59. Wingate, *The Housekeeper* (Aug. 1876): 133.
60. James Ellis Humphrey, "Where Bananas Grow," *Popular Science* (Feb. 1894): 486.
61. Abella, *The Total Banana*, 30.
62. The Bathroom Readers' Institute, *Uncle John's Second Bathroom Reader* (New York: St. Martin's Press, 1989), 113.
63. *Banana Skins*, Sheffield, 1908, 1 roll of 1,712 feet, 35mm, black and white.
64. "Sherlock Junior," Buster Keaton Productions, 1924, 5 rolls, 16mm, black and white.
65. Abella, *The Total Banana*, 30; Lois Gordon and Alan Gordon, *American*

*Chronicle: Six Decades in American Life 1920–1980* (New York: Atheneum, 1987), 36.

66. Widner, "America's Going Bananas," 117.

67. For example, George Booth, *Rehearsal's Off* (New York: Avon Books, 1976), 94–95. This cartoon first appeared in *Playboy*.

68. Debra Barracca and Sal Barracca, *Maxi, The Hero* (New York: Dial Books for Young Readers, 1991). Reviewed in the *New York Times Book Review*, Jan. 5, 1992, 23.

69. Edward Thorpe, *Black Dance* (Woodstock, N.Y.: Overlook Press, 1990), 109.

70. "Mellow Yellow," *Newsweek*, Apr. 10, 1967, 93; "Yes, They Sell More Bananas," *BusinessWeek*, July 8, 1967, 92; and "The Big Banana Hoax," *Science Digest* (Feb. 1968): 62–63.

71. *New York Times*, Oct. 27, 1991, 45.

72. Pamphlet for the International Banana Festival and Schedule of Events printed by the Kentucky Dept. of Travel Development and the International Banana Festival, Fulton, KY, 1991.

73. Typescript sent out by the International Banana Festival organizers, Fulton, Ky., 1991.

74. *Festivals Sourcebook*, ed. Paul Wasserman, Esther Herman, Elizabeth A. Root (Gale Research Company: Detroit, 1977), 225.

75. For examples of banana romanticism, see Edmund S. Whitman, "Banana Nurses," *American Magazine* (Jan. 1937): 54–55; Tom Gill, "Gentlemen of the Jungle," *American Magazine*, serial novel (Oct.–Dec. 1939); Arch. F. Coleman, "Banana Cowboy," *Saturday Evening Post*, May 16, 1942, 19 passim.

76. "New Banana, from an Old One," *Sunset* (July 1962): 170; "Bananas in Sunnyvale? And in Other Bay Area Banana Belts," *Sunset* (May 1986): 278–80; "Nothing Says Jungle Quite Like Banana," *Sunset* (June 1976): 78–81.

77. "Sweet Treat: Bananas," *Good Housekeeping* (Mar. 1982): 178.

78. Widner, "America's Going Bananas," 116.

# Theresa Meléndez

In popular culture, the story of corn in America parallels the image of America itself: from the idyllic land of abundance to the unrefined land of the provincial or savage. This Eurocentric view is in direct conflict with the Native American lore in which corn, or maize, reigns supreme as sacred gift or the essence of humanity itself. Similarly, in world agriculture, corn has been recognized as one of the most beneficent and prolific of all grains. Curiously, its popularity as food and sacred image is found in the Americas alone, while it continues to reap disdain from most modern Europeans and some Americans, as can be seen in common idioms, e.g., corny and cornball.

Corn, or maize (from the Taino *mahiz*, 1555), is arguably one of the foods most identified with American culture worldwide. From the beginning corn evoked both awe and distrust among the Europeans, who encountered it by reason of "The Columbian Exchange," as Alfred W. Crosby has so diplomatically characterized the consequences of the Old World/New World encounter he studied. The New World seemed a cornucopia of dubious merit, one muddying familiar classifications of flora, fauna, and human beings. It is within natural history that we find the earliest instances of mixed sentiments toward maize, but the array of cultural meanings available to us today appears in the multiple discourses of myth, vernacular language, popular culture, advertising, art, and architecture.

## For Mexicans and Pigs

Some twenty years ago as a typically homesick graduate student in Spain, finishing my dissertation on ballad processes, I would scour the vegetable markets and grocery stores for any corn product. As a Chicana in Madrid, I hungered for the corn dishes of my native Southwest, and, not expecting to find Mexican products, I had at least hoped to obtain corn meal or flour, fresh or canned corn—just *the basics*, I thought to myself about the Mexican triad of corn, beans, and squash—but all to no avail. My *Madrileño* friends and colleagues had congratulated me for "returning to my origins," for finally rejecting my "American" ways by living in Spain and by studying Spanish oral traditions. Having lived on the Texas–Mexican border most of my life, I didn't have the heart to tell them I was raised with tales of the arrogant *gachupin* (a derogatory term for Spaniard) and had never thought of Spain as the motherland, but more as the wicked stepmother whose lost embrace we celebrated every September 16. When I lamented the lack of corn to a friendly Madrid neighbor, she laughed at me and said, "Corn? Why would you want corn? Corn is for Mexicans and pigs!" Well, so much for my "origins," I thought.

This contemptuous regard for New World grain is not shared by other American foodstuffs, such as the tomato or potato, both of which figure prominently in gazpacho and the Spanish tortilla. Aside from paella, it is these dishes that are highlighted in the Spanish national cuisine. Among the new Spanish dishes, gazpacho and the tortilla, along with the chocolate drink, were developed to showcase Spain's acquisitions in Mexico and Peru, and became fashionable in European circles in the early post-discovery years.[1]

Why and how does maize *(Zea mays)* come to carry this connotation of scorn and contempt? The phrase "corn is for Mexicans and pigs" embodies a wealth of perspectives and motives, not only toward American peoples and foods, but also toward the New World itself.

The generation of meanings and values exists on a semantic as well as a cultural level. The eating of corn functions in this phrase to equate Mexicans and pigs as inferior, contaminated beings, but in turn the association of corn with Mexicans and pigs also pollutes the connotation of corn. The false analogy between Mexicans and pigs exists because a category is created: "creatures who eat corn," the obvious implication being that both pigs and Mexicans are animals. (The connotation of pig with a "dirty" animal is of peculiar import in the previous anecdote, given the history of the Jew in Spain.) Obviously, "creatures who eat corn" originates as a new category in Europe with the encounter of the two worlds. For both the plant and the human being, this classification has been marked as less than worthy.

The idea of America as a land of unequaled opportunity but with a suspect humanity and inferior nature has a long history. Antonello Gerbi in *The Dispute of the New World* discusses the European view of the inferiority of all "living nature" of the Americas based on the belief of the "newness" of the continents where nature was both "immature" (in embryo) and "decadent" (rotting).[2] The postlapsarian world was always in the process of decay, according to Christian ideology, but the New World more so than the Old. This meant that, for Europeans, the New World's natural resources were problematic. The "discovery" of America was met with high enthusiasm at first, but it began to dissipate as more was learned of its peoples and civilizations.

Hugh Honour's *The New Golden Land: European Images of America from the Discoveries to the Present Time* (1975) wonderfully constructs the view of the Americas as both land of promise and subsequent betrayal or disillusion through both written sources and art works.[3] Europeans saw Indians as savages, people without law, government or religion. For some, such as Bartolomé de las Casas, whose influential *History of the Indies* (1527–60) praised Indian cultures at the expense of the Spanish treatment of them, saw the American peoples as living in a state of innocence, primitive but idyllic. For, in spite of the famous papal bull *Sublimus Deus* of 1536, which declared Indians to be "truly men," most Europeans, including Spaniards, saw the "primitive" as in a state of bestial and corrupt behavior. Gonzalo Fernández de Oviedo, whose admirable *Historia general y natural de las Indias* (1535) praises much of New World flora and fauna, still perceived the Indian as treacherous and shiftless. In the oft-cited phrase by English philosopher Thomas Hobbes, the life of the savage was considered "solitary, poor, nasty, brutish, and short."[4]

The cultural view of corn is part of the referent or situational context of New World ideology, as are any of the foodstuffs new to Europeans. The connection of corn with its indigenous or Native American roots (pun intended) from the beginning of the encounter is what gives corn its primary "entitlement," Kenneth Burke's phrase to explain the symbolic action of giving identity, or a "title," to an undefined situation.[5] Corn, perhaps because of its primacy to American peoples, is associated with the New World in a way that the tomato or the potato is not. It is the daily bread, the grain of sustenance for most indigenous peoples on both American continents. Corn is equivalent to "New World" for the European, and, depending on the cultural motive, the meaning of the term shifts along with ideological aims and behaviors.

It is Columbus himself who first identifies the plant, finding corn on all the larger islands of the West Indies and mistakenly calling it *panizo*, or panic grass, in the log of his first voyage (October 16, 1492): "This island is very large, and I have determined to sail around it, because, as I understand in, or near it, there is a mine of gold . . . . It is a very green island, and level and very fertile, and I have no doubt that year round they sow and reap panic grass and all other things too. And I saw many trees very unlike ours, and many of them

Fig. 3.1. Mexican god sitting on rattlesnakes with corn, peppers, squash, and subjects below, c. 1585. From the Florentine Codex.

have their branches of different kinds, and all on one trunk . . . that it is the greatest wonder of the world."[6] In his characteristic manner of overlooking the most significant, Columbus only incidentally mentions the grain in his overriding search for gold. But this first inauspicious mention of corn, later called *maiz* or *mais* in imitation of the Arawak pronunciation, is couched in the early figurative images of America as a land of abundance and fabled wealth. In his journal and letters, Columbus emphasizes the green and fertile land, the balmy air, the beauty of bird song, the diversity of plants and animals, and always the promise of gold.

The Edenic traits of the natural abundance of food and the perennial fertility of the land help to develop the connotation of the fantastic and bizarre in New World lore. Nicolo Syllacio's Latin pamphlet, the second publication on the New World after Columbus's letter of 1493, includes corn among a description of what the newfound peoples eat. Along with "human flesh" and *asses* (yams) with the flavor of the "manna of the Jews," there is "a prolific kind of grain, as large as the lupine and round as chick-peas, from which a flour of a very fine texture is produced. It is ground like wheat and makes bread of admirable flavor. Many humble folk chew the grains. [These are found growing, along with other] sylvan fruits, amid shady forests and sacred groves. The young crops never suffer damage nor are they ever threatened by tares, vetch, and unfruitful wild oats."[7] It is important to note that it is from this document that scholars believe Peter Martyr, that most famous of popularizers of America, derives his description of corn in his *De Orbe Novo Decades,* appearing as "maizum" in 1516, and thus widely disseminating a similar perspective. Another detractor of maize is the Italian Jeronimo Benzoni whose *Historia del Mondo Nuovo* (Venice, 1565) was published extensively in Latin, French, German, Flemish, and English, and who wrote disparagingly of corn as food.[8]

Again, in this instance, the category "creatures who eat corn" is delineated. The classification is literally "humble folk," but the nonchalant inclusion of corn among other alien foods—human flesh and manna of the Jews (yams)—converts or modifies the category. The attributes of corn, although "of admirable flavor" and thus overtly praiseworthy, are identified by the attributes of the people who eat it: in this instance, cannibals, Jews, and Indians. Following Kenneth Burke, who suggests that "language is equipment for living" and who shows how the use of categories in particular situations constitutes strategies for handling these situations, we can see the development of corn as a label implying baseness. For Burke, the mere act of defining through such labeling implies certain attitudes and behaviors appropriate to that definition.[9]

Corn begins to function as a kind of trope, a figure of speech in which "meaning is changed or enhanced."[10] While metaphor may be the most common or best-known trope, here corn operates more as metonymy, a relationship based on contiguity or association rather than on similarity, as in metaphor.[11] David Sapir states that "metonymy replaces or juxtaposes contiguous terms that occupy a distinct and separate place within what is considered a single semantic or perceptual domain."[12] As the term corn is grouped with the strange or the savage, the semantic domain of corn as metonymy becomes one of brutality, of subhuman or base norms. The semantic meaning of corn, what corn "entitles," is the prejudicial perception of New World peoples. In Burke's view, this process summarizes the moral essence of the situation and defines possible actions toward it.

As the conquests in the New World continued into the sixteenth century, corn was imported first from the West Indies and then Mexico and Peru. Its early use spread through central Europe into the Balkans, and it was also taken to India, the East Indies, and into the mainland of eastern Asia.[13] At the same time, significantly, corn production began in North Africa, where it became an important commodity for provisioning ships for the slave trade. In this way, it became one of the essential mechanisms for the success of the Atlantic slave trade, and, as such, along with other New World plants, became a central element in the formation and development of capitalism. Without a speedy and productive food crop to feed its labor force, colonial commerce would have expanded much less quickly.[14]

In 1542 corn appears in its first illustration, a fairly accurate woodcut, in the famous herbal of Leonard Fuchs, *De historia stirpium* (Basel). Fuchs wrote that corn had originated in Asia, and since western Asia was dominated by Turks, the plant should be called "Turkish corn." This is the beginning of the seeming confusion over its origin and its name, but I believe this confusion is already marked by the perspective on the New World. Maize was also called "Welschen korn" or "strange grain" by a contemporary of Fuchs, Jerome Bock (1539), and for the next two centuries herbalists continue to believe in two varieties of corn, one from Asia and the other from America. In English, it was called Turkey corn or wheat, or Indian corn, depending on its supposed origin.[15] The terms "Turk" and "Welsh" not only indicated the incorrect beliefs about its native origin, but also indicated contempt for the plant, for surely no one believed the plant had come from Wales. Turks and the Welsh were regarded as uncultured individuals by the European, who thus identified anything coarse, rough, or barbaric with these epithets.

The *Oxford English Dictionary* (1989) traces the use of the term "Turkey wheat" to describe corn from the late sixteenth through the nineteenth century and also defines the meaning of "Turkish" as "like or resembling the Turks, their character, or that attributed to them; cruel, savage, barbarous." For example, someone of Irish descent was called a "Turk" derogatorily to describe his "behaving as a barbarian or savage." Similarly, the usage of "Welsh" defined "speech that one does not understand" or anything foreign or crude, such as "Welshcomb," meaning "to comb one's hair using one's thumbs and fingers," or the "Welsh ambassador" to mean the cuckoo bird or a fool. Partridge's *Dictionary of Slang* (1984) gives us "turkey-merchant,"

*Fig. 3.2. The first illustration of maize, called Turkish corn. From* De historia stirpium *of Leonard Fuchs (1542).*

meaning a chicken thief, and "Welsh cricket," a louse (sixteenth through eighteenth century). Thus in addition to confusion over the origin of the maize plant, its being labeled Turkish or Welsh continued the biased view of corn.

As for its food value, only some of the early herbals regard corn as nutritious; the majority, according to Paul Weatherwax, believe it to be "unpalatable and indigestible, decidedly inferior to the other cereals, and to be recommended as food only in case of extreme necessity or for those doing the hardest kind of work."[16] This belief that corn was an inferior foodstuff has some basis in fact, since depending on maize alone as the primary diet results in pellagra, a disease that was not found in New World cultures that had invented the process known as "nixtamalization." This preparation, which involves soaking the grains and cooking them with lime, enhances the protein value, as does its combination with beans; unfortunately, these food habits did not accompany maize into Europe.[17] Perhaps the most illustrative of the poor opinions of maize is found in John Gerard's *The herbal or generall historie of plants:*

> Turky wheat doth nourish far lesse than either Wheate, Rie, or Otes. The bread which is made thereof is meanely white, without bran: it is hard and drie as bisket is, and hath in it no clamminess at all; for which cause it is hard of digestion, and yeeldeth to the body little or no nourishment. Wee have as yet no certaine proofe or experience concerning the vertues of this kinde of Corne, although the barbarous Indians which know no better, are constrained to make a vertue of necessitie and think it a good food; whereas we may easily judge that it nourisheth but little, and is of hard and evill digestion, a more convenient food for swine than for man.[18]

So there it is once again, corn is only for Indians (read Mexicans) and pigs!— a perceptual domain that has survived some four hundred years.

For the Spaniard, who presumably knew its origin and could not name it otherwise, this connotation was not so apparent in the early sixteenth century. In the region of Catalonia, however, corn was identified not only as "blat de les Indies" ("wheat of the Indies"; Spain continued to refer to the Americas as the Indies much longer than other countries), but also as "blat de moro" or "moresc" (wheat of the Moor), again an identification with "foreign" or undesirable people.[19] Most of the early Spanish naturalists looked upon corn favorably. Oviedo in the chapter "Del pan de los indios" from his *Historia general y natural de las Indias* writes about corn farming and notes that it was all learned from the Indians and that corn is planted in the same way by the Christians who live in that land. He says that corn is fed to "caballos e bestias de que se sirven" as well as to "los negros e indios esclavos, de que los Christianos se sirven" (horses and other beasts which they use . . . the blacks and the Indian slaves, of whom the Christians make use). The category "creatures who eat corn" is marked by servitude, either as domestic animals or slaves. However, in other places, Oviedo notes that the "Christians" have improved upon the bread and he finds it delicious.[20] José de Acosta's chapter on the bread of the Indies from his 1590 *Historia natural y moral de las Indias* discusses corn as the principal grain of sustenance, noting it is called Indian wheat in Castile and Turkey grain in Italy; on the whole, he finds it beneficial: "de manera que para bestias y para hombres, para pan y para vino, y para aceite, aprovecha en Indias el maiz" (so that for animals and men, for bread and for wine, and for oil, corn in the Indies is useful).[21] In this case the association of corn as food for animals and humans seems to emphasize its versatility rather than its baseness.

But in spite of the contempt for the plant, its amazing abundance could not be overlooked, a feature which both Acosta and Oviedo document. The English also found this aspect of corn wondrous; in Thomas Hariot's *Narrative of the first English planting of Virginia* (1590), he states: "It is a graine of marvellous great increase: of a thousand, fifteene hundred and some two thousand folde."[22] In *The Columbian Exchange*, Alfred W. Crosby describes its productivity: "Its supremely valuable characteristic is its high yield per unit of land which, on world average, is roughly double that of wheat. For those to whom famine is a reality, maize has the additional benefit of producing food fast. Few other plants produce so much carbohydrate, sugar, and fat in as short a growing season."[23] Corn as the symbol of abundance and foodstuffs of America was highlighted among "Twenty Discoveries That Changed Our Lives" in a 1984 anniversary issue of *Science*. The article celebrates the Native American contributions to corn production and also the technology derived from the study of corn that has "made it possible to feed the world." The United States, of course, leads the world in corn production (about half) as well as utilization (approximately one-third).[24] This view of corn, of its prolific and rapid growth, is the other part of the semantic domain of the term. However, most of the favorable images of corn are strictly American.

## Corn at Home

For the indigenous people of the Americas, maize had always been the most important and widespread cultivated food plant since its domestication in 5000 B.C. It has been noted by many that the greatest cultural development among indigenous societies was made possible by the increased food production occurring in corn-producing cultures.[25] More rituals of traditional peoples have been associated with maize than with all other cultivated plants combined. Planting rites, harvest rites, work songs, marriage and funeral symbols have all derived from the centrality of corn in these cultures. The Aztecs or, more accurately, the Mexica performed numerous seasonal rituals with dance, song, and human sacrifice for the agricultural deities, male and female gods of corn. The Corn Dance of North American Indian cultures addressed the deities for the germination and the growth of the seed and in thanks for the harvest. The most famous of these is perhaps the Green Corn Dance of the Pueblos, a highly ritualized and partially secret ceremony. It has even been suggested that the introduction of maize may have caused a change in social organization toward matrilineal descent, for example, in the cultures of western Pueblos in which women farm and grind corn together.[26]

Certainly one of the most important consequences of introducing agriculture into human activities was the devising of calendars and advancement of the knowledge of astronomical data needed for sowing and harvest processes. For the Mayas and the Mexicas, who developed the most accurate calendars of their time, Paul Weatherwax, the renowned corn geneticist, says that "the primary incentive was the necessity of knowing exactly when to plant corn."[27] These two great civilizations were based, at least in great part, on the cultivation and worship of corn. The basic diet of Central America since 900 B.C. has been corn, beans, and squash, but clearly corn's symbolic power created its central role in the mythological structures of indigenous cultures. Perhaps this fierce attraction is due to the symbiotic relationship corn has with human beings because it cannot sustain itself as a maize plant in the wild. It requires the intervention of the planter in order to reproduce. This intimacy between the human and the plant is noted in the numerous instances in which corn plays a sacred role in Náhuatl myth. It is originally the great culture hero/god Quetzacóatl who brings the precious grain to his people, but the potent mother goddesses are closely associated with the maintenance of the plant. In one of the sacred hymns of the Mexica, the mother goddess in her aspect as Seven Cobs of Corn, to emphasize her relationship to the plant, is petitioned to protect the crops:

> Oh Seven Cobs of Corn . . . arise now,
> awaken. . . . You are Our Mother!
> You would leave us orphans;
> go now to your house, Tlalocan.[28]

In the *Popol Vuh*, the great narrative text of the Quiche Maya from the highlands of Guatemala, a creation myth explains the birth of humanity from maize. In the beginning, when there was only water and sky, the gods created the sun, the moon, the stars, and the land. They also wanted to create human beings who could think and give offerings to them. In their first attempt, they created imperfect beings who could not talk or worship; these beings became the ancestors of all animals. The next two attempts, people of clay and people of wood, were considered failures because they had no souls or minds. When a great flood covered the earth and destroyed them, the birds and other animals began to recite their grievances against humanity to their gods: it was decided that humanity would be made of maize. Four animals, the fox, the coyote, the parrot, and the crow, led the gods to a land of abundance where food of all kinds grew and to a mountain filled with yellow corn and white corn. One of the gods ground the corn and mixed it with water to create four human beings:

> the making, the modeling of our first mother-father,
> with yellow corn, white corn alone for the flesh,
> food alone for the human legs and arms,
> for our first fathers, the four human works.

And because these "mother-fathers" are intelligent, sensitive, and grateful to the creators, they become the ancestors of all people living today.[29] These poems and myths demonstrate the close relationship between plants, animals, land, and water and humanity; all are needed for the creation of what is human.

In North American Indian tales, the role of corn is also sacred. The Navaho have a similar creation narrative of imperfect human beings created before the Holy People decide to lay two ears of corn, white and yellow, on the ground, cover them with buckskin and the feathers of an eagle, and watch the wind blow upon the corn: "And lo! the ears of corn had disappeared./In their place there lay a man and there lay a woman."[30] Other stories from indigenous American traditions explain the special import of corn in their societies by relating how corn came to exist. In the tale of the origin of corn, from the Abanaki, a young Indian man, hungry, lonely, and without the knowledge of fire, is visited by a young woman with long light hair. When he tries to come close to her, she eludes him until she gives him this mission: he is to rub two sticks together, burn the ground, and drag her over it. He at first refuses, but is finally convinced that he must do so. Out of the ground grows a plant with seeds and silk the color of the woman's hair, to remind him of her care. This tale has many analogues among the Iroquois, Huron, Seneca, Cherokee, Pawnee, Zuni, and the Seminoles.[31] The central theme is one of sacrifice and generosity, the death and resurrection of the hero (male and female, old and young in the different cultures), for the grain cannot grow unless one is willing to give up the present, known and beneficent, for the uncertain future. It is the metaphoric analogy of the life cycle of corn: its cob, the hoard of seeds, must be destroyed in order to plant the individual seed.

## Corn in Popular Culture, the Arts, and Everyday Life

In African American and Euro-American folklore, we hear reverberations of the early theme of amazing fertility and abundance in the tall tales recorded by Zora Neale Hurston, among others, who relate stories of land so rich that ears of corn grow from stalks set in the ground overnight. When a young man sits on the corn to prevent it from growing so fast, he reports that he passed through heaven selling roast ears to the angels.[32]

Corn has always played a part in mainstream American culture as well, featured in many art works of the nineteenth and twentieth centuries. Early corn scene painters were William Sidney Mount, George Inness, Seth Eastman, Nathaniel Currier, and James Ives, as well as Winslow Homer with his famous illustrations of corn scenes in *Harper's Weekly* and Andrew Wyeth with *Corn Seed* and *Winter Corn*. Among the most prolific artists of corn was native Iowan Grant Wood, who produced at least seven paintings on corn and four walls of murals in the Corn Room of a hotel in Council Bluffs, Iowa.[33] The noted Chicano poet and muralist, José Antonio Burciaga, has created a fifteen-by-twelve-foot mural at a Stanford University residency hall, featuring the mythology and history of corn, in which the images of a man and a woman emerge from a central sun surrounded by figures of corn and indigenous peoples and animals.

Maize has two museums devoted exclusively to it: the recently opened Museo de Maiz in Matamoros, Mexico, and the magnificent Corn Palace in Mitchell, South Dakota. Here one may find large, changing mosaics made of actual corn, depicting corn culture.[34] The eminent corn scientists, such as Paul W. Weatherwax and George W. Beadle, are fascinated not only with its genetic history, but with its cultural and artistic manifestations as well. Paul Christoph Mangelsdorf (1899–1989), the geneticist who devoted his entire life to the study of corn, called it "a cereal treasure of immensely greater value than the spices which Columbus traveled so far to seek" and donated his considerable thirty-year collection of corn-abilia to the North Carolina State University at Raleigh, a permanent exhibit ranging from plastic corn-shaped harmonicas to a sixteenth-century Chinese ivory ear of corn. Another botanist, Walton Galinet, professing "Corn is my religion, and this laboratory is my church," sends Christmas cards illustrated with corn stalks with the message: "The birth of maize—a rebirth for man." It was Galinet who strove and succeeded, in perhaps the most iconic of American symbols, in creating a breed of corn that produced red and white stripes with blue dots on each kernel for the 1976 bicentennial. Corn-belt states have placed corn shucks on official state seals, and ears of corn adorn the columns of the national Capitol building. In fact, on the four-hundredth anniversary of Columbus's landing, maize was adopted as the national flower of the United States.[35]

This entitlement of corn, especially in its public use as national or state icon, acknowledges the primacy of corn agriculture for North American historical development. What American child is not aware of the legend of the first Thanksgiving feast with the Indian gifts of turkey, corn, and pumpkin squash?[36] This harvest festival in its present form symbolizes the importance of native foods (including the cranberry) and not insignificantly the role of native peoples as well, a feature not found in any other U.S. national holiday. However, native foods did not enter American cuisine in the cookbooks until the publication of *American Cookery* in 1796, featuring "Indian pudding" and

"Indian slapjacks" made of corn; the previous books were really English cook-books published in America.[37]

As corn made its way onto the American dinner table, another issue arose that speaks to the unease associated with corn: How do you eat an ear of corn politely? This topic is still debated in books of etiquette. What guidance is offered by the complex of values known as *table manners*? Some insert tiny forks in each end; others slice the kernels off the ear and then eat them. Still others simply pick it up with their hands and chew it right off the cob. The symbolic importance is that the ear of corn occasions an act of self-identification with either the elite or the hoi polloi.

American folk songs document the ambivalent attitude toward corn. In these two examples, from "Lane County Bachelor," the protagonist pines for a better life:

Farewell to Lane County, farewell to the West,
I'll travel back East to the girl I love best,
I'll stop at Missouri and get me a wife,
And live on corn dodgers, the rest of my life.

and from "An Arkansaw Traveler," the complaint:

He fed me on corn dodger that was hard as any rock,
Till my teeth began to loosen and my knees began to knock.
And I got so thin on sassafras tea I could hide behind a straw.
You bet I was a different lad when I left old Arkansaw.[38]

As we see from these examples, corn can represent either poverty or abundance, but in whatever state its role in popular song appears to be comic. In the first song, its use is ironic: even if the young man must live on corn, he will return, while in the second, eating corn is part of the suffering the traveler undergoes. But as the country developed, the idea of linking corn with abundance began to dominate. Along with the spirit of nationalism and Manifest Destiny, corn was increasingly linked to county fair and state fair exhibits that advertised and flaunted abundance. Americans took pride in the vastness of their continent. Along with this attitude came practical jokes, tall tales, boasting, and exaggeration. Farmers bragged about the giant size of their corn. Popular multicolored postcards began to appear with improbable portrayals, such as a huge ear of corn filling a single railroad flatcar. In local fairs, huge ears in straight rows with absolute uniformity of color won prizes.

Corn was featured at the Centennial Exposition of 1876, at the World's Columbian Exposition held in Chicago, Illinois, in 1893 to celebrate the four-hundredth anniversary of the historic voyages of Christopher Columbus, and at the Louisiana Purchase Exposition held at St. Louis, Missouri, in 1904. This showcasing of corn was evidence of intentional symbolizing of a region and its industry. The period between 1900 and 1920 was the golden age of the corn show. Schools of agriculture and state governments organized corn trains that traveled around giving out the latest scientific information to farmers concerning seed corn and growing techniques. County fairs featured corn-shucking contests and the coronation of Corn Queens.[39]

One of the most impressive influences of corn has been on American regionalisms and slang. *The Dictionary of American Regional English* lists over 130 terms and phrases associated with corn.[40] Many of these deal with agricultural implements or activities, such as festivals or celebrations: corn boiling, corn shucking, corn song, and corn chuck, a minstrel dance. Others cover corn foods, notably cornbread, with fourteen varieties in Texas alone, ranging from corn dodger to hasty pudding.

Aside from these primarily descriptive connotations, the value of corn is noted in expressions such as using the word corn to signify money or a vote (used in the seventeenth century, when balloting was done by casting corn and beans, "corn" meaning a favorable vote and beans the contrary) or "corn freight" as opposed to the less valuable "grass freight." To "feel one's corn" signifies to feel energetic, while to "be corned with oneself" means to be pleased. Several expressions use corn humorously to describe various weather conditions: "corn twister" (drought), "corn weather" (July and August), "corn wind" (no wind), and "corn wagon" (a clap of rolling thunder).

But the most expressive and common usages connote rustic, backward, banal, or clichéd, as in "corny," "cornball," "cornfed," "corn off the cob," and similarly when applied to a person, "corn husker," "corn tassel," "corn cracker." The expressions "corn punk" and "corn sweat" imply fake cures or deceptive practices. Another term derived from corn is the expletive "shucks," used to mean faking or worthless. Derisive terms applied to the human body include "cornstealer" (the hand), "cornsnorter" (the nose), and "cornsheller" (large front teeth). Similar expressions are "cornfield hand," that is, a slave field worker, lower in the hierarchy and thus applied to nonstandard speech, as well as "corn doctor" and "cornfield school." Several phrases employing corn terminology are classified as "underworld" slang: "cornfield clemency" (prison escape) and simply "corn" (to arrest, or bootleg whiskey). Sexual terms include "to cornhole" (anal intercourse) and, perhaps subliminally, "cornswoggled."

In these modern American expressions, clearly corn again is part of a conceptual domain that identifies "creatures who eat corn" contemptuously. These people include seemingly the boorish backwoodsman or farmer, the barbarous Indian, and the shiftless slave; in these usages it is not the European but the American people themselves who convey these interpretations. The use of

Fig. 3.3. Dekalb Acres of Gold advertisement, c. 1940s.

metonymy in this instance would seem not to make sense, given the recognized importance of corn in American culture, but the existence of "corny" presupposes the acceptance of the Old World views.

While recognizing the endurance of latent negative views toward corn as suitable food, we must also note the American crusaders who championed it. The greatest of these were the Kellogg brothers of Battle Creek, Michigan. The older brother was John Harvey Kellogg, a medical doctor who worked out a health philosophy in which food played a major role. Dr. Kellogg embarked on a series of experiments to find a way to make wheat more digestible. He hit on the idea of making wheat flakes, which enjoyed a modest success. Then his younger brother, Will Kellogg, began to develop a product that would become synonymous with breakfast for many Americans—cornflakes. It turned out that Will Kellogg's genius was not as a nutritionist, but as an advertiser. He dreamed up the idea of putting a cornflakes girl, "Sweetheart of the Corn," on every box. Young and beautiful, she embraced a corn shock and suggested a lifestyle of health and wholesomeness. The box of cornflakes with Will Kellogg's own personal signature became an American icon.[41]

If cornflakes suggest wholesomeness and nutrition, perhaps corn's most popularized form—popcorn—suggests entertainment. What could be more American than popcorn and the movies? The secret of making good popcorn is in using the right variety of corn. Different from regular sweet corn, popcorn must have very hard hulls. As the popcorn is heated, the starch inside the skin of the kernel builds up steam until it breaks out in a burst. This heating process will not work with other types of corn because the skin is too soft: the steam will just leak out gradually. In the process of popping corn, the sacred, the nutritious, makes way for the beautiful, in the transformation of corn into its magical cloudlike puffs. Early Amerindians used popcorn to make necklaces and ornaments; today we often string it up to decorate Christmas trees, along with that other American fruit, cranberries. In this form, corn enters the cultural domain of family events and popular entertainments. Another iconic American invention, baseball, is closely associated with popcorn in the form of "crackerjack," as the song "Take Me Out to the Ball Game" says: "Buy me some peanuts and crackerjack/I don't care if I ever get back."[42] In 1893 two popcorn vendors from Germany, F. W. Rueckheim and his brother Louis, wanted to boost their sales at the World's Fair in Chicago. They created a successful product initially called, inconveniently, "caramelized popcorn with peanuts." Three years after its invention, in 1896 a salesman was chewing on a handful, when he explained, "That's a crackerjack," simply a popular slang phrase of the 1890s. The Rueckheim brothers liked the name, and it became official. In those days, the product was distributed loose in huge wooden buckets. Customers could buy as much or as little as they wished. The next big marketing breakthrough came in 1899; it was the idea of selling the product in small, moisture-proof boxes. Then in 1912 came the idea of putting a prize in each box. Children would dig through the box first to find the prize; they would eat the Cracker Jacks later.[43]

If corn were only found in a few brand-name products such as Kellogg's Corn Flakes and Cracker Jacks, then it might be of marginal interest. But corn is found in an astonishing array of products. In her brilliant book *Much Depends on Dinner*, Margaret Visser argues that corn is the "driving wheel" of the North American supermarket. To be sure, Visser was not the first to point out the importance of the supermarket in American culture. In 1955, the *Silver Jubilee Supermarket Cook Book* told us that "the supermarket is a symbol of America's attainment of a high standard of living through democracy, and is so looked upon as one of the greatest institutions of the world."[44] That same year a special issue of *Life* described shopping in supermarkets as "a major weekly ritual of American family life . . . filled with commerce, confusion, and lurking peril [that] swarms with preschool dynamos who crouch among the flour sacks, yip at elders in search of wheat germ, upset symmetrical towers of canned beans or seek to gash themselves on bargain knives."[45]

What Margaret Visser points out is that nearly everything sold there has been touched in some way by corn. Because American livestock and poultry is fed and fattened on corn, meat is largely corn. Corn oil is important in margarine, soap, insecticides, mayonnaise, and salad dressing. Visser explains that corn syrup is the basis of candy, ketchup, and commercial ice cream. Corn starch is found in baby foods, jams, pickles, vinegar, and yeast. Because corn starch is white, odorless, tasteless, and easily shaped, it is found in headache tablets, toothpastes, cosmetics, detergents, dog food, and charcoal briquettes. At the supermarket—aisle by aisle and shelf by shelf—it seems that everything depends, one way or another, on corn.

Given this story of corn, the gold and the dross, we see its vitality as food and symbol in the totality of the Americas. What is important to consider is that because of corn's primacy in American history and in American markets, our view of corn remains linked to a multivalent perspective on the United States itself, a nation peopled by "creatures who eat corn," forever fixing our destiny to that wondrous New World grain.

## Notes

1. Reay Tannahill, *Food in History* (New York: Stein and Day, 1973), 258–59, 286–89. Only in Spain's northwest region of Galicia is corn a common and welcome food, generally found in the form of cornbread.
2. Antonello Gerbi, *The Dispute of the New World: The History of a Polemic, 1750–1900* (Pittsburgh: Univ. of Pittsburgh Press, 1973), 3–34; see also among many others: Howard Mumford Jones, *O Strange New World* (New York: Viking, 1964); the two volumes of *First Images of America:*

*The Impact of the New World on the Old,* ed. Fredi Chiappelli (Berkeley: Univ. of California Press, 1976); Tzvetan Todorov, *The Conquest of America: The Question of the Other* (New York: Harper and Row, 1984).

3. Hugh Honour, *The New Golden Land: European Images of America from the Discoveries to the Present Time* (New York: Pantheon, 1975).

4. Gonzalo Fernández de Oviedo, *Historia general y natural de las Indias* (Seville, 1535). See Margaret T. Hodgen, "The Problem of Savagery," *Early Anthropology in the Sixteenth and Seventeenth Centuries* (Philadelphia: Univ. of Pennsylvania Press,1964), 354–85.

5. Burke, *Language as Symbolic Action: Essays on Life, Literature, and Method* (Berkeley: Univ. of California Press, 1966), 359–79.

6. Cited in Samuel Eliot Morison, *Journals and Other Documents on the Life and Voyages of Christopher Columbus* (New York: Heritage), 72–73. Morison notes that James B. McNair in Botany Leaflets no. 14 of the Field Museum of Natural History (1930) believes this to be the earliest European reference to maize.

7. Ibid., 235; the letter was translated into Latin and published at Pavia, c. 1494.

8. Paul Weatherwax, *Indian Corn in Old America* (New York: Macmillan, 1954), 10–11;13–14.

9. Burke, *Philosophy of Literary Form* (Berkeley: Univ. of California Press, 1957), 253–62.

10. Richard A. Lanham, *A Handlist of Rhetorical Terms* (Berkeley: Univ. of California Press, 1969), 116.

11. See Jonathan Culler, "The Turns of Metaphor," in *The Pursuit of Signs: Semiotics, Literature, Deconstruction* (Ithaca, N.Y.: Cornell Univ. Press, 1981), 188–209, who discusses the uses and definitions of metaphor and metonymy as "response."

12. David Sapir and J. Christopher Crocker, *The Social Use of Metaphor* (Philadelphia: Univ. of Pennsylvania Press, 1977), 4.

13. Weatherwax, *Indian Corn in Old America,* 34–35.

14. See Arturo Warman, *La historia de un bastardo: maíz y capitalismo* (Mexico: Fondo de Cultura Económica, 1988).

15. John J. Finan, "Maize in the Great Herbals," *Missouri Botanical Garden Annals* 35 (1948): 156.

16. Cited in Weatherwax, *Indian Corn in Old America,* 45.

17. Sophie D. Coe, *America's First Cuisines* (Austin: Univ. of Texas Press, 1994), 14–15.

18. John Gerard's *The herbal or generall historie of plants* (London, 1597) cited in Marcus Woodward, *Leaves from Gerard's Herball* (New York: Dover, 1969), 266.

19. Marta Portal, *El maíz; Grano sagrado de America* (Madrid: Cultura Hispanica, 1970), 41–42. She also notes that in Provençal, it was called

"ble de Guinee" or "blad de Barbarie," terms that highlight its use in the slave trade.

20. Gonzalo Fernández de Oviedo, *Sumario de la natural historia de las Indias* (Mexico: Fondo de Cultura Economica, 1950), 169–72.

21. José de Acosta, *Historia natural y moral de las Indias* (Mexico: Fondo Cultural Economico, 1962), 169–72.

22. Cited in Weatherwax, *Indian Corn in Old America*, 25.

23. Alfred W. Crosby, *The Columbian Exchange: Biological and Cultural Consequences of 1492* (Westport, Conn.: Greenwood Press, 1972), 170.

24. "World Corn Supply and Disappearance," *Corn Annual* (1993): 11.

25. Harold E. Driver, *Indians of North America* (Chicago: Univ. of Chicago Press, 1961), 38–39; Olivia Vlahos, *New World Beginnings: Indian Cultures in the Americas* (New York: Viking, 1970), 153–61.

26. Driver, *Indians of North America*, 85–86; 289–90.

27. Weatherwax, *Indian Corn in Old America*, 58.

28. Miguel Leon-Portilla, *Pre-Columbian Literatures of Mexico* (Norman: Univ. of Oklahoma Press, 1969), 31–32, 66. For a study discussing the symbolism of the corn flower in Náhuatl culture, see Doris Heyden, *Mitología y simbolismo de la flor en el mexico prehispánico* (Mexico: Universidad Nacional Autonoma, 1985), 53–67.

29. *Popol Vuh: The Mayan Book of the Dawn of Life*, trans. Dennis Tedlock (New York: Simon and Schuster, 1985), 164.

30. Paul G. Zolbrod, "Poetry and Culture: The Navaho Example," *Smoothing the Ground: Essays on Native American Oral Literature*, ed. Brian Swann (Berkeley: Univ. of California Press, 1983), 234.

31. Stith Thompson, *Tales of the North American Indians* (Bloomington: Indiana Univ. Press, 1929), 51–52.

32. Benjamin A. Botkin, *A Treasury of American Folklore* (New York: Crown, 1944), 599–602.

33. Nicholas P. Hardeman, *Shucks, Shocks, and Hominy Blocks* (Baton Rouge: Louisiana State Univ. Press, 1981), 227–28; for more works on corn, see his extensive bibliography; another useful bibliography is Enrique Florescano and Alejandra Moreno Toscano, *Bibliografía general del maíz en Mexico* (Mexico: Instituto Nacional de Antropología é Historia, 1987).

34. See Robert E. Rhoades, "The Golden Grain of Corn," *National Geographic* 183 (6) (June 1993): 92–117.

35. Hardeman, *Shucks, Shocks, and Hominy Blocks,* 12, 28–29, 212, 227–28.

36. *Encyclopedia Britannica* 21 (1968), 940–41, cites a letter of Edward Winslow of December 11, 1621, who describes the three-day harvest festival ordered by Gov. William Bradford, in which the feast consists of wild fowl killed by the company and deer brought by the Indians. Celebrated since the late eighteenth century, the feast was not declared a national holiday until 1941.

37. Esther B. Aresty, *The Delectable Past* (New York: Simon and Schuster, 1964), 182–83.
38. Cited in Jan Harold Brunvand, "Folk Costumes and Foods," *The Study of American Folklore* (New York: W. W. Norton, 1968), 292.
39. Margaret Visser, *Much Depends on Dinner* (New York: Grove, 1986), 47.
40. Frederic G. Cassidy, ed., *The Dictionary of American Regional English* (Cambridge: Harvard Univ. Press, 1985).
41. Visser, *Much Depends on Dinner*, 421–44.
42. Written by Albert Von Tilzer in 1908, cited in Charles Hamm, *Yesterdays: Popular Song in America* (New York: W. W. Norton, 1983), 325.
43. Linda Shrieves, "Cracker Jack Celebrates Centennial," *New Brunswick (N.J.) Home News*, Aug. 25, 1993.
44. Jane and Michael Stern, *Encyclopedia of Pop Culture* (New York: Harper-Collins, 1992), 492.
45. Ibid., 292.

# Angus Kress Gillespie

"I don't rightly recall whether we had cranberries that first Thanksgiving. Oh, I do love them and all, but my mind was on other things. I'm not even sure we had turkey," said Priscilla Alden in a quotation attributed to her on a prominent plaque at the Cranberry World Visitors Center in Plymouth, Massachusetts. The fact that she could not remember for sure does not affect the basic American mythic and emotional link to the cranberry. Just as New England, correctly or incorrectly, dominates American history, so does the cranberry, deservedly or not, stand out among American plants.

Because cranberries are difficult to grow and largely unprofitable in their natural state, cranberry farmers must be resourceful and ingenious. Thus, cranberry farming is the very essence of Yankee ingenuity. It is true that incredible advancements have been made in the technology that applies to the cranberry industry. It is also true that the cranberry farmer takes full advantage of the research that has been done on soils, weeds, pests, and temperature control.[1] Reading about these advances in the library, I had mistakenly assumed that all of the risks had been taken out of cranberry farming. After a while, I drove down to the sparsely populated cranberry wetlands. What I didn't quite understand was that the fundamental growing of consistently high yields of cranberries is nearly as confounding today as it was one hundred years ago.

Cranberry farmers take pride in their ability to deal with and overcome adversity. One elderly South Jersey cranberry farmer told me, "The only job down here worse than growing cranberries is driving schoolbuses." Farmers complain about the twin problems of weed control and insect control: they struggle with herbicide-resistant weeds and pesticide-resistant insects. But the worst problem in recent years has been coping with an avalanche of regulatory restrictions. Some of the troublesome regulations grew out of legitimate environmental concerns. Others grew out of what farmers see as frivolous environmental nit-picking. Still others arose because of urban and suburban encroachment on agricultural lands.

"If it's not one thing, it's another," says Edward V. Lipman, a second-generation South Jersey cranberry farmer. "There's more to this business than meets the eye." He goes on to explain that, despite the technological advancements that have been made, cranberry farming is still weather-dependent. The growing season in South Jersey runs from May 1 to August 31. The rainfall during this period is crucial. In 1988 there was too little rain; in 1989, too much.[2] For the American cranberry farmer, success is never a given. There are too many variables, too many uncertainties. Perhaps when we Americans think of cranberries, we should think not only about Thanksgiving, but also about the entrepreneurial skills of the cranberry farmer. Indeed, studying the cranberry suggests that overcoming hardships and difficulties is as American as, well, cranberry juice cocktail.

My inquiry into the meaning of the cranberry began with my own recollections of what I learned in grammar school. The story of the American began with the Pilgrims and the Mayflower Compact. A hardy band of English settlers fought to subdue the wilderness. With the aid of God and the help of the Indians, they succeeded. To celebrate their success, the Pilgrims staged the first Thanksgiving in 1621. The historical record is sketchy, but Americans *believe* that the cranberry was served at that event, along with wild turkey, succotash, squash, and cornbread. Like everyone else, I believed it too.

## Legend and Lore

Since more than three hundred years have passed since that first Thanksgiving, it is difficult to sort out the facts from the legend. In many elementary school textbooks, there are romanticized paintings, which can be misleading. Typically, the Pilgrims are shown elegantly dressed. But the ten months of struggle that killed half of the original settlers must have been hard on their clothing also. Typically, the table is set with knives, forks, and spoons. But we know that, except for knives, there were no utensils. It was customary to eat with your fingers from wooden platters or to scoop up food with crude clamshell spoons. Typically, one sees a log cabin in the background. But we know that Pilgrim homes were made from hewn planks.

What we do know with reasonable certainty is that the Pilgrims celebrated their first harvest in 1621 with a three-day banquet, interrupted with tests of skill and games of strength. They had asked their Indian friend and ally Chief Massasoit to join them. They must have been surprised when he arrived with ninety extra uninvited guests, all hungry warriors. Contrary to the sentimental paintings, no Indian women joined the feast. Certainly the event was not easy on Plymouth's five women, who had to serve 145 revelers. Whether or not cranberry sauce was served, it seems certain that they enjoyed eel, lobster, and shellfish—washed down with large quantities of homemade wine.

It was the most important meal at the very beginning of American history. And it took place in New England—the dominant region in traditional U.S. history.[3]

In modern America, it has become an almost universal family custom to serve a Thanksgiving meal that replicates the original Pilgrim celebration. The custom is so widespread that folklorist Barre Toelken chose to delineate it in some detail as a textbook example of an American "folk event." One family whose customs were recorded in detail was the Kimball family in rural central Massachusetts. A typical Thanksgiving dinner, he reported, would have a large turkey, sweet potatoes, small stewed onions, squash, and peas. Plus two kinds of cranberry sauce, fine and chunky. In some ways Thanksgiving makes an ideal event for study, since it seems to be a truly national holiday that transcends religious, regional, and ethnic limitations.[4] From time to time an iconoclast may suggest a change in our holiday customs. For example, Calvin Trillin once facetiously suggested a national campaign to have the traditional Thanksgiving dish changed from turkey to spaghetti carbonara, but no one took him seriously.[5]

When we think of American intellectual history, we think of Emerson, Thoreau, and Hawthorne. For many years, the field of American studies was really New England studies. If we had drawn a map of the United States as it existed in the minds of American studies scholars, New England would have appeared as a huge area, reaching far out into the Atlantic Ocean, with the rest of the country tiny by comparison. We studied New England because it was white, Anglo-Saxon, and Protestant. But most of all we studied it because it was important, or so it seemed.[6]

Because the cranberry was indigenous to America and because of its historical links to the earliest settlers, the cranberry enjoys a unique status. Like the other plants in this book, the cranberry conveys messages and has symbolic meanings. To begin with, the cranberry is inextricably embedded in the history of New England. Even today there is the widespread assumption that the cranberry must be a part of the menu of any New England restaurant that serves authentic local food. One such restaurant is Ma Glockner's in North Bellingham, Massachusetts. It is a great place for those who have a hard time making up their minds: all menu choices have already been made. You get half a chicken, fried in butter, with french fries, salad, and large hot cinnamon buns. Plus, of course, cranberry sauce.[7]

Anyone intrigued by the early history of the cranberry would be well advised to read Fredrika A. Burrows's *Cannonballs and Cranberries*, a brief and accessible account. Burrows points out that long before the Pilgrims landed at Plymouth Rock, cranberries had been used in North America for food and medicine. Scattered references to the cranberry are made in some of the early writings of the sixteenth and seventeenth centuries.

As early as 1550, James White Norwood's diary makes reference to Indians using cranberries. Another early explorer was James Rosier, whose book *The Land of Virginia*, published in England in 1605, contains an account of his coming ashore and being presented with birch bark cups of these berries. Later, in 1640, Roger Williams wrote *Key Into the Language of America*, where he describes cranberries, calling them "bearberries" because they were eaten by bears.[8]

Burrows also recounts a local historical legend, explaining how cranberries came to grow in Massachusetts. According to the legend, the Rev. Richard Bourne, a preacher and early settler on Cape Cod, got involved in an argument with an Indian medicine man. Not surprisingly, each religious leader thought that his own belief system was more truthful and more powerful. To prove his superiority, the irate medicine man cast a spell so that Bourne became stuck in the sand. After much argument, an agreement was reached: the minister would be turned loose only if he could defeat the medicine man in a battle of wits. The contest dragged on for fifteen days. Both men were clever; neither would yield.

During all this fierce debate, Bourne was sustained by a white dove that flew down from time to time, placing a juicy red cranberry in his mouth. In frustration, the medicine man watched the dove render aid to the minister. The Indian tried to place a spell on the dove to prevent the assistance, but his magic would not work. At last, the Indian, weak from fatigue, dehydrated, and hungry, gave up and set the minister free.

According to the legend, during the dove's many flights of mercy, some of the cranberries fell to the ground. There they took root in the sand. Somehow, they flourished and expanded. And so that was the beginning of cranberries in Massachusetts.[9]

To be sure, years later, cranberries would be grown elsewhere, but their legendary and symbolic beginnings were rooted in Massachusetts. Perhaps the earliest full description of the cranberry was written by John Josselyn in his *New England Rarities Discovered* in 1672. The passage gives us proof of the cranberry's value to the early settlers. It describes both the nutritional and medicinal uses of the cranberry:

> Sauce for the Pilgrims—Cranberry or Bearberry (because the Bears use much to feed upon them) is a small trayling plant that grows in salt

marshes that are overgrown with moss. The berries are a pale yellow color, afterwards red, as big as a cherry, some perfectly round, others oval, all of them hollow with sour astringent taste; they are ripe in August and September. They are excellent against the Scurvy. They are also good to allay the fervor of Hoof-Diseases.

The English and the Indians use them much, boyling them with sugar for Sauce to eat with their meat; and it is a delicate sauce, especially with Roasted Mutton. Some make tarts with them as with Gooseberries.[10]

The colonists knew that the American cranberry was a fruit of great potential value. They knew it was superior in size, quality, and taste to its European counterpart. So in 1677, the colonists sent ten barrels of cranberries to King Charles II. The berries were sent "along with two hogsheads of semp [cracked Indian corn] and 3,000 codfish." The shipment was part of an effort to mollify Charles II for having coined the Pine Tree shilling.[11]

A survey of the literature reveals many testimonials—some brief and pithy, others rhetorical and overblown. As an example of the latter, consider the remarks of John Leverett, "Of all the pleasures which ornamented my installation as president of Harvard in 1706, none exceeded in delight the serving of beauteous cranberries."[12]

Not only were cranberries considered beautiful; they were also considered healthful. Barrels of cranberries, packed in spring water, were stored in the holds of New England ships. Sailors learned that including cranberries in their diet helped to prevent scurvy. Just as English "limeys" ate limes to ward off the dread disease, so American sailors ate cranberries. In Herman Melville's *Moby-Dick*, the tyrannical character of Captain Ahab is revealed very early by the remark of one whaler, "Go out with the crazy Captain Ahab? Never! He flat refused to take cranberries aboard. A man could get scurvy, or worse, whaling with the likes of 'im."[13] During the settlement of the American West, scurvy was also found to be a health problem in the logging camps. Before long, loggers as well as sailors were given a ration of cranberries.[14] In addition, cranberries are mentioned in the diaries from the Lewis and Clark expedition to explore the Northwest Territory. When the explorers reached the lower Columbia River, they found cranberries growing wild on the Clatsop Plain, and they arranged to buy some from the Indians.[15]

So the cranberry is fixed in the American memory as both beautiful and healthful, but there is also a dark side, a dangerous side. Like the sirens of Greek mythology, who by their sweet singing lured mariners to destruction on the rocks surrounding their island, the cranberry sometimes tempted men to their doom. John Slocume of Taunton in Plymouth Colony in 1651 could not resist wandering off from his berry-picking party to search for more of the alluring berries. He never returned, and it was generally assumed that he fell victim to a bear or a wildcat.[16]

## Symbolic Fruit

Beauty, health, and danger—a complex significance for a tart, red, marsh berry. Though the cranberry is heavily invested with symbolic and patriotic meanings, it has no official standing as an American icon. At the present time, the United States does have a national bird but no national fruit. Actually, there has been some discussion of such a designation. In 1982 the cherry industry asked Congress to designate the cherry as the official national fruit. All over the country, journalists were delighted to take on this apparently frivolous issue. The apple growers joined the fray, arguing that the phrase "American as apple pie" settled the matter.

Bob Taylor, the editor of *Cranberries: The National Cranberry Magazine*, also got involved in the argument. Taylor wrote, "We have no grudge against the cherry. It can claim a certain association with America. It was a cherry tree that George Washington chopped down, wasn't it? Cherries do make for a great pie. And what would a Manhattan cocktail be without a maraschino? But the official U.S. fruit? No, no. If a U.S. fruit is to be named, the cherry will have to take its place in line, behind the cranberry."[17]

The cranberry differs from the other classic "American" fruits. It is unlike the cherry or the apple, both of which grow on trees and are comparatively bigger, more juicy, more luscious. The humble cranberry grows on low-lying, bushlike vines. Indeed, there are several dichotomies which work to the disadvantage of the cranberry in this comparison: big/little, sweet/sour, soft/hard, tree/vine, orchard/bog. What does history show? Well, the cranberry is as old as America itself. It has been with us a long time. It has been functionally and aesthetically satisfying. If we struggle to make a case for the cranberry as a national fruit, we could point out that the cranberry's identity is what Americans have made it. The apple and the cherry came to us as ready-made symbols, suggesting abundance and ease of cultivation, while the cranberry has required consistent effort over a long period of time.

So the cranberry has not been designated the official U.S. fruit, nor would it be likely to be a heavy contender if Congress were ever able to address the issue. In this chapter, we shall explore briefly the botany and history of the cranberry because of the challenge of the special traditional agricultural methods required for its cultivation. We shall also investigate the problems that had to be solved before the tangy, but very hard, cranberry found its way into our diet. Unlike strawberries and blueberries, which are delicious right off the vine, for most people the cranberry must be treated and processed to become edible. All of this depends on appropriate recipe knowledge and cooking skills.

How did the cranberry win acceptance into the American diet? It helped that the cranberry had appealing taste and color. It helped that the cranberry had physiological benefits. But it is quite clear that the English settlers were most influenced by their exposure to the Indians' eating habits. The necessity of making their way in a new land led them to observe the Indians carefully and to imitate their example.[18]

A cursory survey of the literature indicates that hundreds of cranberry recipes can be located in dozens of serious hardbound cookbooks. Little purpose would be served in reciting them here. However, a few points should be made.

For one thing, the cranberry has a definite place in *American* cuisine. Any cookbook that has pretensions to surveying American cookery must at some point deal with the cranberry. Take, for example, Jeff Smith's best-selling *The Frugal Gourmet Cooks American,* a companion to his thirty-nine-part national television series. Smith is completely open about the content of his book: "It's an attempt at cooking patriotism," he says. The book is organized by regions, so the cranberry section, complete with a historical discussion in addition to the recipes themselves, is grouped with other New England foods like maple syrup and the pumpkin (which is the subject of Tad Tuleja's chapter in this volume). The author feels that most Americans have a culinary inferiority complex, always bowing to Europe, but he constantly exhorts his readers to take pride in American cuisine. Significantly, Smith writes in his acknowledgments, "I offer up a cranberry pie to Mom. (You thought I was going to say apple pie, didn't you? She would prefer cranberry pie.)"[19]

Another category of cookbook is of interest here. I refer to the paperback booklet, devoted exclusively to cranberry recipes. In my research I have come across two of these—a thirty-two-page booklet from Massachusetts and a thirty-six-page booklet from New Jersey.[20] With persistence, I feel sure that others could be located. They do make interesting reading since they show considerable ingenuity and flexibility in the use of the cranberry. They go way beyond mere cranberry sauce. They embrace the entire cranberry culinary spectrum from bread and cakes, through cookies and crisps, through jellies and jams, through muffins and pies, through salads and main dishes, to desserts and beverages.

As I went through hundreds of cranberry recipes, one thing became abundantly clear: the widespread popularity of the cranberry in modern America can be attributed in large part to sugar's way of making the cranberry more palatable. Whether we are talking about the commercial manufacture of prepared and processed cranberry sauce or the lovingly prepared homemade cranberry pie, it is sugar that makes it possible to eat. Anthropologist Sidney W. Mintz has pointed out that refined sugar is the very symbol of the modern and the industrial and that development has meant, among other things, a steady increase in sugar consumption.[21] The rest of the food plants discussed in this book, save pumpkins, can be eaten and enjoyed without the addition of sugar, but not the cranberry.

## Vines and Bogs

Botanically, the cranberry is known as *Vaccinium macrocarpon* Ait. The cranberry is one of only three native American fruits. The other two are the Concord grape and the blueberry, both of which were seriously considered as possible additional chapters for this book. Alas, as in any undertaking like this, certain boundaries must be set. Berries similar to cranberries do grow in many of the swamps of northern Asia and central Europe, but they are described as inferior in size and flavor to those grown in America.[22]

The cranberry grows on low-lying vines, which need acid-peat soil, a top layer of sand, and an ample supply of fresh water. The most celebrated and well-known bogs are, of course, in Massachusetts. At the present time, Massachusetts is the leading cranberry-producing state in the United States. With about eleven thousand acres under cranberry cultivation, Massachusetts produces almost 40 percent of all U.S. cranberries.[23]

Right behind Massachusetts (and gaining) in cranberry production is the state of Wisconsin. With about seven thousand acres under cranberry cultivation, Wisconsin produces 30 percent of the entire U.S. cranberry crop. Soon it may catch up with Massachusetts. The historical record shows that cranberries were well known to the Algonquin Indians of Wisconsin, who called the little red berry "atoqua." They harvested the berries, which grew wild in the marshes of that state. When the first settlers arrived in Wisconsin, some of them were already familiar with the berry, which had also grown wild in Massachusetts. In 1828 a New Englander who had come to Green Bay to make his fortune took eight boats loaded with cranberries from Green Bay to Galena, Illinois. There he traded the berries for provisions to supply an encampment of Indian shinglemakers working at the mouth of the Yellow River in Juneau County.[24]

Third in cranberry production is the state of New Jersey. New Jersey produces about 10 percent of the U.S. crop. Other producers include Oregon, Washington, and British Columbia. Long before there were white settlers in the area of what is now New Jersey, the Leni-Lenape Indians used the wild berries for food and medicine. One of the earliest references to cranberries in New Jersey appeared in a letter written by an early settler in Burlington, New Jersey, to his brother in England. The letter, written by Mahon Stacy, was dated April 26, 1680. Among other things, Stacy wrote: "We have from the time called May until Michaelmas a great store of very good wild fruits as strawberries, cranberries, and hurtleberries. The cranberries, much like cherries for color and bigness, may be kept until fruit comes in again. An excellent sauce is made of them for venison, turkeys, and other great fowl and they are better to make tarts than either gooseberries or cherries. We have them brot to our homes by the Indians in great plenty."[25]

Though New Jersey is only third in cranberry production, it is the state that I know best. Before launching this investigation into the meaning of the cranberry in American culture, I was already familiar with the cranberry cultivation in New Jersey because of my field work in the Pine Barrens of New Jersey. Even so, I write on the New Jersey cranberry with some trepidation, since several of my friends and colleagues have already done so, with considerable style and insight. However, it is only fair to point out that the topic that has dominated most recent research on cranberries in New Jersey has been the environmental issue. My own aim differs in that I am trying to set the cranberry into a broadly cultural context. Nonetheless, I will summarize some of the regulatory battles that cranberry growers find themselves constantly fighting. To do so, we must first describe the Pinelands National Reserve.

## Cranberries and the Pine Barrens

In 1978 the U.S. Congress set up the country's first National Reserve in the Pine Barrens of New Jersey. This was an entirely new concept. The Pinelands National Reserve is different from National Parks, Forests, or Monuments. What it tries to do is to protect natural and cultural resources while allowing patterns of compatible human use and development. There is a fifteen-member Pinelands Commission, which attempts to manage the million-acre area by coordinating the actions of local, state, and federal governments. Human ecologists have argued that cranberry cultivation is a traditional nineteenth-century use of the land and therefore should be considered a compatible use. Others have argued that any human agricultural use is disruptive and should therefore be curbed. This is an important argument, highly political, with lasting consequences, but the scope of this chapter allows us only to review the literature briefly.

Let us begin with the work of Jonathan Berger and John W. Sinton, who have pinpointed the major stress point in environmental planning for the New Jersey cranberry region. Cranberry growing has been one of the traditional land-use patterns in the Pine Barrens. While cranberry growing is gentle on the landscape, it does have some impact. With considerable sympathy to both points of view, Berger and Sinton sketch the conflict between those who prefer a wilderness and those who would allow an indigenous industry to survive:

> People involved in outdoor recreation have an interest in clean water. Outsiders rely on the clean rivers a few days a year, hoping they will always remain free flowing and clean. Coming for a day's canoe trip on the Oswego, they see the Pine Barrens as "pristine"—uninhabited, wild, and clean except for litter. They want the Pines to remain exactly the same, but as a Piney said, "If you don't want 'em to change, better take a photograph, for they'll be different tomorrow." The insiders have a far different perspective.
>
> Outsiders are not the only ones who use the waters that flow in and out of the rivers. There are also residential and commercial users downstream in hamlets and towns, and there are the agricultural uses. "Clean" water is a relative concept, and "pristine" is a loaded term that scientists, lawyers, and planners on the Pinelands Commission have translated into

a precise standard, namely, water with a very low (.17 ppm) nitrogen concentrations suggesting little or no human activity in the area.

The major users of water in the Mullica/Batsto/Wading watersheds are cranberry growers, who need clean, but not pristine, water for their bogs. They must use pesticides and herbicides, so they contaminate the pristine quality of water flowing out of the bogs as does any farming enterprise. The water from cranberry bogs is still clean, meaning potable and capable of sustaining the unique habitats of the Pines, but cranberry growers have no use for outsiders' concepts of a pristine, uninhabited, and wild landscape.[26]

The cranberry bog landscape has been effectively described by folklorist Mary Hufford of the American Folklife Center. In an essay published by the Library of Congress, she points out that canoeists and hikers often perceive the cranberry region as a wilderness area, when in fact it is a working landscape. Cranberry bogs are subtle landscape features, so embedded in their surroundings that the outside viewer may not realize that they are humanmade. Of course, the truth is that a great deal of work is involved in constructing the bogs. Hufford summarized the findings of fieldworkers for the Pinelands Folklife Project. Here are the steps they reported:

1. Pick a spot near a stream.
2. Survey the property for elevations, to facilitate conservation of water.
3. Locate the reservoir at the top of the property.
4. Plan the bogs.
5. Ditch the first bog, using the sand to make dikes, which also serve as roads for machinery.
6. Push the trees out with large machinery. Salvage the cedar and pine.
7. Burn off useless vegetation.
8. Eliminate competitive root systems by inverting turf. Use turf to line the dikes.
9. Grade the bog. A bog should be within a half-inch of level for conservation of water.
10. Put in underground pipes for irrigation.
11. Plant the vines, forty to seventy thousand per acre.[27]

After these steps have been completed and the cranberry bog is in production, it appears to the casual observer to be almost entirely natural. The cranberry bog is so gentle on the landscape that it is almost invisible. It is unobtrusive in a way that crops like corn and tobacco, which are planted in rows, can never be.

With this concept of the "natural" bog in mind, let us turn to the work of

Mary Ann Thompson, a cranberry bog owner and manager of a company started by her great-grandfather more than one hundred years ago. A lawyer and political activist, no one knows better than Thompson the need for hard work and vigilance in keeping the water for her bogs clean and usable. In the last twenty years, Thompson has spoken out on the need for government intervention to help preserve the cranberry landscape. Not all of her neighbors and fellow bog owners agree. Some of them would prefer to avoid the inevitable hassle and red tape that government regulation always entails. Suffice it to say that it is an ongoing argument.

Thompson has described the cranberry region not as a wilderness, which it is not, but instead as a special cultural landscape with much planned-for open space. It is a place that has been created and managed by a few families over many years. She has lovingly described the historic villages and structures that one encounters there:

> The structures built for the cranberry industry became an integral part of the environment. As the swamps were cut off to set out bogs, the growers used the cedar wood for fences, shingles, siding on buildings and gates for dams. New impoundments for reservoirs insured water for remaining cedar swamps. The characteristic pine of the area, *Pinus rigidia*, was used for door and window frames, flooring and cranberry boxes and barrels. The buildings in the cranberry villages were spaced in order to achieve the maximum protection from numerous forest fires which swept through the Pine belt. . . .
>
> The prime example of integral buildings are the cranberry packing houses or sorting houses. Originally most cranberry sorting houses were located away from the bogs in town. Horse and mule-drawn wagons transported the berries from the woods into town where they were sorted. . . .
>
> Cranberry sorting houses are to cranberry villages what cathedrals were to medieval villages. Cranberry villages were centered around the packing house where everyone worked. Along with the screenhouse were workers' houses, tool sheds, storage barns, garages, and sometimes a company store. Workers' housing was available in multi-family and single cottages. The foreman lived in the best house. Generally multi-family structures were only used to house workers temporarily during the harvest season. The growers often referred to the housing as camps.[28]

There are 127 known varieties of cranberries, but the vast majority of these are selections from the wild berry with the scientific name *Vaccinium macrocarpon* Ait, mentioned above. Cranberry growers proudly point out that the bright red berry contains vitamin C and low amounts of sodium. They also state, "In its natural state, it is low in calories." This claim is perfectly true, but the cranberry is almost never eaten in its natural state. As pointed out earlier, the preparation of cranberries in actual recipes for consumption almost always requires the use of sugar.[29]

In any foodways research, a central question is always why people eat some plants and not others. In a book like this one, the question lurks in every chapter. One food consultant said, "What people eat is what food is available and what they've been taught to eat by their mothers."[30] Certainly this question was very much on my mind when I visited Cranberry World in Plymouth, Massachusetts, in the late fall of 1988.

## Cranberry World

Before my visit, I had feared that Cranberry World would be a tacky, commercialized tourist trap, with no redeeming educational value. The very name "Cranberry World" invoked the image of an amusement park with mechanized rides and costumed cartoon characters. I was wrong. The Cranberry World Visitors Center located on Water Street, just a half mile north of Plymouth Rock, is a carefully conceived, well-maintained mini-museum with a knowledgeable and helpful staff. The museum exhibits and artifacts, along with related displays and captions, tells a coherent story.

The Cranberry World Visitors Center, as it turned out, was an ideal place to continue my study of the cranberry and its cultivation. The museum tells the story, with pictures and words, of the environment, early history, harvesting, processing, and marketing of the cranberry.

One of the first growers was Henry Hall of Dennis, on Cape Cod, described as "a farmer-seaman-fisherman-saltmaker."[31] About 1810 Hall observed that the wild cranberries on his land grew better when sand from the beach blew over them. So he began transplanting the cranberry vines, taking care to protect them from his cattle by erecting fences. Then he would cover the vines with sand. The method worked. Gradually, others learned of Hall's success. And for the rest of the nineteenth century, many other Cape Cod residents took up cranberry farming.

The growth in cranberry acreage escalated after the Civil War. There was an economic depression in New England, brought about by the replacement of the old wooden sailing ships by iron steamships, the growth of rail shipping at the expense of sea shipping, and the decline of fishing. With the decline of ship building and fishing, the people took a new look at their bogs and marshes. What had been worthless land was now cleared and drained. When planted with cranberry vines, the land began to produce an income. One old ship captain, delighted with his new employment and ready cash, expressed his joy in poetry.

> There's nothing to me in foreign lands
> like the stuff grows in Cape Cod sands;
> there's nothing in sailing of foreign seas

equal to getting down on your knees
and pulling the pizzen ivy out.
I guess I knew what I was about
when I put by my chart and glass
and took to growing cranberry sass.[32]

Through a process of trial and error, drawing on Yankee ingenuity, the early growers learned how to perfect techniques of cranberry cultivation. Later, immigrants from all over the world, especially from the Cape Verde Islands and Finland, took part in developing the industry. Some of their descendants still live and work in Massachusetts. In 1988 the Cape Cod Cranberry Growers Association made a documentary video that is available at Cranberry World. The video featured some of these descendants, including two brothers, Wilho and Eino Harju of South Carver, whose parents had come from Finland in 1902. Also featured was Domingo Fernandes of Carver, whose grandfather had come over from the Cape Verde Islands.

Other exhibits at Cranberry World explain the evolution of the harvesting process. At first, cranberries were picked by hand. Cranberry scoops were the main implements. Workers got down on their knees in the bogs, in a long line across the section being harvested. Laboriously, they would push the scoops before them, gently combing the wooden teeth through the vines, removing the berries. The work was uncomfortable, awkward, and difficult. It was especially hard on the knees.

The harvesting exhibits make it clear that inducements had to be offered to the cranberry pickers beyond simple wages for picking. Employers tried hard to make the cranberry harvest into a social event. Nineteenth-century growers had to provide a dance hall and had to furnish at least part of the music for the pickers. Special trains were provided with reduced fares to bring pickers from the city to the bogs. Boardinghouse accommodations were provided. The recruiting literature tried hard to project a hospitable image. One Wisconsin grower in an 1884 poster promised, "We will pay as much as others do for the same kind of work. We will try to make our patrons as comfortable as we can."[33]

In the twentieth century, cranberry farmers continued to be resourceful and inventive in coming up with better harvesting methods. Everyone knew that cranberry scooping was dreadfully difficult work. The scoops were replaced by mechanical dry harvesting. Several types of mechanical harvesters were developed. Typically, the dry pickers look like large lawnmowers. These self-propelled machines are directed over the bogs, gently combing the berries from their vines by means of rotating metal teeth. The berries are carried by a small conveyor belt to a box or bag at the rear of the machine. Such berries picked at harvest time are usually marketed in their natural state as fresh fruit. Today cranberry scoops are most often used as items of rustic living-room decor rather than for actual scooping.

In modern times, dry harvesting still exists, especially for whole fruit. The dry harvesting method gives whole fruit a better shelf life. In most of areas of the United States, consumers can still buy whole fruit during the winter holiday season. Normally, it comes in small cellophane bags in the grocer's refrigerator. However, dry harvesting has mostly given way to wet harvesting, a method developed in Wisconsin. Growers prefer wet harvesting because it is more efficient. Using the water supply already available for irrigation (and frost protection), growers flood the bogs to a depth of one or two feet. Workers then guide self-propelled water reels, nicknamed egg beaters, around the bogs in a systematic pattern. The water reels stir up the water with considerable force. The turbulence loosens the berries, which then float to the surface, forming a brilliant red mass, ready for collecting. The resulting scene is most photogenic. Imagine a crisp autumn day with a clear blue sky above a crimson-colored lake, bordered with bright evergreens. It makes an unforgettable picture. Harvesters round up the berries bobbing on the surface with floating booms. Large conveyor belts then lift the berries into waiting trucks. The meaning of the evolution of the American cranberry harvesting techniques is quite clear. It is a tribute to the Yankee efficiency of the American farmer that he is now able to harvest more cranberries with less effort than ever before.

Once the cranberries are harvested, they must be processed. Several exhibits at Cranberry World explain what happens to the cranberries during this stage. At the receiving station, the berries are sorted. The good berries are separated from the bad ones. The basic separation process was discovered by

Fig. 4.1. Workers guiding self-propelled water reels, nicknamed "egg beaters," around a cranberry bog. Photograph by Angus Kress Gillespie.

an early *bricoleur*, John Webb, a New Jersey schoolteacher. Webb began moving wild cranberries from the swamps to humanmade bogs in 1843. It seems that Webb developed his own system for sorting cranberries. According to the story, which has been told and retold so many times that it might properly be considered a legend, he stored them in a loft, but his bad leg prevented him from carrying them down the stairs. The cranberries bounced down. At least the good berries bounced down: the rotten berries stayed behind. This makeshift sorting device became the basis for the later, more sophisticated machinery. In today's machinery, each berry has several chances to bounce over a four-inch-high wooden barrier. If the berry is bruised or rotten, it will not bounce. Such berries fall into a disposal bin.[34]

The very best cranberries are sorted out early in the process and sold as fresh fruit. Most of the rest of the cranberries are used for juice. Such berries enter large presses that squeeze out the juice, which contains high amounts of natural color, eliminating the need for artificial coloring. The remaining berries are generally cooked in large kettles and made into cranberry sauce or relish.

## Taming the Wild Berry

In the early days, the main problem was learning how to cultivate cranberries. After all, the Indians never even tried to cultivate them; they simply took advantage of the ones that grew wild. It took more than a hundred years of patient Yankee trial and error to learn how to cultivate the cranberry. There were times when cranberry growers became discouraged. Many of them felt that the cranberry was inherently a wild plant, and it could never be fully domesticated. The struggle was nicely summed up by Cornelius Weygandt in his book *Down Jersey* in 1940: "The cranberry submits to cultivation, but it retains that savour of wildness that is its by birthright. It cherishes that as a cat its spirit of independence. There are little things as well as great that cannot be tamed, cranberries and cats, as well as winds and waters."[35]

I had assumed that by the mid-twentieth century the cranberry grower's main problem was no longer growing cranberries. I theorized that the number-one problem would have been marketing the crop. In point of actual fact, my assumptions were only partly correct. Growers did recognize the importance of marketing. Gradually, the farmer's cooperative, Ocean Spray, became more and more important. Ocean Spray is owned by a group of independent farmers who have pooled their resources to market their fruit in an effective manner. The cranberry growers who own the Ocean Spray cooperative agree to deliver their fruit, and, in return, they receive research, marketing, processing, and distribution services. In other words, the growers delegate responsibility for marketing to the cooperative and its hired marketing specialists.

So the actual work of growing cranberries remains tricky and difficult. But there was a recognition on the part of the farmer that the job was not over when the cranberries were delivered to the processing plant. At this point marketing specialists took over. These experts reached the conclusion the only way to market bigger crops was to build a greater consumer demand. How they went about achieving that goal, and the setbacks they encountered, makes for a fascinating story.

Marketing experts discovered that cranberry festivals can attract broad audiences. Typically, such festivals were not indigenous harvest celebrations, but rather contrived, commercialized events. The historical record of early cranberry festivals is sketchy. The first such festival may have taken place in Wisconsin in 1936.[36] In any event, such festivals became increasingly popular and widespread, so that by 1948 there were quite a few, each with its own Cranberry Queen. There was the National Cranberry-Harvest Queen, the National Cranberry Week Queen, the Southwestern Oregon Queen, the Wareham (Massachusetts) Queen, and so on.[37]

At first, conservative cranberry growers were skeptical about the value of such festivals. Letters to the editor of the most important trade publication, reasonably enough, questioned the need for festivals. But the early promoters were quite clear about their objectives. Clarence J. Hall, editor of *Cranberries* wrote in 1951: "The primary purpose of these affairs in the various cranberry states is to publicize cranberries widely, through the medium of the press, radio, by word-of-mouth and in every way, that cranberry sales will be stimulated."[38] Part of the role of the trade press seemed to be that of mediator between conservative growers and the more flamboyant marketing types. In retrospect, Hall's analysis seems overly simplistic. Both growers and promoters may have hoped that festivals would stimulate sales of cranberries, but was that really "the primary purpose"? Most people probably attended out of other motives, including the simple impulse of gregariousness.

Though cranberry festivals got started in the 1930s and 1940s, they seem to have reached their peak during the 1950s. Typically held in the fall, such festivals often were held in conjunction with pre-existing daytime events, such as local high school football contests or Indian pow-wows. There might have been a reading of a proclamation from the governor. In the evening, there was a stage show and dancing, plus prizes, including "the popular cranberry guessing contest, in which the number of berries in a glass jar is estimated."[39] Sometimes, there were elaborate firework displays.

Some cranberry festivals also featured parades with floats, high school bands, and drum majorettes. There were food fairs, with hundreds of cranberry dishes—cranberry breads, salads, and deserts. A 1951 festival in Wisconsin featured "fifteen thousand pieces of cranberry pie, made of 1200 pounds of flour, 1600 pounds of sugar, 53 pounds of salt, 43,000 cups of cranberries plus water and a few other ingredients."[40] Usually the highlight of the affair was the coronation of a new Cranberry Queen at the Coronation Ball. The Queen and her princesses (other contestants) would be given a number of gifts from the local chamber of commerce. Then the Queen might be awarded a trip to New York, where she would be a guest on the Arthur Godfrey radio program.[41]

Because the cranberry festivals of the 1950s now strike us as corny, trite, and unsophisticated, we might suppose that they have all died out. But this is not the case. A recent guidebook lists two that are still very much alive. One is the Massachusetts Cranberry Festival, begun in 1948, which is held in South Carver on the last weekend in September and the first weekend in October at the Edaville Railroad Park. There is also a cranberry festival in Warrens, Wisconsin, which is held during the last weekend in September.[42]

Though the trade press rationalizes the continuance of cranberry festivals in terms of promotion and marketing, I still believe that other strong motivations are at work. To be sure, in a capitalist society, festival organizers often feel the need to explain attendance behavior in marketing terms because those terms seem to be rational and logical, not to mention they are appealing to corporate sponsors. I would argue that the people who actually attend cranberry festivals are responding to a more atavistic need. Fall harvest festivals like these are basic to agriculture and are in keeping with the spirit of America. It is part of the legacy left to us by Thomas Jefferson. Deep down, we share his belief that farm life is satisfying, wholesome, and virtuous. Attending a cranberry festival allows us to participate, however briefly, in that life.

Let us discuss in some detail the New Jersey Cranberry Festival, the one with which I am most familiar. It was first held in 1984. Back then, it was a one-day event that drew a crowd of about 5,000 people. The fair originator and organizer was Mary Ann Thompson, mentioned earlier in this chapter. In 1985 she decided to expand and enlarge the festival to make it a two-day event. The attendance quadrupled. Then in 1986 the festival drew an estimated crowd of 35,000—almost double the figure of 1985.[43] In 1987 the festival attracted 50,000 visitors, which is amazing when you consider that the figure represented a tenfold increase over the first festival in 1984.[44] To me there is a meaning to be read between the lines of these attendance figures. It seems certain that, while the earlier cranberry festivals may have been produced by local people for local people as an expression of local pride, the contemporary cranberry festivals are produced by local people for outside visitors.

Every fall the New Jersey Cranberry Festival takes place at Chatsworth, New Jersey, a town described as the "Capital of the Pine Barrens." The heart of Chatsworth is at the intersection of New Jersey Routes 532 and 563. On one corner is Buzby's General Store; on the diagonally opposite site is the Griffin Auto Service Shop. It is truly a "blink-and-you-miss-it" kind of town—unless you happen to be passing through the area on the weekend in October when the festival is taking place. On that occasion, cars line the sand shoulders of Route 563 for about a half mile before you reach the town proper. The grounds for the festival are provided by the DeMarco Brothers, who are cranberry growers in the area.

Fig. 4.2. Cranberry cake booth at the Chatsworth Cranberry Festival, Chatsworth, New Jersey, Oct. 1988. Proceeds from the cranberry festival go to a nonprofit group that works to preserve the Pine Barrens history and culture. Photograph by Angus Kress Gillespie.

The festival covers both sides of Route 532 between the Chatsworth Firehouse and Buzby's General Store. Opposite the firehouse sits the White Horse Inn, the future (pending renovation) home of the Pine Barrens Museum and the Chatsworth Community Center. Surrounding the inn is the outdoor "Cranberry Cafe," which includes tables selling cranberry bread, cranberry strudel, and muffins. One can also purchase tickets for bog-harvesting tours, festival T-shirts, the Cranberry Festival Cookbook, hot dogs, hamburgers, turkey sandwiches with cranberry sauce, and cranberry ice from Leo's Yum-Yum of Camden. The Cranberry Cafe is run by members of Chatsworth Club II, and all proceeds from the stands are said to go toward the renovation of the inn.

The stalls on the other side of the road, in front of and next to the firehouse, are filled with various craftspeople, antique dealers, and only a few cranberry-related attractions. Except for one or two dealers who sell antique cranberry barrel labels, it is the sort of stuff that you might expect to find at any southern New Jersey flea market. There is a lot of old junk cleared out from basements, garages, and attics. Some of the "craft" items appear to be made from commercial kits. It can be disappointing to the visitor looking for authentic indigenous handmade items. However, in fairness, it should be pointed out that the largest cranberry and the runners-up were on display at one stand, as well as the winners of a craft contest whose theme called for the use of cranberries in a project. Most of the projects displayed were floral arrangements with cranberries and their vines.

Among the more interesting exhibitors at the festival was Mr. Karl Flato, a talented rebuilder of old agricultural engines and early farm equipment. He was able to rebuild not just the average worn-out engine, but the kind of thing found lying in the woods in ruined condition. Mr. Flato of Brown's Mills, New Jersey, took pride in collecting these engines, tearing them apart, and building them back up until they were completely operational. The engines are gasoline powered and were used mostly in farm machinery such as saws and grinders.

Another worthwhile exhibitor I found at the festival was Mr. William Kelly, a builder of a traditional South Jersey boat called the Barnegat Bay sneakbox. Mr. Kelly is one of five sneakbox builders within a seven-mile radius of his hometown, West Creek, New Jersey. The Barnegat Bay sneakbox is a boat built exclusively for duck hunting, and it is believed to have originated in 1836 in West Creek. The point is that, despite the lack of an overall programming concept for the festival, some of the exhibitors actually manifest the fabric of traditional life in the area.

One of my students from Rutgers, Ellen Gulczynski, who is keenly interested in Jerseyana, attended the Cranberry Festival at my urging. She browsed among the stalls of antiques and junk at the festival until she found one that had stacks of old cranberry magazines. She figured, quite correctly, that the magazines could be helpful in her research. As she looked through the piles, she noticed that some magazines cost ten cents, while others cost twenty-five

Fig. 4.3. "The Little Cranberries" solicit donations for the restoration of the White Horse Inn at the cranberry festival in Chatsworth, New Jersey, Oct. 1988. Photograph by Angus Kress Gillespie.

cents. Ellen asked the proprietor of the stall the reason for the price difference. She was told that the twenty-five-cent magazines had recipes in them, while the ten-cent ones did not. Ellen thought that this was amusing and said so, while she continued to look through the magazines. Another woman who was buying magazines heard her comment and said, "That's how they usually do it. Why else would you want an old magazine?"[45]

## Berries and Juice All Year Long

As intriguing as cranberry festivals can be, there is some doubt as to their effectiveness in marketing cranberries. To be sure, these festivals are important as ritual celebrations of the abundant American harvest. They give people an opportunity to gather together as an outlet for local pride and gregariousness. Undoubtedly, such festivals do build residual good will toward the industry. Whatever the merits of these festivals, let us now turn our attention to some of the other concerns that clearly involve marketing. The fundamental, underlying problem of the growers was that, for years, everyone had associated cranberries with the consumption of turkey at Thanksgiving. But in the late 1940s, there were a number of bumper crops, supplying enough cranberries to provide for a year-round market. But no such market existed. Traditionally, cranberries sold well in the fall and winter, but sales fell off drastically during the spring and summer. A solution to the problem had to be found.

In 1948 growers came up with an advertising campaign for "Chicken and Cranberry." The growers made advertising funds available to grocers who would agree to set up sales displays for cranberry sauce in the meat department, next to the chicken. Almost immediately, sales of cranberry sauce increased. Not surprisingly, sales of chicken also increased, bringing even greater cooperation from grocers. In 1951 cranberry growers came up with another idea—national advertising in magazines and newspapers built around specific holidays with no historic connection to cranberries, holidays like Valentine's Day and Easter. An effort was made to get the consumer to associate the purchase of chicken with the purchase of cranberry sauce. Gradually the market for cranberries was being expanded.[46]

Buoyed by their successes in these early advertising campaigns, cranberry growers began to rely more and more heavily on the advice of market consultants. By 1953 the marketing blitz became increasingly brazen. In August of that year plans for "OPERATION SELLMOR" were unveiled in Chicago by an emcee, assisted by "Cranberry Dan," a forty-seven-inch midget, costumed to represent the Eatmor Cranberry Man trademark. Prizes were offered to consumers, retailers, and distributors. Consumers had a chance to win a Cadillac convertible by selecting the most appropriate first and last name for the "Cranberry Girl" and telling in twenty-five words or less why they liked Eatmor cranberries. By today's standards, the campaign seems to have had something to offend everyone—materialism, sexism, even "size-ism."[47] But to be fair about it, this was the same era when diners served blue-plate specials, when cars had lots of chrome, and when suburbanites put pink flamingoes on their front lawns. It was a period of optimistic consumerism.[48]

As the 1950s drew to a close, it seemed to cranberry growers that sales would just keep increasing indefinitely. It seemed that the sky was the limit. Then in November of 1959, the sky fell down on the growers. Sales for the 1959 crop were proceeding in an orderly fashion, when on Monday, November 9, there was bad news. The new problem was political in nature rather than agricultural. Arthur S. Fleming, secretary of the U.S. Department of Health, Education, and Welfare, made a startling announcement. Some shipments of cranberries from the West Coast were contaminated with the pesticide and weed killer amino-triazole. The announcement was circulated by newspaper, radio, and television. It happened at the worst possible time, just before the Thanksgiving sales peak.[49] What problem could be worse than this? But cranberry growers were accustomed to dealing with adversity. This problem, too, in time, was overcome.

The cranberry industry tried to fight back. Marketing representatives went on television to defend the reputation of the business. Political support was enlisted among the congressmen and senators from affected states. Cranberry sales for this period were down 78 percent for canned cranberries and 63 percent for fresh fruit. Growers were quick to label the event a disaster. They began to make plans to seek government assistance to recover.[50]

After a lengthy lobbying campaign, cranberry growers did get partial government redress in 1960: an allocation of $8.02 per barrel for unsold cranberries, less than the market value, but better than nothing.[51] The "cranberry scare" of 1959 has become a classic textbook case of the problems of government regulation. Subsequent investigation showed that less than three-tenths of one percent of berries were found to be tainted. These came only from about ten growers from all over the country.[52] No wonder the cranberry growers were outraged.

Still, in fairness to the government, what is a regulator to do? On the one hand, if the public health is endangered, the prudent thing to do is to condemn the entire crop. On the other hand, growers argued that there was no sudden threat to public health, that the compound amino-triazole had been found in minute quantities in a few cranberries. They went on to argue that the compound is found naturally in some common foods, including radishes, broccoli, turnips, and cabbage. Growers claimed that a person would have to have eaten 2,200 pounds of heavily sprayed cranberries in order to consume as much amino-triazole as would have been found in one turnip.[53]

The immediate result of the cranberry scare was that the industry quickly banned the use of amino-triazole on cranberries completely. The ban was a hardship on some growers, since it made weed control difficult, but they obeyed the law.[54] The long-term result of the cranberry scare was that the industry relied even more heavily on advertising and marketing. An editorial in *Cranberries* for May of 1961 stated: "But today our biggest problem is not really the growing of cranberries efficiently and abundantly. It is marketing. The supply potential runs ahead of cranberry consumption. That is where obviously lies our problem. We can grow 'em, but can we induce people to eat all we can produce? Some how, some way, we must."[55] Ironically, while there was an oversupply of cranberries in the 1960s, this has not been consistently the case ever since. In some periods, notably the late 1980s, there were not enough cranberries.[56]

It was about this time that Ed Gelsthorpe took over as chief executive officer for Ocean Spray, the growers' cooperative. Gelsthorpe steered this group of independent, cooperating farmers toward a new marketing direction. In an interview for a documentary video, Gelsthorpe explained:

> When I came in, in that environment, for some time Ocean Spray had been selling a product called cranberry juice cocktail, but they had been selling it only in New England. We tasted the cranberry juice cocktail, and we could understand why very few people drank it. It had actually been formulated to meet the taste of cranberry growers.
>
> If you've seen cranberry growers, they can pick up a handful of cranberries off the vine and eat them. And that's about the way cranberry juice cocktail tasted, so we did the not so brilliant thing of putting more water and more sugar in it. It then became a very palatable drink, and we initially marketed it across the country. And that really started to turn the business around.[57]

The new improved cranberry juice cocktail, introduced in 1962, was a tremendous marketing success. Building on this success, Ocean Spray kept introducing new products, including a Cran-Grape drink, a Cranapple drink, even a Cran-Raspberry drink. The drinks have been marketed in cans and bottles. Prior to 1962, most cranberries were sold as either fresh cranberries or as canned sauces. But by the late 1970s, more than two-thirds of sales were in juice and juice drinks.[58] Increasingly, there was a comfortable balance between cranberry supply and cranberry demand.

In 1981 Ocean Spray began using the "paper bottle," a single-serving, rectangular, air-tight package. The hope was to make additional sales for school and office lunches, as well as for trips and picnics.[59]

A fascinating historical footnote to the development of blended cranberry juices can be found in the archives of the University of Massachusetts. It seems that when apple and cranberry juice are simply mixed together, the resulting concoction is not very appetizing. An enzyme in the apple juice destroys the red cranberry pigmentation, leaving the mixture a repulsive purple-brown color. As with so many other problems in the past, the situation seemed hopeless. The amazing thing about the cranberry industry is that nearly every time an impasse is reached, another Yankee tinkerer steps forward with a solution. The cranapple color problem was solved in the later 1940s by Kirby Hayes, then a graduate student at the university.

Hayes made an important breakthrough: he found that heat treatment would get rid of the pigment-destroying enzyme without altering the taste or nutritional value of the apple juice. The heat-treated apple juice could then be mixed with cranberry juice to produce a drink that had real eye appeal. Eventually, the new drink found its way to our supermarket shelves. Although Hayes may have been a talented food scientist, he was certainly no marketing genius. The name Hayes had suggested for his new product? Crapple![60]

The enormous profits made in the sale of cranberry juice have created some problems in the industry. From time to time, unscrupulous companies have been tempted to adulterate the product. One such case came to light in 1986. A small New Jersey company, Minot Food Packers, was certain that some of its competitors could not possibly produce cranberry juice at their low-selling price and still make a profit.

The firm hired a detective agency that provided blind samples of the suspected products to scientists at Oregon State University, known for their expertise in detecting food adulteration. Researcher Ron Wrolstad concluded, "Some samples had as little as three percent cranberry juice and many had only 15 percent. We calculate that the advantage to the criminals could be as much as $2 a case (12 one-quart bottles) if they used 10 percent cranberry juice instead of 25 percent. I feel that there are three groups being ripped off: consumers, cranberry growers, and legitimate processors."[61] Legitimate processors have to be vigilant and aggressive in going after the cheats in order to stay in business.

In the late 1980s, yet another problem arose for the cranberry juice industry—a major labeling controversy. In the late 1970s, Ocean Spray had taken the initiative to print nutritional labels on its products. Since cranberry juice is relatively nutritious, this was no problem. But in 1989, the Food and Drug Administration began to consider the possibility of requiring the percentage of juice content to be printed "in fairly large letters" on the front of all fruit juice labels.[62] Since cranberry juice has large amounts of water added in order to make it palatable, the processors would be at a competitive disadvantage with other fruit juices, such as apple juice.

As this chapter was being written, the labeling controversy had not been fully resolved. The cranberry industry basically took the position that they were opposed to large product labels giving the percentage of juice unless they were accompanied by equally large product labels giving the facts on nutrition. Ocean Spray claimed that it was only trying to level the playing field. The company went on to point out that one six-ounce serving of its cranberry juice cocktail (admittedly only 15 percent juice) contained 100 percent of the U.S. recommended dietary allowance of vitamin C.[63]

What new marketing gimmicks lie ahead for the 1990s and beyond? One recent product innovation was the craisin, a sugar-infused, dried fruit. In addition to being marketed as a casual fruit snack, craisins can also be used in baked goods and cereals. Rich O'Brien, national sales manager for Ocean Spray, says,

> Other fruit will not hold up as well to infusion and air drying. The cranberry has a strong cell structure needed for the process.
>
> The bright, red berry color makes craisins an ideal ingredient for cereals, baked goods, and dairy products.
>
> Major companies in these categories want a way to communicate clearly to consumers that they have real fruit in the product. Now we can offer a contrast to the browns and beiges which most fruit and nuts provide.[64]

The raisin industry was not amused when Ocean Spray introduced the craisin. In 1989 the California Raisin Advisory Board in Fresno asked the California attorney general to determine whether or not Ocean Spray can legally use the word "craisin." As this chapter was being written, a final determination had not been made, but the controversy did draw widespread interest. Craisins do resemble red raisins. They are sliced cranberries, which are sweetened in cranberry juice.

Having spent a great deal of money to promote its product over the years, the raisin industry feels that the cranberry industry is trying to cash in on its success. Says Ernest Bedrosian, president of the National Raisin Company, "We've spent millions of dollars building the raisin image up as a healthy, natural fruit of the sun. Now they put a c in front of it and call it a Craisin. We made it so popular, they just want to shirttail on our success."[65] "If it's a cranberry, why don't they call it a cranberry?" inquired California Advisory Board member Don Martens.[66]

Certainly, there is a risk for the cranberry industry in introducing too many new products. In its zeal to market the cranberry in any number of new forms, there is a risk of losing sight of the original product and its original power in the American imagination. Interestingly enough, the marketing types at present are way out in front of the growers. During the period from 1984 to 1990, there was a consistent supply deficit.[67] In other words, growers have been unable to supply enough of the hard-to-grow cranberry to keep up with demand. This basic limitation may serve, for a few more years, to put the brakes on excessive marketing innovation.

Let us conclude with one last marketing ploy—the development of a cranberry catsup. The product was introduced at the Sunburn Penguin Restaurant in West Hartford, Connecticut, as a condiment served with turkey burgers. Shortly thereafter the restaurant began to sell bottles of the cranberry catsup to their patrons. Besides cranberries, the new product is made with several spices and flavorful ingredients, including mustard seed, orange and lemon zest, garlic, anchovies, tamarinds, and chili pepper. To give the product even more zip, white wine, distilled vinegar, and dry sherry are added. The catsup is bottled at a factory in Rhode Island, where it is mixed in 250-gallon batches before bottling.[68] The making of cranberry catsup represents the end of a long line of development. Originally a native plant growing wild at the perilous border between land and sea, it has lost some of its original innocence. Increasingly, it is becoming a malleable product of commercial agriculture put to uses limited only by the capitalistic imagination of entrepreneurs.

## Notes

The research for this study was partially funded by the Fellows Opportunity Fund of Douglass College at Rutgers—the State University of New Jersey. My thanks to David A. Libby, who warmly and hospitably showed me around Plymouth, Massachusetts, in 1988. Thanks also to Jeanne O'Brien, Miriam Weinstein, and Ellen Gulczynski, students at Douglass College who did some initial research on this topic. I am especially indebted to Robert Blake Truscott and Edward V. Lipman, both of whom made numerous helpful suggestions.

1. For a comprehensive account of cranberry biology, ecology, cultivation, economics, and history, see Paul Eck, *The American Cranberry* (New Brunswick, N.J.: Rutgers Univ. Press, 1990).
2. Interview with Edward V. Lipman, New Brunswick, N.J., Aug. 14, 1990.
3. For a discussion of the problems of fact and myth surrounding the first Thanksgiving, see *American Folklore and Legend* (Pleasantville, N.Y.: Reader's Digest Association, 1978), 14, which features J. L. G. Ferris's 1915 painting, *The First Thanksgiving.* See also Thanksgiving calendar customs explained in Benjamin A. Botkin, *A Treasury of New England Folklore* (New York: Crown Publishers, 1964), 418–22.
4. Barre Toelken, *The Dynamics of Folklore* (Boston: Houghton Mifflin, 1979), 123–49.
5. Calvin Trillin, *Third Helpings* (New Haven and New York: Ticknor and Fields, 1983).
6. Michael Aaron Rockland, "The Concord Complex: Some Remarks on the American Geographical Imagination," *Connections 2* (Summer 1976): 28–31.

7. Jane and Michael Stern, *Goodfood: The Adventurous Eater's Guide to Restaurants Serving America's Best Regional Specialties* (New York: Alfred A. Knopf, 1983), 39–40.
8. Fredrika A. Burrows, *Cannonballs and Cranberries* (Taunton, Mass.: William S. Sullwold Publishing, 1976), 55.
9. Ibid., 52–53.
10. Ibid., 56.
11. Ibid.
12. Cranberry World plaque, Plymouth, Mass.
13. Ibid.
14. Burrows, *Cannonballs and Cranberries*, 58.
15. Ibid.
16. Cranberry World plaque, Plymouth, Mass.
17. Bob Taylor, *Cranberries: The National Cranberry Magazine* (May 1982): 5.
18. J. Solms, D. A. Booth, R. M. Pangborn, and D. Raunhardt, eds., *Food Acceptance and Nutrition* (New York: Academic Press, Harcourt, Brace, Jovanovich, 1987).
19. Jeff Smith, *The Frugal Gourmet Cooks American* (New York: William Morrow and Company, 1987), 71.
20. "All-Time Favorite Cranberry Recipes," Lakeville-Middleboro, Mass.: Ocean Spray Cranberries, Inc., n.d.; and "Cranberry Festival Recipes," Chatsworth, N.J.: Chatsworth Club II, 1985.
21. Sidney W. Mintz, *Sweetness and Power: The Place of Sugar in Modern History* (New York: Viking Penguin, 1985).
22. Burrows, *Cannonballs and Cranberries*, 51.
23. "Cranberries in Massachusetts," three-page Ocean Spray handout, Vertical File, Restricted Reference, Plymouth Public Library, Plymouth, Mass., 02360.
24. "Cranberries in Wisconsin," three-page Ocean Spray handout, Vertical File, Restricted Reference, Plymouth Public Library, Plymouth, Mass., 02360.
25. "Cranberries in New Jersey," three-page Ocean Spray handout, Vertical File, Restricted Reference, Plymouth Public Library, Plymouth, Mass., 02360.
26. Jonathan Berger and John W. Sinton, *Water, Earth, and Fire* (Baltimore: Johns Hopkins Univ. Press, 1985), 73.
27. Mary Hufford, "Culture and the Cultivation of Nature: The Pinelands National Reserve," *Folklife Annual* (Washington, D.C.: Library of Congress, 1985), 21.
28. John W. Sinton and Sandra Hartzog, eds., *History, Culture and Archeology of the New Jersey Pine Barrens: Essays from the Third Annual Pine*

*Barrens Research Conference* (Pomona, N.J.: Center for Environmental Research, Stockton State College, 1982), 193–97.

29. Mintz, *Sweetness and Power*, 74–150.
30. Comment made by Arthur Odell and quoted by Jack Star, "Why You Choose the Foods You Do: The Psychology and Physiology of Eating," *Today's Health* (Feb. 1973): 34.
31. Cranberry World exhibit.
32. Burrows, *Cannonballs and Cranberries*, 71.
33. Cranberry World exhibit.
34. John T. Cunningham, *Garden State: The Story of Agriculture in New Jersey* (New Brunswick, N.J.: Rutgers Univ. Press, 1955), 150.
35. Cornelius Weygandt, *Down Jersey: Folks and Their Jobs, Pine Barrens, Salt Marsh and Sea Islands* (New York and London: D. Appleton-Century, 1940), 147.
36. *Cranberries* (Oct. 1951): 13.
37. *Cranberries* (Nov. 1948): 9.
38. *Cranberries* (Oct. 1951): 13.
39. *Cranberries* (Oct. 1950): 10.
40. *Cranberries* (Oct. 1951): 10.
41. *Cranberries* (Dec. 1950): 14.
42. Alice M. Geffen and Carol Berglie, *Food Festival: The Ultimate Guidebook to America's Best Regional Food Celebrations* (New York: Pantheon Books, 1986), 176–81.
43. *Cranberries* (Jan. 1987): 14.
44. *Cranberries* (Apr. 1988): 14.
45. Ellen Gulczynski, research report, submitted to the author, Nov. 1, 1987.
46. *Cranberries* (May 1951): 19–21.
47. *Cranberries* (Sept. 1953): 19.
48. Angus Kress Gillespie and Michael Aaron Rockland, *Looking for America on the New Jersey Turnpike* (New Brunswick, N.J.: Rutgers Univ. Press, 1989), 38–39.
49. *Cranberries* (Nov. 1959): 11.
50. *Cranberries* (Dec. 1959): 15.
51. *Cranberries* (Apr. 1960): 15.
52. *Cranberries* (Mar. 1960): 15.
53. *Cranberries* (Jan. 1960): 15.
54. *Cranberries* (July 1960): 15.
55. *Cranberries* (May 1961): 19.
56. Interview with Edward V. Lipman, Aug. 14, 1990.
57. "The Crimson Harvest" (Marstons Mills, Mass.: Cape Cod Cranberry Growers Association, 1988).
58. *Cranberries* (June 1985): 8.

59. Ibid.
60. *Cranberries* (Oct. 1985): 5.
61. *Cranberries* (July 1986): 16.
62. *Cranberries* (Mar. 1989): 3.
63. Ibid.
64. *Cranberries* (Apr. 1989): 9–10.
65. *Cranberries* (Aug. 1989): 5.
66. Ibid.
67. Interview with Edward V. Lipman, Aug. 14, 1990.
68. *Cranberries* (June 1990): 3–4.

# David Scofield Wilson

Peppers invite superlatives. Consider several recent expressions: "Eating chile peppers is like gustatory skydiving";[1] or, "Bell peppers are probably the most attractive vegetable in the produce section";[2] or "The chili . . . peppers . . . were the Americas' most important contribution to the world's spices."[3] Whether judged by standards of gustatory daring, visual beauty, or world commerce, peppers stand out, and yet they remain relatively exotic or unknown to many Americans. Granted, "sweet" bell peppers have achieved popular status, along with tomatoes and sweet corn, as staples of midsummer, middle American salad and picnic fare, but these fat and sweet bell peppers have been drawn so far away from their heritage through cultivation as to remove them from serious consideration by true pepper lovers. At least so one champion of wild peppers would have it; Gary Paul Nabhan calls sweet peppers "freaks of nature, or better, freaks of nurture."[4]

True peppers, those which Columbus "discovered" for Europe as a substitute for their precious black pepper (no relation), own an essence and presence unique to American life. They have retained their pungent presence at the heart of certain local and ethnic foodways (Cajun, Latino, Southwest Native American, Hungarian, Italian, Thai, Szechwan, etc.) and have lent a touch of wildness to domestic fast food fare (chili con carne, BBQ, pizza, nachos, etc.) How these peppers may both mark boundaries and feed the melting pot cuisine is a story to be told and understood.

Botanically, peppers are apposites, brothers to tomatoes.[5] Symbolically, they are opposites. Tomatoes are fleshy, full, juicy, soft, and pendant; peppers are leathery, hollow, dry (often dried), tough, and often erect on the plant. Tomatoes thus strike many Americans as feminine and peppers as masculine. Bell peppers are an exception; listen again to Nabhan: "sweet peppers" show "a prolonged immaturity, staying green and fleshy for many more days than a wild chile would ever dare to. The domesticated chiles are mostly pendant, rather than being erect on the stem. . . . Whereas [wild bird peppers] ripen quickly and stick out above the foliage like sore thumbs, domesticated *Capsicums* like bell peppers hang to the ground below the plant's foliage, like a silicon-injected monster too awkward to behave properly."[6]

Nabhan's discernment of the male tenor of bird peppers draws on his ethnobotanical fieldwork among native peoples of the Southwest. But the masculine value of the pepper appears throughout Euro-American popular and folk culture as well. The shape, the "heat," and the erect posture of (some) hot peppers, as well as their valence as spicy foreign fare, assure a role for them in performances of masculinity, such as jalapeño-eating contests or the barstool bravery of "popping" red peppers from the Polish-sausage jars behind the bar.

Peppers have become potent players on the stage of American culture. What they contribute varies from cultural setting to cultural setting, to be sure, but so "lively" are they that they seem sometimes less to be contained by context than to be agents of meaning and of change themselves. Like tricksters, peppers pop up in different but compelling stories, acting different roles: healing, amusing, burning, exciting, or drawing us into festive community display.

## Hot Peppers, Cool Cuisine, and American Culture

CAYENNE PEPPER, *n.* A very pungent pepper, the produce of some species of Capsicum.
CHILLI, *n.* The pod of the Cayenne or Guinea pepper.
GUINEA PEPPER, *n.* A Plant, a species of *Amomum or Capsicum.* The fruit of some species is used for pickles.

—Noah Webster, *An American
Dictionary of the English Language,* 1848

Noah Webster included only three entries related to hot peppers in his mid-nineteenth-century *American Dictionary of the English Language:* "cayenne pepper," "chilli," and "guinea pepper." Evidently, mid-nineteenth-century, English-speaking America understood peppers to be foreign. They came from black Africa (Guinea) or Latin America (Cayenne in French Guiana), and their origins, combined with their "bite," consigned them largely to pharmacological rather than gustatory uses.

Not native to Europe, hot peppers remained uncommon in northern Europe and Anglo-America long after their acceptance elsewhere. Even black pepper was "rare and costly in northern Europe well into the modern period," according to Raymond Sokolov, and consequently northern Europeans and Anglo-Americans enjoyed or endured a relatively "cool cuisine."[7] And despite some late-twentieth-century additions of hot peppers to sauces and to special dishes, our cuisine remains cool for the most part—one need only survey the contents of supermarket frozen food cases, shelves of canned goods, and bins of produce to confirm the continued marginality of "hot" and the centrality of "cool" in mass-market American foodways today. Our tradition of lumping black pepper *(Piper nigrum)* and capsicum peppers together in English under one word, *pepper,* documents a culturally inherited lack of experience or interest in distinguishing one "hot" from another. Perhaps that collapse of all peppers into "pepper" contributes even still to keeping hot peppers from easy acceptance as vegetable fare.

In Webster's day, most of what we call the Southwest today was still literally foreign, but even following political inclusion, the cuisine and culture of its Native American and Mexican American peoples remained symbolically outlandish. Their foodways did not impinge much on American cuisine for another century. When J. G. Bourke wrote his long essay on folk foods of the Southwest for the *Journal of American Folklore* in 1895, he clearly cast his remarks on *Chile, Chilchipin, Chile con carne, Enchiladas,* and *Tamales* as a report on foreign foodways.[8] "No Mexican dish of meat or vegetables is deemed complete without" the *chile,* he claims, and of the *chilchipin,* he says, "It is used in the green and ripe, or red, state."[9] "*Chile con carne* is meat prepared in a savory stew with chile colorado, tomato, grease, and . . . garlic," he reported, in language not meant to invite American imitation. Mexican was foreign still in 1895.

Two short stories in *Overland Monthly* in 1915 and 1923 exhibit chili con carne and chili respectively as markers of Mexican ethnicity.[10] Speaking of her parents, the "Chili Cherub" of one story explains to her aunt that "its [sic] Mamacita that's got the *Chili* looks, but its [sic] Papacito that's got the *Chili* ways. . . ." In the other story we learn that a man is "her jailer! her tyrant!" and "a *chili* devil."[11] Both stories are by Anglo authors.

As late as 1943, William Brandon, in a story for the *Saturday Evening Post,* invokes the little, very hot "Chillipiquin" for a title and the name of a little red pony in the story.[12] "There is a poem in Spanish about small women being best," Brandon writes, "small jewels being best, and small peppers being hottest."[13] Whatever else one might make of this amalgam of gender, jewels, and peppers into a poem, it clearly "spices up" the story with its exotic flavor.

As recently as 1896, Fannie Merritt Farmer, in the first edition of her soon to be standard American cookbook, called cayenne "the powdered pod of capsicum grown on the eastern coast of Africa and in Zanzibar," and included it only as a spice.[14] She did call for "a few grains" of cayenne in deviled scallops, Welsh rarebits, Scotch Woodcock, minced mutton, and chafing dish recipes. But it is clear that hot peppers did not count as vegetables with her, though artichokes, asparagus, beans, beets, Brussels sprouts, cabbage, carrots, cauliflower, celery, chiccory [sic] or endive, corn, chestnuts, cucumbers, eggplant, greens, dandelions, lettuce, onions, oyster plant (salsify), parsnips, peas, "Stuffed [green] Peppers," pumpkins, radishes, spinach, squash, tomatoes, turnips, truffles, and mushrooms did. There were no recipes for hot peppers; none even for frying peppers. The only *chili* in Farmer's index leads one to a recipe for a "Chili Sauce" that calls for tomatoes, vinegar, sugar, salt, cloves, cinnamon, allspice, nutmeg, and generic "peppers," which, in the context of her recipes, signifies bell, not chile, peppers. It bears no relationship to any "chili" that is kin to chili con carne.[15]

Cookery aside, cayenne pepper played a role in nineteenth-century medicine. Homeopathic practice especially drew on tiny doses of this or that plant for its pills and concoctions, and cayenne was a regular item in its *materia medica*. It was self-evidently powerful, and things that tasted "bad" or "burned" going down seemed to advertise their medicinal virtue.

Cayenne pepper was exploited by doctors like John C. Gunn, who found its pungency a handy stimulant in addressing various weaknesses: Quinsy, Debility of the Stomach, Dropsical affections, weak Digestion, Pains of the Womb, obstructed Menstruation, etc.[16] Certain of his recipes appear more heroic than homeopathic, as with this prescription for sudden colds: "Every old lady in the country knows, or ought to know, that, in sudden colds, a tea made of Cayenne Pepper is an excellent remedy; or 1 tea-spoonful of Cayenne, mixed with Molasses or Honey, and taken in broken doses, is a valuable remedy in Coughs."[17] Or that for the "No. 9, Gargle in Scarlet Fever": "Take Cayenne, 1 tea-spoonful; common Salt, 2 tea-spoonfuls; 1 teacupful of Vinegar and Water, bring to the boiling point, then let stand and cool, and then strain. Use as a Gargle, cold, in Sore Throat and in Scarlet Fever. An excellent remedy."[18]

Gunn's mission was "home medicine": that mix of lore and handbook recipes by which self-reliant Americans drew on the wild and tamed herbs and on household stores for the potions, liniments, teas, poultices, and pills. While Gunn identified cayenne as South American, West Indian, and African, whence the stronger and better species, he took it nevertheless to be a common item in the cupboard if not on the board of American households in those days. Cayenne did not need to be grown locally, for it dried and powdered and lasted well. Gunn's "ministry" lasted from the Jacksonian era well into the twentieth century; the last printing of his work appeared in 1920, before it was reprinted in a scholarly edition years later.[19] Gunn's book was a monument of American home medicine. Mark Twain made "Dr. Gunn's *Family Medicine*" one of the markers of mid-South gentility, along with Henry Clay's *Speeches* and *Friendship's Offering,* in his description of the Grangerfords' parlor.[20] Medical historian Philip M. Hamer called it "one of the most famous" medical books of its day written for laymen.[21]

Noah Webster's and John Gunn's perception of peppers as both useful and exotic ought to alert us to the more widespread if less articulate "reading" given peppers by the wider American public. In part, the exotic valence of peppers derives from their history, from the facts of "The Conquest," of subsequent trade, and of diffusion along those trade routes. Peppers left the New World in Spanish and Portuguese bottoms and became "acculturated" in Africa, whence they returned to the United States as alien imports. Or they entered southeastern Europe with the Ottoman Turks and as paprika became a marker of Hungarian cookery. And they reached to India, Indochina, and China, whence they returned to America in recent decades. Add to this economic history an underlying mistrust of things "foreign," and the suspicion with which many Americans look on peppers makes sense. Such stuffs may pass as medicinal but not as comestible.

In the face of such inexperience with peppers and strong bias against "hot" ("dirty," "foreign," "dangerous") foods, the recent shift of Americans from taken-for-granted avoidance to conditional embrace of peppers reveals a cultural dynamic at work. The story of how this cousin to the tomato achieved "resident alien" status at first and fuller integration in time reveals a good deal about American culture and certain twentieth-century accommodations to ethnicity.

The larger story within which the tale of the pepper's looping progress out around the world and back is told by Alfred Crosby in *The Columbian Exchange,*[22] but that "emigration" and "acculturation" abroad does not much bear on our story, except as witness to the pepper's appeal to all manner of peoples. The pepper's widespread acceptance elsewhere serves to relativize Anglo-America's dismissal of peppers. It is only in terms of its "cool cuisine" that a taste for peppers may seem an affectation or idiosyncrasy to be accounted for by reference to ethnic origin, to cosmopolitan experience, or to vain displays of vulgar or heroic hubris. In contrast, the wider regard for peppers abroad suggests that perhaps the cultural curiosity meriting explanation is the relative absence of hot peppers in Anglo-American cuisine. In any case, just as "primitive man in America must have found wild peppers an interesting addition to his diet" and must eagerly have sought them out,[23] Americans have now joined post-contact Asians, Africans, and Europeans in finding peppers beautiful, delicious, and exciting to grow. The cuisines of many nations have so incorporated capsicums that we can hardly imagine otherwise: Hungary without paprika, Thailand without tiny "Thai peppers," Korea without kimchee, curry without cayenne, northern Chinese cookery without hot stir fry.

The "discovery" of America aside, the development of peppers as food began well before European contact. Hot peppers evolved in Mexico from the mother pepper, *Capsicum annuum* var. *aviculare*.[24] Called "bird peppers," these wild chiltecpin ("flea peppers") grow wild in the dry Sonoran regions of Mexico and Arizona and are immensely popular with those who know and love peppers. "I know of no cultivated Mexican chile," Gary Nabhan says, "that is 'pulled' across the border by a demand of equal strength."[25] Early people very likely spread seeds as the birds did. Further selection produced in time a plenitude of cultivars.[26] But

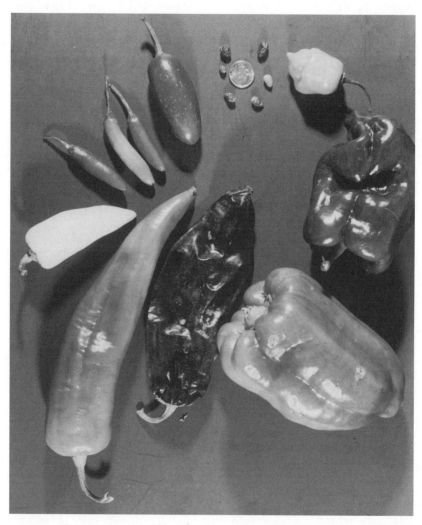

*Fig. 5.1. Chiles, clockwise from the top: chiltecpins, habañero, pasilla, bell, California dried pepper, Anaheim, Fresno, serranos, and jalapeño. Photograph by David Scofield Wilson.*

this, too, is beyond our scope except as the recipes and produce from these other lands and cultures enter American life.

In the United States today, a handful of varieties fulfill the demands of the dominant culture. Jalapeños have become popular enough to be pickled and canned for use beyond their growing range and seasonal availability. Serranos appear by the handful in pricey northern markets and specialty stores, but only as exotic fare. Bells, of course, dominate the home garden scene across America, on a par almost with tomatoes as indices of summer opulence and as emblems of one's ability and virtue in the garden. Cayennes commonly show up ground into powder; less pungent "reds" as crushed "red pepper" to sprinkle on pizza.

Red and Green Chilies in the Southwest (called Anaheims in California) furnish the bulk of peppers for salsas and sauces needed in "Mexican" and "New Mexican" cooking. Recently farmers' markets in middlewestern states as well as California and the Southwest have begun to offer fresh, locally grown hot peppers in season. Even mainline supermarkets in the West, at least, now carry a half-dozen fresh hot peppers, including the extremely hot, orange-colored habañeros.

In Latin America and Asia, by contrast, appreciation for the plenitude and variety of tastes and pungencies available seems catholic.[27] Such variety may well be an artifact of the dispersed agriculture in these so-called underdeveloped countries, but the attenuated offering of American industrial agriculture surely derives in part from the standardizing tendencies of nationwide markets on production and distribution. In this light, the rather recent passion for growing diverse varieties takes on a special revisionist motif. Pepper enthusiasts have "adopted the gene pool," so to speak, and have set about replicating something like the natural diversity of capsicums in private kitchen gardens and boutique truck gardens.

The "otherness" of hot peppers in Euro-American culture has found expression in the folklore as well as foodways and medicine. One informant claims that "hot and sweet peppers planted together will all be hot"; the hotness, one infers, symbolically invades and takes over the sweetness of the mild, popular vegetable pepper.[28] This symbolic symmetry gains plausibility from the genetic dominance of the gene for hotness. Another folk belief from Texas reports that "if you cuss your peppers while they are growing, you will have a good crop."[29] And from Utah: "If you want to raise a lot of strong pepper, make a person with a strong temper mad and get him to plant the seeds. But don't let the person know or suspect your design; catch him off guard."[30] Like the dark side of the nightshades, peppers belong to the profane realm and so may be assumed to thrive on what would rightly wither gentler plants.

But by far the most common mention of hot peppers in the archives of folklore and popular belief that I have visited alludes to the jump-rope game "Red Hot Peppers." This well-known schoolyard diversion features two girls twirling a rope and one girl at a time jumping over it each time it touches the ground in time to the rhyme, "Mabel, Mabel, set the table/Don't forget the red hot peppers!" The "beat of the jump rope was regular, specifically when the rope was at the closest point to the ground and the jump roper was in the air in the process of jumping," one informant explained, "as the words 'hot peppers' were said, the rhythm and pace of the jump rope increased . . . until 'someone messed up,' tripped or fell." Others explain that, following the speed-up, onlookers counted "One, Two, Three . . ." till the jumper failed, and that indicated the number of babies she would have. The informant accounts for the presence of peppers in the jump-rope rhyme by explaining that jumpers get hot and hot peppers make you jump around. That kind of surface explanation does more to hide the meaning than to expose it.[31]

Assume that the "how many babies" motif looks ahead to a relatively imminent stepping over a line from childhood to motherhood. And that the rope, like a line in the sidewalk or a boundary in culture, establishes a distinction of crucial character, the difference between in and out, OK and failed, adept or inept. Perhaps the slap of the rope on the pavement, then, counts cadence to the jumper's and her playmates' rehearsal of a drama of competence and maturity over and against ineptitude and childishness. What looms just ahead is a female fruitfulness both frightening and rewarding, but above all unpredictable. What better, then, should the girls invoke than the pepper. They both take on the pepper by employing it and risk "getting burned" by it.

Hot, wild, dangerous, and masculine, the pepper's potency may owe as much to redundant patterns of cultural association and interpretation as to the capsicum's actual pungency. Hot peppers admirably suit the deeper agenda of the play. It is the symbolic pepper that gets invoked and made the marker of the escalation between the girlish part of the game and the "full tilt," headlong, no-time-out character of the denouement.

## Into the Melting Pot

Chili sauce, chili powder, a "NuMex Big Jim," "TAM Mild Jalapeños," and Tabasco sauce—what do these five products have in common? Each illustrates a familiar American strategy for "naturalizing" putatively "foreign" foodstuffs by "taming" them and making them convenient, comfortable, affordable, and a treat. Rather than enter the foodways at the center as dishes, they contribute to dishes (or drinks) by adding to them. And they work into American foodways along paths of mass production, advertising, and agribusiness, even though some may have once been "homemade" and sharply regional in character and origins.

Consider the case of chili sauce. It has almost nothing to do with chile peppers, but simply retains a similar name. Hot peppers seldom figure in chili sauce, only green ones. Fanny Farmer called for only one green pepper to twelve tomatoes and some salt, pepper, cinnamon, cloves, allspice, nutmeg, and vinegar in 1896.[32] The *Better Homes and Gardens New Cookbook*[33] and the long standard *Joy of Cooking* are a little bit hotter: in the latter, to a peck of tomatoes making eight quarts of sauce, one tablespoon of "dried hot pepper pods" is to be added.[34] Evidently, chili sauce as it is made in American kitchens essentially bows to the chili pepper without embracing it. Chili sauce appropriates the name but not the substance of chile peppers. Like wieners, hamburgers, and French fries, chili sauce may be *sui generis* and now integral to American foodways, but it is hardly more tied to hot peppers or to Latin foodways than wieners to Vienna, hamburgers to Germany, or French fries to France. Chili sauce appropriates the name of chiles the way fraternities and sororities do Greek letters or football teams ethnic epithets like "Redskins," "Indians," "Braves," etc.

Chili powder enacts a different naturalization. Chili powder, like curry powder, is concocted of several spices and may be quite mild or very pungent. Made from Anaheim-like red peppers, garlic powder, oregano, cumin, cayenne, and paprika, the balance of hot and mild and amounts of cumin or cayenne may vary. Today commercial chili powders appear on supermarket shelves— as American as cans of seasoned salt, pumpkin pie spice, and pickling spice. Unlike chili sauce, chili powder boasts an author. Willie Gebhardt, a German American from New Braunfels, Texas, invented it in 1892, and it is the "basis of fabled chili con carne."[35] More on chili con carne later. The point here is that in pre-packaging chili powder and thereby standardizing the mix of ingredients, commercial food companies established an American frame within which hot pepper is made accessible at secondhand and useful as a flavoring but without the unadulterated fire of the peppers neat. One may sprinkle chili powder on deviled eggs or into stews or onto fried fish without ever really encountering much capsicum flavor or pungency. Indeed, cumin, oregano, garlic, and allspice contribute more than peppers do to the taste of most commercial powders. Chili powder, like chili sauce, may well enrich American cookery, but it thoroughly contextualizes capsicums as it accepts them into the menu, not unlike the way stage-Irish blarney, Jewish humor, Chinese sagacity, Native American stoicism, and Italian brotherhood spice up the comedies and dramas of mass media entertainment without ever forefronting the gritty details of everyday life among such populations in America and without learning anything new from their "alien" experiences and perspectives.

In 1951 *Science News Letter* announced that Paul G. Smith of the University of California at Davis had crossed the tiny Chilipiquin of Mexico with peppers already on the market. He predicted that this would "intensify the color of American manufactured red pepper, paprika, and chili powder."[36] Some "seventy five percent of the chile grown—some 15 to 20 million pounds a year—goes . . . for pigments used in food coloring and cosmetics."[37] Roy Nakayama, late of New Mexico State University at Las Cruces, continued such agribusiness-inspired alteration of the pepper, creating several new cultivars, but most notably the NuMex Big Jim, a capsicum milder than the native Red Chiles. Not only a new kind of chile but also one with a pod more than a foot long, the NuMex Big Jim might be taken as an icon of American commercial horticulture: its pungency tempered and its size inflated.

The pepper's size bars it from canning and from TV dinners, Nakayama admits, but with pods "weighing 7 to 9 ounces, . . . twice as many tons can be processed in one day and pay growers the same rate—but without increasing the price to the consumers."[38] He articulates the rationale of academic horticulturists, the same that drove tomato researchers and engineers in California to square the tomato. So far, "chile must still be harvested by hand, an arduous and tedious task that adds as much to the cost of producing the crop as all the other aspects of growing it."[39] Hoping to alter the plant to suit the machine, Nakayama sought "the development of a chile plant that grows at just the right height, with its pods clustered at just the right density, out-thrust slightly upward at just the right angle, for machine harvesting."[40] Henry Ford and Luther Burbank still reign as the patron saints of corporate, commercial agriculture.

For many Americans the Jalapeño pepper has become the prototypical hot pepper. The 1987 *Park Seed Flowers and Vegetables* catalogue puts "Tam Mild Jalapeno" seeds at the top of its "Hot Pepper" column:

> 5267-9—Tam Mild Jalapeno. 70 days. Now enjoy all the extraordinary flavor of Jalapeno Pepper without all the heat. Only mildly pungent, Tam Mild Jalapeno has a sweet flavor that increases as the dark green 1 x 2 $^1/_2$ inch fruits turn red. A heavy yielder, ideal for nacho or pizza rings, sauces, pickling or to serve sliced with cheese. Mosaic resistant.

Somehow this condensed text says it all. Just as the tilde has been left off the *n*, de-ethnicizing the name, capsaicin—"the pungent principle in capsicums"[41]—has been cleansed from the pepper, and all in the cause of tempering the pungency so that the pods may now be used popularly on pizza and nachos, two American fast foods with only problematic connection to Italian or Mexican, or even New Mexican, cuisines. This accomplishment neatly disentangles flavor found in the skin from the pungency lying in the placenta (the "veins"), cherishing the one and banishing the other. Americans easily distinguish flavor and pungency, and opt for flavor as if it were a quality to be valued and react to pungency as if it were an accidental flaw to be banished. What they lose, or abandon, is any regard for the whole complex oral experience, for the subjective integrity of eating-tasting-feeling-biting-smelling all at once. One is reminded of the sacrifice of succulence and juiciness to meatiness and toughness in the square tomato (see chapter 9 below).

More than any other of the hundreds of bottled pepper sauces, Tabasco sauce has found a transethnic and transregional niche in American foodways and saloons. While "essence of capsicum" and "cayenne vinegar" condiments are not new, appearing as early as 1861 in Mrs. Isabella Beeton's *The Book of Household Management*,[42] the American commercialization of pepper sauce dates from Edmund McIlhenny's 1868 and B. F. Trappey's 1898 ventures into the hot sauce business.[43] That is a history all its own, and one well told recently by Richard Schweid in his light-hearted but well-researched *Hot Peppers: Cajuns and Capsicum in New Iberia, Louisiana,* in which he especially fixes on the regional and ethnic resonances of hot sauce.

It is the de-regionalized and de-ethnicized acceptance of Tabasco especially that fits into this melting-pot section, for it documents one final way in which capsicums have been embraced selectively, if not unreservedly, by the wider American public; in this state, capsicums are adopted as an indispensable if infrequently employed seasoning somewhat on a par with capers, anchovies, and Worcestershire sauces. The McIlhenny Company spoke to this place on the kitchen shelf with its blurb on the back of the bottle: "Try TABASCO in your recipe for spaghetti, chili, salad dressings, barbecue sauce, gravy and soups. Or add a 'Gourmet Touch' at the table to hamburger, eggs and tomato juice." Recently the company has replaced that text with one reading "Ask for it when you eat out, too. TABASCO sauce is in most restaurants. Just ask for it. Enjoy the condiment you like at home." To be sure, while Tabasco does indeed seem to be *in* most restaurants, apart from the South and Southwest one frequently must ask for a bottle, since it does not automatically appear on the table along with the sugar, salt, and pepper.

Tabasco had really "come out of the kitchen" a couple of decades earlier with the boom in popularity of the Bloody Mary, a vodka and tomato juice eye-opener laced with Tabasco. "It is my view that the use of Tabasco Sauce in Bloody Marys is what led to its introduction into today's American kitchens," Walter McIlhenny told Schweid.[44] "Almost every bar in the United States now keeps a bottle of hot sauce on hand," Schweid reports.[45] While there is nothing "tame" about the pungency of Tabasco or Trappey's Red Devil Louisiana Hot Sauce, their matter-of-fact location on backbars, in kitchen cabinets, and on many restaurant tables lends them a taken-for-granted place in the American consciousness if not in the day-to-day cookery; these sauces are not ghettoized so much as granted a niche. Tabasco's place in Cajun American cookery and in Mexican American booths is of a different order, somewhat akin to the way in which bagels may serve either as a marker of Jewish foodways or as an elective "bread" at sandwich bars—hence "healthy" whole-wheat bagels, cinnamon bagels, and raisin bagels.

What is lost by all this taming of the chiles is the natural variety of tastes and of gustatory experiences, including but not limited to the heightened state of consciousness resulting from "mouth surfing," the artful "riding" of a crest between bland and too hot.[46] What is gained, one must allow, is a multivalent American cookery that allows wide choice and furnishes to all who care an immense range of menus, dishes, ingredients, and methods of cooking and serving, from patio barbecues to tailgate picnics to chiliwich lunches and tacos on the run or nachos at a bar stool. Neither ethnic template nor historic practice stymies an ethic of making do and doing what one pleases. Discovering a new ingredient often leads to widespread adoption or co-option by the ever-eager and ever-dissatisfied cooking and eating public. Similarly, kiwi fruits ("Chinese Gooseberries") have recently been made into pies, jellies, salads, and even wines. Peppers began their assimilation much earlier and now have begun to be relished for what they are in their native settings.

## As American As Apple Pie

Chili con carne, rather than apple pie, might well be America's favorite dish.

—Craig Claiborne, *New York Times Magazine*, 1981

More American than apple pie.

—Connie Welch, *Parents*, 1983

"Chili con carne?" To one American it will mean the classic do-it-yourself, stovetop concoction, made up out of some ground or chopped meat, onions, tomatoes, beans, and chili powder. Any number of touches may be given it by this cook or that, but the core structure remains essentially unaltered. Some omit beans, some, tomatoes, but "chili" is the upshot, nevertheless: a home-made, vernacular, staple of American cuisine. And anyone can do it. "A man barely smart enough to steal a horse can whip up a tolerable mess of it," claims Richard Starnes in *Outdoor Life*.[47]

To other Americans, chili means public lunch counters and cheap, good fare. Many will share H. Allen Smith's warm memories of cafe chili. As a ten-year-old boy in Decatur, he reminisces, he used to spend his lunch allowance at "Chili Bill's joint a couple of blocks from the school." For ten cents he "got a bowl of steaming chili, six soda crackers and a glass of milk." "That was livin'!" he sighs in print.[48] Others met their first chili in the pool hall, still others in the school cafeteria, but all these public chilis shared a handmade quality or, sometimes, mediocrity.

To still others, chili purely comes out of a can. No making, just can-opening and heating, and then eating with saltines or oyster crackers. Crackers "on the side" or "crumbled in the bowl" may dress the chili; a shot or two of hot sauce, spice it up, but with canned chili a whole different eating experience emerges, an experience that has only a remote link to that of downing the homemade or cafe kind. And it is not that the others are superior, only eating of a different sort.

Whereas handmade chili carries the imprint, or at least the aura, of one cook making-it-up again, canned chilis exhibit uniform qualities of color and consistency and taste that abide unaltered over years, even decades. I can count on a can of Hormel's tasting just as it did in Minneapolis fifty years ago when I heated a can up for lunch during a half-hour break from stacking cans and bagging groceries at National Tea. While homemade and cafe chili may well bear a close resemblance, canned chili is really a comestible of a separate sort. Designer chilis and cook-off chilis are beside the point here. They entered American foodways after 1967, but they document a kind of mock-gourmet posturing and self-consciousness absent in the vernacular tradition. They belong better in the discussion of chili festivity and ritual below.

To make chili takes time; to make it good takes more simmering time than many are willing or able to give to it except on weekends. Enter industrial mass production, quality control, national marketing, and brand loyalty. Like so many other formerly homemade and now mass-produced foods—bread, pizza, tacos, soup, ice cream—chili has become big business. "Chili has evolved substantially from its putative origins as 'son-of-a-bitch stew,'... prepared by the washerwomen who followed around the 19th-century armies of Texas, into big business," according to Robert H. Bork Jr. in *Forbes*.[49] "The canned chili industry reached 240 million pounds" in 1984, "grossing $254 million," he continues, and then lists the major makers of canned chili: Hormel, with 28.77 percent of the market, worth $73 million in sales; followed by Quaker Oats at 14.73 percent ($37.4 million); Dennison, with 13.55 percent ($34.4 million); and Armour, with 7.51 percent ($19.1 million). That is big business, big cookery, big eating. But it says little about what chile peppers mean to Americans.

Millions of Americans may cook up chili con carne; millions more eat it in a restaurant or out of a can and never confront a chili pepper undisguised. It is this absorption of the chili pepper into an enveloping chili powder and then further into a contextualizing "stew" that testifies most eloquently to the way Americans have "naturalized" the pepper. A kind of barely conscious, collective conspiracy to take over and tame the pepper and put it to everyday domestic service seems to have driven a nation of anonymous cooks to design a simple, democratic, all-in-one national dish. So thoroughly has "chili" become the nickname for the dish, that chile pepper lovers have taken to distinguishing chili the dish from "chile" the vegetable. It must be as well that the recent upsurge of interest in "winning chilis" and chili cookbooks reflects just such an understanding of how little chili has had to do with chile peppers or their "heat" as a rule.

"More American than apple pie"? If so, what it enacts of a spirit that speaks to many Americans differs significantly from whatever values and meanings apple pies realize. Apple pies are made by cooks adept at crusts and seasoning and baking, not by just anybody "barely smart enough to steal a horse." Experience and culinary wisdom and taste lie realized in even a merely passable apple pie. Chili, on the other hand, tolerates slapdash kitchen practices and allows continuous corrective treatments, more liquid, more chili powder, more beans if it gets too hot. An apple pie is a triumph of synthetic art, achieving a finished masterpiece of pastry and fruit and spices and juices caught just in time, before overcooking, before leaking, and the like. Chili has no neat beginning, middle, or end. Rather, it accrues character, picks up flavors, and its ingredients become progressively less separately identifiable as simmering continues. There is a point, to be sure, before which it is "not done," but no point where it is finished the way a pie is. If people are late to dinner, the chili can go right on bubbling and is none the worse for it. Common lore has it that chili even keeps on improving after it is decanted and placed in the refrigerator. It is "better the next day." Chili, then, is apple pie's iconic opposite, a syndetic rather than synthetic and an invocative rather than virtuosic creation, to borrow the categories of anthropologist Robert Plant Armstrong.[50]

Pie is a treat, and a treat at the end of a meal. Chili not only presents itself as "main dish" to pie's dessert, it largely denies that meals even need courses. Often chili is the whole meal. Pies are festive, special; chili, ordinary, unpretentious. Pies have generally presented women's skills and experience and roles; chili has no particular gender. Men make it as well as women. Nothing about the composition of chili con carne says "feminine or masculine." It does not boast of a kill or celebrate wifely achievement. "Can she bake a cherry pie, Billy Boy, Billy Boy?" the old song goes, enunciating one test of a girl's suitability as a wife. Nothing about ordinary chili con carne leads one to take it as a test of gendered virtue. Chili, then, speaks of the irrelevancy of artificial lines between experienced and novice cookery, between soup course and main course, between meat course and vegetable, making even the need to wield the right fork or any utensils but a spoon irrelevant. Chili proves that elegant and adept procedures and sequences need not tyrannize cooking and eating. Dinner may be "on time" or not, pick up as well as sit down, and there is no need for different dishes to arrive ready at the same time; there is only one dish. And diners need not even sit down together all at once. Men equally with women and even children may make a "tolerable mess" of chili. Chili is the melting pot, melting down distinctions of class, gender, taste, polite dining, family hierarchy, cuisine, and even competence.

If chili con carne realizes a leveling and integrative cultural strategy applied to cookery, drawing all ingredients into its melting-pot vortex, the recent embrace of hot peppers, in particular, and ethnic cuisines, in general, demonstrate a contrary, "salad bowl" model of adaptation and incorporation of separate and distinct ingredients allowed to retain their separate character. From a tripartite armature of soup-or-salad/main course/dessert schema, ingenuity reaches out to ever more exotic garnishes and finishing to "spice up" the meal and make the day-to-day cooking more interesting for the man or woman charged with it.

## Spicing Up the American Cookery

Things began to change. Writing for the *American Mercury* in 1925, Burton Kline complained that "in spite of a plethora of all things eatable, American cookery lags the very last of our arts."[51] He calls for Americans to throw over the "Puritan stomach" along with "the Puritan mind." For those like Kline who take cookery as an art, the drudgery of cooking taken-for-granted fare can oppress. No wonder then that those charged with it scour cookbooks, monthly magazines, and weekly newspaper columns for inspiration.

One source of inspiration was "foreign cookery" from neighboring Mexico and the Southwest. Sarah Gibbs Campbell assured readers of her 1931 column "Foreign Cookery: Recipes from Mexico and the Southwest" in *Ladies Home Journal* that "American housewives can easily acquire skill in this delightful cookery of Mexico if they select their material carefully and remember the necessity for long, slow blending and cooking."[52] "Chile-Pepper Paste," "Chile Con Carne," "Sopa de Arroz," "Arroz y Gallina à la Valencia," "Mexican Pecan Candy," and "Cafe" are the recipes for foods "commonly served in Mexico" which Campbell includes. In 1939 Edith Barber offered the readers of *Good Housekeeping* magazine thirteen recipes "Tested by Good Housekeeping Institute," among them one for "Mexican Rice" but calling for no peppers, and others for Tomato Sauce, Mexican Salad, and Frijoles that called for a teaspoon of chili powder each.[53] These recipes, while "tested" and tamed down "for American Meals," clearly open ways for American "housekeepers" to spice up meals, to add a dash of exotic piquancy to otherwise generally "cool" cookery. Whereas chili con carne may have become an all-American dish, Barber and Campbell turned a corner. They introduce exotic cookery *as such* into "American meals." Granted, they "translated" for their readers, and their kitchen tested their translations, but spice up American meals they did.

A similar spicing up, this time of American snacking, occurred following World War II. It drew its inspiration from the Italian American foodways of the Northeast. Troops stationed at or passing through Fort Dix and encountering the "pizza pies" of New York and New Jersey became missionaries for pizza. It spread steadily out across the nation, appearing first in bars, then generating its own separated restaurants, and finally fast-food franchises. Meanwhile, people learned to make pizza at home from scratch, and later from kits as they became available, and finally to pop frozen pizzas into the oven. While pizza does not feature hot peppers any more than chili con carne does, it may contain pepperoni and spiced sausage meat and does seem to invite patrons to sprinkle crushed red pepper over it. Many were induced into their first pepper experience by the same route as Naomi Wise, with "a slice of pizza on which a boyfriend shook too much crushed red; she couldn't eat it, so he did."[54] Pizza opened the door to even hotter ethnic American foodways for America.

Perhaps the stationing of troops in the Southwest and West helped open the way to wider exploitation of a heretofore mainly regional and ethnic cookery. Off-duty munching of tacos in bars or of eating inexpensive combination plates of enchilada, tamales, chiles rellenos, rice, and beans initiated palates into an additional food to go with drink. And when mustered out, these veterans went back to Minnesota or Detroit and looked for ingredients to replicate some of the salsa and snacks they had enjoyed earlier. Raymond Sokolov recalls his own initiation, but I take his story to be the type specimen for hundreds of others similarly deposited in family foodways: "During World War II, my father was stationed for a time in El Paso, Texas, near the Mexican border. Although he brought away little else of value from this stint at Fort Bliss, he did return to Detroit with a taste for fiery jalapeño peppers. For me those pale green tongue burners, lurking in ambush among cocktail snacks, were a test of manhood. But when I managed . . . to gulp one whole . . . , I discovered that I had been initiated into a tribe. . . . I was forever doomed to be a hot person in a cold culture."[55]

What began as vernacular snacking and dining soon found expression in the food columns of the popular press. Poppy Cannon addressed the developing national taste for "Tex-Mex" eating in a 1953 *House Beautiful.*[56] "In this packer-blessed era, your key to 'Tex-Mex' eating is the trusty can opener," Cannon assures her readers. Chili sauce, Tabasco, green chiles, beans, and even tortillas may be bought in cans, she explains. Cannon addresses a national audience, one that transcends the South, the Southwest, and California, and one drawn to the modern kitchen architecture and furnishings pictured in the article and characteristic of postwar affluence (a world of stoves, ventilators, dishwashers, refrigerators, and open counter space).

Meanwhile, in the Southwest and California, *Sunset* magazine took another tack, touting an amalgamated cookery that echoed native and Mexican foodways prepared from fresh, local ingredients.[57] "Peppers: Mild, Hot, Hotter" tells how to handle, wash, and prepare hot peppers, and gives recipes for three dishes: a Green Peppers Florentine (nothing hot), Chiles Rellenos (using eight long green chile peppers), and a Lime and Chile Pepper Loaf (the lime from "lime flavored gelatin")! The amalgamation continues with Poppy Cannon's 1957 "Mexican Magic for American Tables," in which she advises readers on "American" substitutes for ingredients such as pasilla, jalapeño, ancho, and poblano chiles—she substitutes "bell or sweet green peppers."[58]

In the decades that followed these first rather timid embraces of hotter regional and ethnic alternative to cool cuisine, publishers discovered a market for articles about and recipes for all manner of cooking. Magazines like *Woman's Day* and *Family Circle* produced luscious-looking, color-illustrated articles on foods for shoppers to pick up on impulse as they waited at supermarket check-out counters. Later, *Woman's Day Encyclopedia of Cookery*, a twelve-volume, illustrated, two-thousand-page compendium, appeared with sections featuring exotic national cuisines as well as regional American emphases: "American Cook book," "South American Cook Book," "Southeast Asian Cookery," "Southern Cookery," "Southwestern," and "Western Cook Book."[59] The *Encyclopedia* not only glosses *Capsicum frutescens* and explains chili con carne and chili sauce, it includes thirty-four listings in its index under "Pepper, Green" and eight under "Pepper(s), Capsicum," including recipes for a pepper butter, for pepper and corn relish, and hash, in Pipérade with potatoes (pepperoni con patate), and roasted-pepper sauce.[60] Under "Chili," the index lists over forty recipes for sauces, salsa, and hot dishes using hot peppers. Travel and leisure magazines began to address the interest: *Holiday, Sunset, Southern Living, Health, McCalls, Look, Farm Journal,* the *New York Times Magazine, Natural History, Gourmet,* and *Bon Appétit* all take up the cause of hot cooking. *Sunset* pictured and explained the differences between Anaheim, Pasilla, Yellow Wax, Hungarian Yellow Wax, Fresno, Jalapeño, and Serrano chiles in a piece called "Chiles Mild to Wild."[61] In the same year the magazine explained how to use "fresh jalapeño chile peppers" to apply "Jalapeños' Fire to Ribs, Beans, Spoonbread."[62]

This popular press documents a remarkable change in the symbolic significance of chiles in American cookery. A century ago few would have raised an eyebrow at Rousseau's matter-of-fact dismissal of pepper eating as savage. The savage's touch and taste will remain as coarse as his hearing and sight are keen, he deduced, and presumed that such coarse senses explain why they "stimulate their taste with red peppers, and drink European liquors like water."[63] A corollary to such a "truth" would be that eating hot peppers likely harms one's taste or erases it. Compare this traditional Euro-American suspicion with the developed taste for peppers that is at the heart of the new taste for Thai food and other hot cuisine.

Raymond Sokolov, food writer for *Natural History Magazine,* eloquently sums up the cultural dissonance between those on opposite sides of what he calls "the great hot pepper divide": "Weaned on a cold cuisine, we have no background in hot tastes and are so struck by the intensity of the experience that we have trouble sorting out the different strains of flavor that can be supplied by the multifarious hot seasoning mixed up in a well-prepared hot dish. We also tend to look down on hot cuisines because they have so often originated in nonindustrial or nonwhite cultures."[64] He notes that "otherwise discriminating eaters" will dismiss complex and highly spiced cookery because it "anesthetizes the tongue." "One also frequently runs into the culture-bound view," he continues, "that all hot food is just crude stuff, an assault on the body that no civilized cuisine would permit." If culture and nature are seen as contending realities, peppers would seem to these alarmed eaters to belong to nature.

A contrary view is that held by the indigenous peoples of the New World, he explains, invoking Claude Lévi-Strauss, who, as Sokolov points out, "concluded in his analysis of the myths of preliterate America that *the hot pepper is the symbol of civilized eating* among them." He quotes Lévi-Strauss as follows: "It is striking, indeed, that the majority of American societies view rotted food as the prototype of precultural nourishment and consider the hot pepper, which is their principal condiment, as *the element that separates nature and culture* [emphasis added]."[65]

## Chili Hokum and Chili "Sivilized"

Frank X. Tolbert recounts a mock ritual of chiliheads in a piece on chili con carne for the *Saturday Evening Post* in 1962.[66] Lyndon Johnson was in Washington, D.C., as vice president; Dallas was the brash capital of the Texas Southwest boom, but still a year away from its shame as the city in which President Kennedy had been assassinated. The mock seriousness and even self-mockery of the chiliheads in Tolbert's piece set the tone for much of the chili hokum that flourished during the Johnson years and after, but the precedent had been set earlier in 1952 when "a Dallas advertising man, the late Joe Cooper," had written and published "the society's bible": *With or Without Beans; Being a Compendium to Perpetuate the Internationally Famous Bowl of Chili (Texas Style) Which Occupies Such an Important Place in Modern Civilization.*[67]

A question of "civilization" is the fulcrum this mock ritual and the later cook-off festivals teeter upon. The base rests on a bed at least three centuries deep of seaboard Brahmin distrust of unwashed and undisciplined enthusiasts of the interior, first in the Connecticut Valley and upcountry Carolina, later in Pennsylvania and the Ohio River watershed, later still in the Old Southwest, and eventually in the cattle and mining West of the nineteenth century. Reciprocally, inhabitants of the interior cursed the East as corrupt and effete or "worked them," as Mark Twain would have put it, by "putting them on," by acting more boorish and ignorant than they were so as to trap them into making fools of themselves when they took the westerners at false face value, when they had, in the phrase of the day, "been sold."

Literary humor of this ilk reaches back at least as far as Benjamin Franklin's 1765 letter to the editor of a newspaper on "the grand Leap of the Whale . . . up the Fall of Niagara."[68] Appropriately, the great chili cook-off phenomena of the post-Johnson era has its origins in just such a genre. Joe Cooper's inflated encomium to chili, "the aroma of good chili should generate rapture akin to a lover's kiss," sets a tone and establishes a mock-heroic strawman for H. Allen Smith to "'front" half a decade later.[69] Writing for *Holiday*, Smith throws down the gauntlet in his title, "Nobody Knows More About Chili Than I Do."[70] In the tradition of tall bragging so common to the genre, Smith claims that his chili is "light years beyond" any other and that all other chili is "such vile slop that a coyote would turn his back on it."[71]

Wick Fowler, a Texan from Austin, who butchered out, he claimed, "at better than 250 pounds," picks up the challenge, and the upshot is the now traditional Terlingua, Texas, chili cook-off.[72] Fowler boasted that his chili had been known "to open up eighteen sinus cavities as yet unknown to modern medicine" and puts down "Soupy" Smith's chili as "on the sissy side": "'The maternity wards in Texas hospitals,' said Mr. Fowler, 'have to warm up Smith's formula before feeding it to newborn babies.'"[73]

As much as this posturing and bombast radiates a mock-macho air and turns on putting women and children out of the picture—as Starnes puts it, "First, drive all women and children from the kitchen"—the deeper target is "sissy" culture and its cooking for children. It is accidentally sexist more than meanly so.[74] This is important since an equal proportion of the participants in the chili cook-offs I have observed have been women who got equally into the spirit of slapdash, anti-sissy dress, cookery, and semiotics. The peppers which "real men" put in the pot are one key to the distinction between Texas chili and effete slop; the beans Smith and others "dilute" their chili with, the other, beans signifying a vegetable that diminishes the essential sauce.

As with Lévi-Strauss's "sauvages," hot peppers function again as "the element that separates nature and culture" and are "the symbol of civilized eating" among Americans. But the separation has now two faces. On the one side, beans "finish out" the chili con carne for those of an eastern and northern persuasion, tempering the chili wildness, as it were. On the other, Texans take beans as the stuff upon which chili may be spooned to make them fit to eat. Hot peppers mark a new cuisine for "modern civilization," but a "civilization" not too "sissy" or childish; in short, a "natural, manly" civilization. This theme is compacted into the last sentences of *The Adventures of Huckleberry Finn:* "I reckon I got to light out for the territory ahead of the rest, because Aunt Sally she's going to adopt me and sivilize me, and I can't stand it. I been there before."

Since the 1960s, chili cook-offs have spread, back into the Midwest and out to the Pacific Coast, have become common in cities as well as in rural small towns, but while the literature is abundant and entertaining to savor, it takes us away from a focus on hot peppers. Chili cook-offs have more to do with chopping and cooking meat and certain "secret" ingredients than with chiles per se. They are high-spirited affairs, featuring a good deal of light-hearted self-mockery and playful showing off. Goofy aprons, punning signs, silly names, and free-flowing beer characterized the only one I have yet attended.

At the 1987 First Annual Chili Cookoff in Woodland, California, for example, booths offered "Duckblind Chili," invoking the local male hunting ethos; "Okie Dokie" chili, celebrating the "ethnic" heritage of the performers and many other Californians; and even "Uffda Chili," proving that "even Norwegians make chili." One cook wore a "Farkle Family" T-shirt and another a T-shirt featuring a farting hillbilly, alluding apparently to the notorious windiness of beans. Clues of dress, physical appearance, talk, humor, and iconography suggest that this rural cook-off drew on lower middle- and working-class "Anglos" for many of its performers and customers.

*Fig. 5.2. UFFDA chili booth at the First Annual Chili Cookoff, 1987, Woodland, California. Photograph by David Scofield Wilson.*

The Fourth Annual (1987) Chile Fiesta in Berkeley, California, on the other hand, drew a cosmopolitan crowd and took the chile pepper instead of chili for its focus. Booths erected by "leading restaurants, delicatessens, and cafes" offered exotic, spicy fare. They were mobbed. Other booths offered chile-inspired jewelry: earrings, pendants, buttons, necklaces. A Salsa band performed. A Nicaragua banner made it plain that solidarity with Central America was part of the meaning of this event. Crowded and popular as this gathering obviously was, I would rank its cooking as "haute cuisine" compared with the "bas cuisine" of the Woodland cook-off.

The meanings of these two events diverge politically, aesthetically, and socially. The Woodland cook-off plays out and plays off the "good old boy" (and "gal") motif seen in Texas affairs. At the Berkeley festival, "with it" citizens rather than "good old boys" both patronized Latino liberation and bought into the hot (in the sense of fashionable) new cuisines of California. But the two share one quality: they flaunt chili or chiles as signs of their self-conscious distinction from whatever they take to be "mainstream" American life.

Festivals make their cultural point by altering or affronting conventional norms of behavior, and cook-offs belong to this family of non-everyday social behavior. Rituals, on the other hand, commonly affirm core values by enacting them in special and elaborated ways. The tenor of a number of recent articles and books on hot cuisine suggests that a kind of seriousness appropriate to ritual has come to characterize that American cookery which aims to boost peppery dishes into *haute cuisine* status. Carolyn Dille and Susan Belsinger explain peppers and present recipes to the readers of *Gourmet* for "Tequila Diablo," "Sweet Potato and Jalapeño Enchiladas with Tomatillo Sauce," "Anaheim Pepper Timbales with Tomato Salsa," "Corn and chili Pepper Soufflé," "Chicken, Scallop, and Asparagus Sauté with chili Peppers," and a "Mango and Hot Pepper Sorbet," among others, calling for such special ingredients as tomatillos, mangos, dark rum, ancho and pasilla peppers, avocados (preferably Haas), and "*achiote* (annatto, available at Hispanic markets)."[75] That is taking the peppers seriously. Often these essays teach the proper names to call chiles by and recount a history of the cuisine. Others set out to integrate the chili cookery into one of the subsets of modern American cookery, as with *Health*'s presentation of recipes for "tofu Chili," "Eggplant chili" "chili Honolulu," "Mushroom Chili," and "Fish Pozole."[76] *Southern Living* reports as well that ristras, those handsome, hanging ropes of red chiles usually seen in the Southwest, are "now showing up all over the South," proving that chiles are "in" as decor as well as food.[77] *Bon Appétit* passes along Chef Robert Del Grande's recipe for "Quail with Poblano Sauce and Tomato Salsa" and explains that "chiles work well together, too . . . like grapes in a blended wine."[78] And *Gourmet* offers the reader recipes for a Southwestern Thanksgiving, thus linking spicy cookery to a ritual feast as American as Norman Rockwell: "Roast Cornish Game Hens with Chili Gravy," "Pine Nut, Pinto Bean, and Scallion Pilaf," "Stewed Zucchini and Red Bell Peppers," and "Pumpkin Bread Pudding with Coffee and Whipped Cream." "This melting pot harvest celebration reflects the cultural mix of the American Southwest," we are told.[79] When a holiday meal "reflects" a region's putative demography and pulls together its indigenous produce and peoples' palates, we can feel justified in concluding that a sort of ritual ratification of foodways and other cultural matters is afoot. Finally, pulling together regional and ethnic foodways and tempering it with the recent fad for *nouvelle cuisine*, Suzanne Kimball reports on the "Nueva cocina Mexicana" of Mexico City's "classiest restaurants" for the *Arizona Republic.*[80]

Jessica B. Harris integrates capsicum hot cookery with black pepper cookery from around the world, legitimating, as it were, the full citizenship in world cuisine of New World pepper cookery in her book, *Hot Stuff: A Cookbook in Praise of the Piquant.*[81] She explains the history of hot cookery, the botany of *Piper nigrum* and *Capsicum* species, the properties of pepper varieties and pepper products, and offers "chile caveats" and recipes to "put out the fire." *Totally Hot* (1986) similarly narrates history, explains the chemistry, and address the question "Why do we eat chile?"[82] Best of all, the recent (1990) *Whole Chile Pepper Book,* by Dave DeWitt and Nancy Gerlach, recalls the history of peppers, explains the qualities of diverse cultivars, includes beautiful color plates of over two dozen peppers, and includes nearly two hundred recipes for Southwestern, East Asian, African, South American, and other dishes using hot peppers. With these and other full-length cookbooks and articles in gourmet magazines, chiles may be said to have become, if not central to American cookery, at least an ingredient with unique qualities that make it essential to certain fully legitimate dishes and cuisines.[83] And more, capsicums have become one more item on the palette that any cook with pretensions to staying abreast of current cuisine must come to terms with. As if rotated 180 degrees, peppers have become the "symbol of civilized eating" and a marker of culture, and peppers have gone from symbolically "savage" to being indices of "taste."

## The Capsicum Cult

While folklore archives house shards of popular belief and recipes relevant to people's use of peppers, and commercial magazines circulate lore and narratives about peppers and handsome images of peppers, surely the greatest store of pepper lore, pepper use, pepper tales, tastes, recipes, and warnings exists outside of the public sphere and in private kitchens, home gardens, and around the family table. I was lucky to have some of this opened to me accidentally. I had written a brief note to *National Gardening* about my interest in peppers and asked for any lore. The magazine printed my letter in the "Seed Swap" section instead of in "Member's Mailbox," where I meant it to go. As a consequence I receive seventy letters in thirty days, mostly asking for seeds but some also sending seeds and accounts of what the writers had grown and how. A few passed on jokes or superstitions about planting, but most did not "know any lore," as they saw it. To me their narratives and reports of practices were exactly what I needed to complement what I had gleaned from archives, from published compendia of beliefs, and from the popular press.

A woman from Mississippi wrote at length:

> The South has long been a user of peppers of all kinds, especially of the hot variety. I am 42 years old and have always eaten them in some form. Even as a child I remember relatives making hot pepper Chow-chow and relish. Our table also always had what we refer to as pepper sauce in some form or another depending on the frame of mind of the preparer at the time it was made. I, myself grow hot peppers and also make the sauces, relish and chow-chow. My husband and I love to eat hot peppers. I "pickle" all of the extras to save for winter use that are not eaten during the growing season, I grow several varieties: Cayenne, Jalapeño, hot banana, sweet banana, Bell pepper and we have a mystery pepper (our name for it) that appears to be a cross between a cayenne and ? It is some what lighter in color and is hotter than the hot banana but not as hot as the true cayenne. It is a very good table pepper (what we Southerners call a pepper that is

just washed and put on the table in a bowl and eaten a bite at a time along with your meal). Most all of the people that I know also eat peppers in this manner and also make sauces relishes and etc. with the recipes varying from household to household. Most of the recipes have been handed down in each family for generations.[84]

And an old man from Tennessee contributes both lore and his historical framing of hill cuisine:

> White people started moving into our Tennessee hills during the 1770's and came in larger numbers just after The Revolution. From that time until about 1945 the area was a poverty pocket. The food was coarse and monotonous, and the only spice the people could grow was capsicum. Cayenne is the variety they started with, and they are slow to change. I remember my grandparents and some of the great-grandparents who would never come to dinner without a big pod of cayenne.
>
> Back in 1911 my mother, named Tony, was six years old, and was the favorite of her grandmother, named Mary. Mary had many grandchildren, but she always wanted Tony to select the pod of pepper for grandma's dinner. Tony could look at a large string of dried pepper and select the hottest pods in the string. Mom told me years later that she was picking the pretty, waxy, shiny pods. She was selecting pods because they were pretty, and they also happened to be hottest. Now, look at de arbol chili and you'll see a small, very waxy cayenne which is somewhat hotter than long red cayenne.[85]

He tells us also that "my father's mother was unusually successful with peppers, and she . . . insisted that to get peppers to come up you had to be angry as the devil when you sow the seed."

And a woman from Massachusetts takes pride in her horticulture and cooking:

> In my garden I have about six hundred plants of hot peppers, all different. I live in the Italian section of Malden, where everyone has a back yard and garden. Its fun to see my men friends and neighbors looking over my fence in *awe* because I have so many. I dried them on a string, I also roast them and freeze for the Winter. I also pickle the hot Cherry. . . . We have a pepper joke out here every time we have a party. "'Auntie Glo' (that's me) is coming with her hot peppers," and they laugh, but they all eat them and Love them and joke about the after effects a pepper will give.[86]

And from Mississippi:

I can remember seeing a pot or a plant in a special place in the flower garden that had peppers that were similar to cayenne and could have possibly been cayenne. These peppers were allowed to ripen and turn red. As they ripened they were added to a string of peppers hanging in the kitchen. The string would be very full with peppers sticking out on all sides. The string would be from 18 inches to 3 feet long. I have seen these strings of peppers hanging in kitchens all my life but have never made one nor have I witnessed anyone use a pepper from these strings to cook with or season. I went to the expert, Mammaw who is 82 said she and her Mother also made strings of pepper. Nothing was done to the pepper just strung and allowed to dry. She said the string was like crochet thread or sometimes the thread used on the old 25 or 50 pound bags of flour. She said they always strung several to use in sausage when they killed a hog also. I was wrong they were used.[87]

Performers share stories and jokes and admonitions:

Only two quips come to mind about peppers. One is, "Those peppers are so hot you'll have to use the bathroom in the creek to keep from setting the house on fire." I have heard that all my life and did clean it up a might [sic] as what was done in the creek was more graphically stated! The other is more modern and was told to me be a friend. Do you know where the phrase "Burning ring of fire" came from? It came out in a song after Johnny Cash spent a few weeks in South Texas eating some Mexican hot sauce. One who eats alot of hot peppers does not need to analyze that to understand its meaning. I've also heard that peppers are supposed to help keep your arteries clear of plaque and lower your blood pressure and also keep you from being so at risk for colo-rectal cancer. According to my husband (who is a county deputy coroner) Mexicans are supposed to have a lower incidence of colo-rectal cancer.[88]

Another correspondent admonished me to tell people not to pick their noses or play with themselves after cutting-up hot peppers.

In the context of our noted American "cool cuisine" and historic marginalizing of peppers, these chatty accounts of easy familiarity with hot peppers brought me up short. Evidently there is, and has been, a set of Americans (northern and southern, rural and urban) for whom peppers are both an everyday matter and valued as special.

## Peppers' Presence

My correspondents made me recognize that across the land there exists a kind of "enclave," not one enclosed in space amidst outsiders, but a cohort of "believers," as it were, of pepper insiders who carry on a capsicum culture of jokes, warnings, narratives, recipes, and foodways. I take the outpouring of letters and seeds and SASE's for seeds in response to my *National Gardening* query as an instance. I found that I was told family history, even beyond the subject of peppers, invited to drop by for pepper tales and beer, directed to be sure to write to another savant, and treated generally as an insider, not simply because I am a fellow member of the National Gardening Association, but a fellow pepper lover. To love peppers appears to signal to others that you expect and deserve intimate treatment. Similar enclaves may exist among sweet corn growers and surely between tomato fanciers. Somehow, in electing to invest energy and money and self in peppers, one appears to demonstrate a loyalty to a set of values that sets him or her off from the mass of the public.

If I read my informants correctly, many of them interact with their peppers in an intimate, more than personal, dramatic way. They characterize themselves as "fanatics," "lovers," and "enthusiasts" of peppers. They give them pet names: "Hades Hot," "Indian Hot Hot," etc. They relish the "bite" the pepper gives them back and joke about its "burning at both ends" if they unwisely abuse it. They grant the peppers' presence.

Furthermore, they interact with peppers in a way that mimics dialogue, give and take, respect and amusement. A person and a pepper may play out patterned exchanges: One picks a pickled pepper up in a special way and does not

*Fig. 5.3. Chiles de arbol as Christmas tree ornaments. Photograph by David Scofield Wilson.*

wipe his eyes after, and the pepper squirts and snaps back or heats lips as expected. Peppers become more than mere produce. They often are kept in sight as a presence in the living quarters as well as in gardens, perhaps as an "affecting presence," which makes visible and constant the special genius of the capsicum, its "intensivity" and "discontinuousness," to use the language of Robert Plant Armstrong again.[89] Each pod is distinct and whole, shiny and smooth, collapsing in on itself with age, collecting itself and concentrating its essence (capsaicin), hence "intensive"; but each is distinct and even different, hence "discontinuous." Recall the woman from Massachusetts and her "six hundred plants of hot peppers, all different." She can hardly have had six hundred separate kinds; perhaps each was individual to her, but what is important to note is the value she places on their separateness, their discontinuous presence.

A persuasive confirmation of the pepper's "affecting presence" is that gorgeously presented in a recent poster which gathers on one sheet likenesses of thirty-one cultivars (fifty-one pods), each "shown actual size."[90] Each one is richly colored (red, green, yellow, orange, or black) and so smooth that highlights dramatize every swelling and each convolution. Beneath each separate portrait the pepper's name ("Poblano Verde," "New Mexico Red," "Orange Habañero") appears, as well as its place of origin and use in cookery. A number from 1 to 10 codes each pepper's piquancy (3 for the Poblano, 10 for the Habañero).

Assembled in syndetic ristras, or strings, peppers own additional power and presence. Ristras of reds hang in ramadas and patios and porches, being "with us" more than, say, a sack of pinto beans or a bushel of potatoes. Lately, ristras have been used to decorate delis and restaurants, along with braids of garlic. In both instances the again-and-againness of the assemblage invites admiration and cautious respect. In the Parkers' case (above), the family kept the "string of peppers" inside and continually added to it, but almost never "used" it. It was, it appears, more one of the family than merely a food resource.

As members of the family, peppers are "personal" and unpredictable. In engaging them, we invite a kind of mutual intercourse. As players in the kitchen or as actors at the table they may promise and surprise, trick and delight, one. Cooking with peppers amounts to a kind of play, behavior within rules in which boundaries are tested and "moves" or "stories" are invented and played out. "You can always put peppers in but you can't take them out," one informant warned, voicing a meta-rule for pepper play. One may cook automatically, by rote, but even habitual cooking has built within it a kind of necessary slack. Peppers differ. It does not work to "add three tsps minced Serrano peppers" the way one would "1 T of chili powder" or "cup of flour." Either you follow the exact recipe and concede that what you get may be too hot, just right, or too mild, or you test and taste in continuous negotiation with the dish to create a finished, mutual, and satisfactory performance.

What all these pepper lovers acknowledge by their consent to capsicums is the power of the vegetable to act on one's consciousness as well as on one's palate. Whether as a ristra, as a chile necklace, or as a condiment, the hot pepper asserts its pungent presence too strongly to overlook. The "rush" that pepper eaters experience when eating hot peppers "brings on a high state of consciousness," according to A. Weil, "a physician who studies the effects of psychotropic plants."[91] Less grandly, I have found that paying attention to peppers and their place in American life, its popular beliefs, home cures, and foodways has enriched my sense of the interconnections between Old World beliefs and New World conditions. My study has also alerted me of the degree to which learnéd culture, mass culture, and folk culture converge on certain resonant "texts." And especially of the lively, ongoing texture of culture when looked at up close and in detail.

## Notes

1. Chris Schlesinger, with John Willoughby, "In Praise of the Pepper: You Can't Beat the Heat," *Metropolitan Home* (Nov. 1990), 59.
2. Alan Goldman, "Beyond Aesthetics," *California Living Magazine*, Apr. 15, 1984, 31–33.
3. C. B. Heiser Jr., "Peppers," in *Evolution of Plant Crops*, ed. N. W. Simmonds (New York: Longman, 1965), 265.
4. Gary Paul Nabhan, *Gathering the Desert* (Tucson: Arizona Univ. Press, 1985), 129.
5. Both are "nightshades," along with potatoes and eggplants, tobacco and black nightshade, bittersweet and petunias, jimsonweed, mandrake, and belladonna.
6. Nabhan, *Gathering the Desert*, 265.
7. Raymond Sokolov, "Some Like It Hot," *Natural History* 83 (Apr. 1974): 64.
8. J. G. Bourke, "The Folk-Foods of the Rio Grande Valley and of Northern Mexico," *Journal of American Folklore* 8 (Jan. 1895): 41–71.
9. Ibid., 46.
10. L. E. Smith, "Chili con Carne: (Meat With Hot Sauce)," *Overland Monthly* n.s. 66 (Sept. 1915 ): 224–27; A. M. Chase, "Chili Cherub," *Overland Monthly* n.s. 81 (Nov. 1923): 28–29, 39.
11. Chase, "Chili Cherub," 28, 39.
12. William Brandon, "Chillipiquin," *Saturday Evening Post* 216, July 10, 1943, 19.
13. Ibid.
14. Fannie Merritt Farmer, *The Original Boston Cooking-School Cook Book 1896* (New York: Crown, 1973; facsimile of the 1896 ed.).
15. A word about nomenclature. Some authors, in seeking to regularize spellings and meanings, have sought to reserve *chili* for that concoction of meats

and spices and tomatoes sometimes added to beans to form chili con carne. They call the peppers "chiles," but there has not yet arisen out of all the rationalizing efforts a standard usage. In the context of this chapter on capsicum peppers, "peppers" or "chiles" for the vegetables and "chili" for the popular dish should forestall confusion; and "chili sauce" or "Cincinnati chili" for other concoctions and "bell pepper," "frying pepper," or "Italian pepper" for nonhot but edible capsicums should dissolve any ambiguity.

16. John C. Gunn, *Gunn's New Family Physician, or Home Book of Health* (Cincinnati: Wilstach, Baldwin & Co., 1874), 824. Beliefs about the medicinal virtues of red pepper persist into the twentieth century in folk beliefs. *Popular Beliefs and Superstitions: A Compendium of American Folklore From the Ohio Collection of Newbell Niles Puckett* (hereafter referred to as *Popular Beliefs and Superstitions. . . Ohio)*, ed. W. D. Hand, A. Casetta, and S. B. Thiederman (Boston: G. K. Hall and Company, 1981), records medical uses of red peppers for hoarseness (no. 10184), menstrual cramps (no. 10531), neuralgia (no. 10626), rheumatism (nos. 10984, 11014, and 11023), and for whooping cough (no. 12687). These uses would seem to draw upon the physiologically stimulating properties of the pepper. Others nod to their metaphysical "strength": worn as an amulet against evil (nos. 25576, 27465), sprinkled under the rug to keep evil away (no. 22984), and "to avert witches" (no. 25964). None of these listings address the presence of red pepper in cuisine. *Popular Beliefs and Superstitions from Utah* (hereafter referred to as *Popular Beliefs . . . Utah*), collected by Anthon S. Cannon, ed. Wayland D. Hand and Jeannine E. Talley (Salt Lake City: Utah Univ. Press, 1984), similarly records using red pepper to stop thumb sucking (no. 1148), in one's shoes to keep feet warm (no. 1721), to stop internal bleeding (no. 2992), for ulcers (no. 4185), sore throat (no. 4003), heart attack (no. 3599), varicose veins, and colds (no. 3187). The "logic" behind these medicinal uses and the association between caloric heat and piquant "heat" in no. 1721 are of a pattern with the Ohio beliefs. *The Frank C. Brown Collection of North Carolina Folklore,* vol. 6 of *Popular Beliefs and Superstitions* from North Carolina (hereafter referred to as *Popular Beliefs . . . North Carolina*), ed. Wayland D. Hand (Durham, N.C.: Duke Univ. Press, 1961), note treatments for rheumatism (nos. 1997,1992, and 1998), to induce labor (no. 29), for delirium tremens (no. 1273), flu (no. 1748), pneumonia (no. 1939), toothache (no. 2362), chills (no. 1070), to treat a "felon," or infection of the finger (no. 1407), chills (nos. 1071 and 1069), measles (no. 1821), and frostbite (no. 1529). As in *Popular Beliefs . . . Ohio,* a number of magical uses are noted as well; similarly in *Folk-Lore from Adams County Illinois,* rev. 2d ed., ed. Harry Middleton Hyatt (Hannibal, Mo.: Western Printing and Lithographing Co., 1965).

17. Gunn, *New Family Physician,* 824.

18. Ibid., 774.

19. Charles E. Rosenberg, ed., *Gunn's Domestic Medicine* (Knoxville: Univ. of Tennessee Press, 1986).
20. *The Adventures of Huckleberry Finn,* chap. 17.
21. Philip M. Hamer, *The Centennial History of the Tennessee State Medical Association: 1830–1930* (Nashville: Tennessee State Medical Association, 1930), 19. For more on Gunn, see Rosenberg's introduction to *Gunn's Domestic Medicine.*
22. Alfred W. Crosby Jr., *The Columbian Exchange: Biological and Cultural Consequences of 1492* (Westport, Conn.: Greenwood Press, 1972).
23. Heiser, "Peppers," 267.
24. Nabhan, *Gathering the Desert,* 127; Jean Andrews, *Peppers, the Domesticated Capsicums* (Austin: Univ. of Texas Press, 1984), 54, 113.
25. Nabhan, *Gathering the Desert,* 126.
26. The five cultivated species include the following: *Capsicum pubescens,* found mainly in the Andes today and in highland Mexico; *C. chinense,* common to tropical America and cultivated in Africa, where it has become "reportedly the most pungent of all the peppers"; *C. frutescens,* found largely in lowland tropical America, but including the Tabasco cultivar grown in the United States and Central America for the production of hot sauce; *C. Baccatum,* confined largely to Bolivia; and, *C. annuum,* the most important economic species today and the one most familiar to North Americans. This species includes both the "sweet" bell, banana, tomato, and paprika peppers and the "hot" chilies: cayennes, serranos, Anaheims, jalapeños, poblanos, chiltecpins, and the like.
27. An article by Madhur Jaffrey, "Tastes of Thailand," *Gourmet* 38 (Oct. 1986): 18–23 passim, shows a Thai market with a display of a couple dozen kinds of peppers for sale.
28. *Popular Beliefs . . . Ohio,* no. 32709.
29. Folklore Archives, Kroeber Hall, Univ. of California, Berkeley, Calif.
30. M, 54, Midvale, 1964, *Popular Beliefs . . . Utah,* no. 13087.
31. Folklore Archives, Kroeber Hall, Univ. of California, Berkeley, Calif.
32. Three generations later, the tenth edition (1965) calls for no more green pepper and no hot pepper, but adds half a teaspoon of black pepper and doubles the sugar, while halving the other spices. *All New Fannie Farmer Boston Cooking School Cookbook,* 10th rev. ed. by Wilma Lord Perkins (Boston: Little, Brown, 1965), 545.
33. *Better Homes and Gardens New Cookbook,* rev. ed. (n.p.: Meredith Publishing Company, 1965), 149.
34. Irma S. Rombauer and Marion Rombauer Becker, *The Joy of Cooking* (Indianapolis: Bobbs-Merrill, 1967), 784.
35. Andrews, *Peppers,* 70–71.
36. *Science News Letter* (1951): 89.
37. John Neary, "The Big Chile," *Horticulture* 55 (Mar. 1977): 70.

38. Ibid.
39. Ibid.
40. Ibid.
41. Andrews, *Peppers,* 56.
42. Isabella Beeton, *The Book of Household Management* (London: S. O. Beeton, 1861; facsimile ed., New York: Farrar, Straus and Giroux, 1977).
43. Richard Schweid, *Hot Peppers: Cajuns and Capsicum in New Iberia, Louisiana* (Seattle: Madrona Publishers, 1980), 47.
44. Ibid., 128.
45. Ibid., 126.
46. Andrews, *Peppers,* 73.
47. Richard Starnes, "The Great Chili Cult Conspiracy," *Outdoor Life* (July 1977): 10, 12, 16.
48. H. Allen Smith, "Nobody Knows More About Chili Than I Do," *Holiday* 42 (Aug. 1967): 68.
49. Robert H. Bork Jr., "Give Me a Bowl of Texas," *Forbes* 136 (Sept. 23, 1985): 184.
50. See the chapter "Synthesis and Syndesis," in Robert Plant Armstrong, *Wellspring* (Berkeley: Univ. of California Press, 1975), 128–50, and the chapter "The Powers of Invocation, the Powers of Virtuosity," in his *Powers of Presence* (Philadelphia: Univ. of Pennsylvania Press, 1881), 3–20.
51. Burton Kline, "American Cuisine," *American Mercury* 4 (Jan. 1925): 69–70.
52. Sarah Gibbs Campbell, "Foreign Cookery: Recipes from Mexico and the Southwest," *Ladies Home Journal* 40 (Jan. 1931): 70.
53. "Mexican Dishes for American Meals," 109 (Oct. 1939): 176–77, 219–20.
54. Michael Goodwin, Charles Perry, and Naomi Wise, *Totally Hot!* (Garden City, N.Y.: Doubleday, 1986), xvi.
55. Sokolov, "Some Like It Hot," 65.
56. Poppy Cannon, "Open a Can and Make Yourself Famous for Good Texas Food," 95 (Oct. 1953): 222–25.
57. "Peppers: Mild, Hot, Hotter," *Sunset Magazine* 113 (Aug. 1954): 103–5.
58. Poppy Cannon, "Mexican Magic for American Tables," *House Beautiful* 99 (Sept. 1957): 122, 126–27.
59. *Woman's Day Encyclopedia of Cookery* (New York: Fawcett Publications, 1966), 18–79, 1702–09, 1710–17, 1718–25, 1726–32, and 1924–33.
60. For the respective listings, see ibid., 1: 64, 10: 1541, 6: 879, 9: 1359, 6: 1359, and 11: 1738.
61. "Chiles Mild to Wild," *Sunset* 159 (Sept. 1977): 82–85.
62. "Applying Jalapeños' Fire to Ribs, Beans, Spoonbread," *Sunset* 159 (Oct. 1977): 218, 220.
63. Jean-Jacques Rousseau, "Discourse on the Origin and Foundation of Inequality Among Men," *The First And Second Discourses,* ed. Roger D. Masters (New York: St. Martin's Press, 1964), 113.

64. Sokolov, "Some Like It Hot," 65–66.

65. Ibid., 66.

66. Frank X. Tolbert, *Saturday Evening Post* 235, Nov. 24, 1962, 38–39.

67. Ibid., 38.

68. *Benjamin Franklin*, ed. C. E. Jorgenson and F. L. Mott (New York: Hill and Wang, 1936), 317.

69. Tolbert, *Saturday Evening Post*, 38.

70. Smith, "Nobody Knows More About Chili," 68.

71. Ibid.

72. H. Allen Smith, "The Great Chili Confrontation," *Holiday* 43 (May 1968): 34 passim.

73. Smith, "Nobody Knows More About Chili," 68.

74. Starnes, "The Great Chili Cult Conspiracy," 10.

75. Carolyn Dille and Susan Belsinger, "Chili Peppers," *Gourmet* 44 (June, 1984): 48, 136–43.

76. "Chiles: The Top 7," *Health* 17 (Feb. 1985): 42–45, 66.

77. N. McKey, "Ristras Are for Cooking, Too," *Southern Living* 20 (Oct. 1985): 226.

78. "Sizzling Southwest Favorites," *Bon Appétit* 32 (Aug. 1987): 61.

79. "Cuisine Courante: A Southwestern Thanksgiving," *Gourmet* (Nov. 1987): 476.

80. For a persuasive analysis of the cultural and historical roots of *nouvelle cuisine*, see Raymond Sokolov, "Deconstructing Dinner," *Natural History* (Apr. 1987): 74–77; "'Nueva cocina' adds light touch to Mexican staples," *Arizona Republic*, Oct. 21, 1987.

81. Jessica B. Harris, *Hotstuff: A Cookbook in Praise of the Piquant* (New York: Ballantine, 1984).

82. Goodwin, Perry, and Wise, *Totally Hot*.

83. Dave De Witt and Nancy Gerlach, *Whole Chile Pepper Book* (Boston: Little, Brown, 1990).

84. Letter to the author from Judi Parker, July 23, 1987.

85. Letter to the author from Dwight Blankenship, July 22, 1987.

86. Letter to the author from Gloria Di Sano, July 18, 1987.

87. Letter to the author from Judi Parker, July 23, 1987.

88. Ibid. See also *Popular Beliefs . . . Utah*, no. 4186: Mexicans have a lower percentage of ulcers because they eat hot peppers. In order to prevent or cure ulcers, eat hot peppers once a week.

89. Robert Plant Armstrong, *The Affecting Presence* (Urbana: Univ. of Illinois Press, 1971).

90. Mark Millar, *The Great Chile Poster*, produced by Celestial Arts, Berkeley, Calif., 1990, 24 by 36 inches.

91. A. Weil, *The Marriage of the Sun and the Moon: A Quest for the Unity in Consciousness* (Boston: Houghton, Mifflin, 1980); reported in Andrews, *Peppers*, 73.

# Jay Mechling

Early in his powerful autobiography, Richard Wright captures in one small scene both the literal and symbolic hunger he felt as a poor black boy in the South just at the end of the First World War. "Christmas came and I had but one orange," he writes. "I was hurt and would not go out to play with the neighborhood children who were blowing horns and shooting firecrackers. I nursed that orange all of Christmas Day; at night, just before going to bed, I ate it, first taking a bite out of the top and sucking the juice from it as I squeezed it; finally I tore the peeling into bits and munched them slowly."[1] For Richard and for other children in the Western world, the Christmas orange evoked the mysterious and the exotic; its sweet flesh and juice both fed the hungry child and stood for the paradox of the season—the "sunshine" fruit in the midst of winter was as strange and wonderful as the birth of a Savior.

I recall from my own childhood that Santa Claus always left in our stockings, among the candies and nuts and gifts, small tangerines with their stems and a few dark green leaves still attached to the bright orange fruit.[2] I insisted upon continuing this custom through our daughter's childhood, and even now our grandsons are learning the tradition, though most recently we have experimented with substituting special Christmastime German chocolate oranges for the real fruit. The most recent film version of Louisa May Alcott's *Little Women*, which opened on Christmas day of 1994, shows young Amy treasuring her Christmas orange in the midst of hard times for the March women, and the 1995 film, *Once Upon a Time When We Were Colored*, has an equally touching scene in which a small boy receives his Christmas orange.

Why does the orange hold this power? The acceptance of the orange on the American table testifies to a series of marketing campaigns so successful that, to most Americans, a day without orange juice does seem, as the advertising slogan puts it, "like a day without sunshine." Orange juice is a firmly established element in the code of the American breakfast, just as the Christmas orange is firmly established in the code of Christmas customs.[3]

But marketing campaigns work only to the degree that they create persuasive narratives about the consumption of the product being marketed. In primarily oral cultures, speakers rely heavily upon commonplaces (that is, formulaic sayings) to capture the audience's attention and move them from present beliefs to new beliefs.[4] Marketing campaigns in the nineteenth and twentieth centuries also drew upon the power of commonplaces, but the commonplaces now come from mass-mediated, popular culture, as well as from the primarily oral folk cultures of Americans. Which means that commonplaces can appear as any of the genres of folk and mass-mediated culture; commonplaces can be visual or verbal, and they can appear in short genres (such as proverbs or jokes) or in extended narratives. Commonplaces, in this new sense, represent the public culture we assume Americans share even in a highly fragmented, plural social world. Americans "share" a reservoir of commonplaces, then, that represent shared knowledge of sorts.[5] Commonplaces are what make intelligible to wide audiences the various "texts" of public culture, from political cartoons in the newspaper to Pepsi-Cola ads on television.

To inquire into the power of the orange as a symbol in American culture, therefore, is to assemble and analyze the commonplaces, the folk and mass-mediated cultural narratives, of which the orange is a part. This essay aims to discover the commonplaces of the orange in American culture and how those commonplaces became the basis for the creation of a *desire* in the consuming audience. The desire created by these commonplaces was for more than the oranges. Land companies and railroads used the commonplaces of the orange to attempt to create a desire for a place—in one instance Florida, in the other California—and for the lifestyle that the place represented. The commodification of the orange and the place were not without their contradictions and ironies, as I shall show. The point of working through this example of the orange is to show how cultural narratives operate in the commodification of place.

I write on the orange with some humility, revisiting some of the territory described thirty years ago by John McPhee in a justly praised book entitled, simply, *Oranges*.[6] McPhee made his first excursions into Florida to do research for a magazine article about oranges and orange juice, but he became so involved in the topic that he decided that nothing less than a book would suit his purpose. *Oranges* moves back and forth between McPhee's accounts of what he learned by reading about oranges and his fieldwork accounts of conversations with a variety of Floridians, from the waitress who serves him frozen orange juice instead of the fresh juice he requests, through colorful growers, to the colorless bureaucrat who manages the Florida Citrus Mutual. I recommend McPhee's book to the reader and rely upon him a great deal in these early pages, but I should say how my aim in this essay differs from McPhee's. His is a rich, reportorial account of the orange industry in Florida. I have no reportorial base for this essay, though I am a native of Florida and know very well the sights, sounds, tastes, and smells that McPhee recounts. I bring California materials to add to the Florida case, and in both cases my interest focuses upon the ways in which the orange became the centerpiece for creating commodity desire. My subject is the uses of cultural commonplaces about the orange to create a desire to consume not just the orange but the land, the place. The orange and the place become commodities in this process, and I am interested in the formula narratives some Americans used to sell oranges and land to other Americans.

## The Orange of European Commonplaces

Oranges most likely originated in Southeast Asia or southern China in the third millennium B.C. and moved West through India.[7] The Arabs of the Middle East brought the orange into Africa and then into Spain. The Crusaders encountered oranges in Syria in the eleventh and twelfth centuries. The Hindus called the fruit *naranga*, a Sanskrit word closely related to the Tamil word *naru*, which means "fragrant."[8] Muslims took this word in the form *naranj*, which in turn became *naranja* in Spanish, *arancia* in Italy, and *orange* in French.[9] The Europeans also brought back with them the Arabs' medicinal uses of the orange, but most of all the Europeans valued the orange as a seasoning and as a confection. These were the *Citrus aurantium*, the sour orange, for the sweet orange, *Citrus sinensis*, was not known in Europe until late in the sixteenth century, possibly not until 1635.[10] "The taste for confections was propagated in Europe with the introduction of sugar," wrote one historian of the orange, "and this delicate food [oranges] became at once a necessary article to men in easy circumstances, and a luxury upon all tables. It was, above all, as confections that the Agrumi [citrus fruits] entered into commerce, and we see by the records of Savona that they were sent into cold parts of Italy, where people were very greedy for them."[11] Italian lore held that the Hesperides, the daughters of Hesperis and Atlas in mythology, crossed the Mediterranean from Africa and landed on the shores of Italy bearing oranges.[12]

Europeans also valued orange trees for their striking beauty and the sweet aroma of their blossoms, so they were planted for ornamental purposes in the warmer, Mediterranean climes. Accounts both old and new rhapsodize on the dark green foliage laden with orange fruit. Wealthy Europeans so desired the orange that they became determined to thwart nature and grow orange trees where they could not grow naturally. The solution was to construct large hothouses, an "agricultural luxury" (wrote Gallesio) that was unknown until they were built in the mid-fourteenth century specifically for the growing of oranges and other citrus fruits.[13] The most famous orange tree in history was the one named "Francis First," or "Grand Bourbon," kept in the *orangerie* at Versailles and reputed to have lived 473 years.[14] By the beginning of the fifteenth century, the custom of building orangeries had spread from royalty to the merely rich, so that by then one historian could claim that "We now see orangeries in all the civilized parts of Europe, it being an embellishment necessary to all country-seats and houses of pleasure."[15] Imitating the European rich, the American rich began building orangeries for their estates in the nineteenth and early twentieth centuries.

European customary lore long associated oranges and orange blossoms with love and marriage. The simultaneous appearance of flowers and fruit of the tree suggested the wedding of beauty and fecundity. It was "Golden Apples"—oranges—that Juno gave Jupiter on their wedding day and that Paris gave Aphrodite in order to win Helen.[16] Boccaccio's *Decameron*, as McPhee points out, is filled with examples of orange-blossom water and scents connecting lovers.[17] "Orange blossoms were worn by brides among the Saracens," reports one history of these customs, "who regarded the flower as a token of a happy and prosperous marriage. Cretan couples were sprinkled with orange-flower water on their wedding days. Sardinians attached oranges to the horns of oxen pulling the cart that drew the newly married pair."[18] McPhee notes a paradoxical body of folk beliefs that the touch of a woman will kill an orange tree.[19]

European artists employed in their paintings a repertoire of visual commonplaces regarding the orange. Based on the Crusaders' discovery of the orange in Palestine, painters would include orange trees in religious paintings to indicate that the setting was the Holy Land, even though the orange was unknown in the Middle East at the time of Christ.[20] "Benozzo Gozzoli's frescoes in a family chapel of the Medici," explains McPhee, "show Melchior, Balthazar, and Gaspar looking less like three wise kings from the East than three well-fed Medici, descending a hill that is identifiable as one near Fiesole, dressed as an Italian hunting party, and passing through stands of orange trees bright with fruit."[21] In fact, the orange tree was a specific symbol for the Virgin Mary in Renaissance art. This visual commonplace turns up again in American folk explanations for the customary orange in the Christmas stocking, that is, that the orange represents the gifts of the Magi to the Christ child. As was the case with other Old World natives, such as the alligator, the orange carried with it into the New World a large repertoire of customs, customary lore, and visual commonplaces that set the terms for American understanding of the meaning of the orange.[22]

## Florida

The orange orchards of Isabella, a town on the north coast of Santo Domingo, are reputed to be the site of the appearance of the fruit in the New World. Columbus brought seeds from the Canary Islands on his second voyage in 1493 and planted them there. The benefits of citrus fruits in preventing scurvy had become well known to the maritime explorers, so the Portuguese, Spanish, and Arabs had planted what McPhee calls "scurvy prevention stations" in the Azores, on the west coast of Africa, and in the Madeira Islands.[23] Columbus was following routine custom in planting oranges in the Caribbean, as was Ponce de Leon on his 1513 voyage that marks the European discovery of Florida. De Leon wrote to Spain's Charles V from Puerto Rico in 1521, informing the king of his intention to plant fruit seeds near Charlotte Harbor. Those fruit seeds most likely were orange seeds. Narvaez and de Soto also planted oranges on their Florida explorations in 1538 and 1539, respectively.[24] What all of these explorers planted was the sour orange, the only orange known in Europe at the time.

The earliest unambiguous mention of sweet oranges in Florida appears in a letter from Gov. Menendez Marques from St. Augustine on April 2, 1579. Sir Francis Drake cut the St. Augustine orange trees to the ground when he sacked St. Augustine in 1586, but the hardy trees came back. The English took Florida in 1763 and began shipping St. Augustine's oranges back to England in 1776. Settlers began planting more orange groves south from St. Augustine, along the St. Johns River. The Spanish were not much interested in developing the orange trade when they recaptured east Florida in 1784, but when the United States acquired the territory in 1821 the commercial growing and shipping of oranges began to gain national attention.[25]

By most accounts, Captain Dummett's commercial grove established in 1830 on Merritt Island, between the Indian River and the Atlantic Ocean, marked the real birth of the Florida orange industry. Dummett grafted sweet orange buds onto wild sour orange root stock, thereby creating the premium Indian River citrus, which is sweeter and juicier than the citrus grown elsewhere in the state.[26] In 1870 Samuel Parsons, a nurseryman from Flushing, New York, established the first orange nursery in Lakeland and introduced into Florida the Valencia orange, a late-maturing variety that has become the predominant crop of the industry.[27]

The 1880s saw the beginning of the symbiotic relationship between the orange industry, the railroads, and land sales that in some ways is the most important part of the story of the orange. From their origins in 1881, the Florida railroads were connected to commercial orange production. Henry

Plant created the Waycross Short Line that connected Jacksonville with Savannah and the northern states, and Jacksonville soon became the largest orange-shipping port in the world. Over the next decade, small railroads consolidated to create the Atlantic Coast Line (previously Plant's system) and the Seaboard Air Line. Peter Demeus's Orange Belt Line connected Sanford with the Gulf Coast port of St. Petersburg in 1888, and Henry Flagler's Florida East Coast Railway reached the Indian River by the 1890s.[28]

"If any commercial business can be said to have a romantic period," wrote one historian of the orange in Florida, "the decade 1884–94 was that in the orange history of Florida."[29] The great freeze of 1894–95 ended that particular boom, but if we take this historian at his word and focus upon the notion of a "romantic period," we see that this period saw the birth of a formulaic cultural narrative about the orange that was to last into our century.

The Rev. T. W. Moore's *Treatise and Hand-Book of Orange Culture in Florida, Louisiana and California,* first published in 1881 and in its fourth edition by 1892, provides a representative taste of the romantic narrative told about oranges. Moore's book is a technical, how-to book in most ways, but the book is most importantly a booster book, and Moore could not resist framing the cultivation of oranges in its full meanings. "To those engaged in the business," wrote Moore in the Preface to the fourth edition,

> orange-growing is truly fascinating. The beauty of the tree, the beauty and fragrance of the flower, challenge all rivalry among ornamental trees and beautiful flowers. The aesthetic cultivator becomes a true lover of his sweet and beautiful pet, which he looks upon as a relic and reminder of Paradise. But when this beauty is accompanied with useful, golden, and gold-bearing fruit, affording a living, and promising all other material luxuries, then the lover appreciates his orange grove only less than he does his wife, who has brought to him not only the accomplishments of a sweet and cultivated woman, but with herself an ample fortune. And though he may have waited as long as Jacob did for his Rachel, he does not regret the toil and waiting, since the reward is ample. I do not know but that the toil and waiting demanded by the orange does not increase the ardor of the planter, and increase his pleasure when once the tree has been brought to full beauty and bearing, for we love best those that need to be courted earnestly in order to be won. When thus won we feel that the bride is the more fully our own.[30]

"Does the reader wish to know how to win this fair bride," asks Moore, "clad in nature's richest green, adorned with golden globes, crowned with fragrant orange-blossoms—her own fair crown, so often plucked for other bridal wreaths? The object of this book is to answer that inquiry."[31]

Moore's romantic reverie uses several of the commonplaces established for the orange in European culture—the rendering of the orange tree as the female bride, the reference to Paradise, the association of orange blossoms with bridal wreaths. But his reverie also mentions toil, and, a few pages later, Moore adds intelligence to the list of qualities needed in the man who would be a successful orange grower. "Orange culture belongs to the class of *skilled* labor," he explains.

> Hundreds engaged in the business will fail, because success requires intelligence, application, patience, and skill. Hundreds have already failed, from one or all of these causes, and have left the State, never dreaming that they alone are to be blamed for their failure. Men in the very communities thus abandoned have succeeded because they were more prudent in the selection of soil and location, and used their intelligence and the intelligence of others, and persevered in the face of partial failure brought about by ignorance.[32]

To be sure, Moore's dire warning works to make the reader receptive to the advice proffered later in the book, but Moore's discourse here and elsewhere sounds remarkably like that found in advice literature for young men late in the nineteenth century. In fact, these passages resemble Russell Conwell's famous speech, "Acres of Diamonds," which he delivered over six thousand times between 1861 and 1925 to audiences that totaled more than ten million people across the United States and the world.[33] Like Conwell, Moore warns that the riches under our very noses will be harvested only by those intelligent enough to realize what they have and to seek knowledge. The self-made man of the late nineteenth century knew how to recognize and seize opportunity.

Conwell's great speech belongs in the genre of religious oratory, not just for its theme linking capitalism and Christianity, but as much for its structural and stylistic resemblance to oral sermons. One feature of this oral style is the telling of a small story, a parable really, meant to make a central point. Moore employs the same formula, telling the following story that sounds straight from "Acres of Diamonds":

> In no business can a young man with pluck, intelligence, and application, so certainly lay the foundation for a competency and fortune as in orange-growing in Florida. With the exercise of these he may in ten years be what the country would call a rich man.
>
> A young man from Middle Florida borrowed money enough from his father to buy a piece of land. After paying for his land, located a few miles above Palatka, he landed in Palatka with three dollars in his pocket. These he paid for provisions, and went to work growing vegetables on about an acre and a half of cleared land. Six years afterward he sold his

place for twelve thousand dollars cash, without owing a cent for any-thing. Many instances could be given of young men, as well as old men, who have done as well, and of some who have done still better. Young men have frequently written to the author to aid in securing for them a clerkship. His advice has been invariably given, "Go to work raising fruit in Florida, and be *independent* and *have a home.*"[34]

The railroads and land companies picked up these themes of great profits for relatively little work. The land companies and orange-growing companies published attractive prospectuses, filled with the visual imagery and language promising the romance of owning an orange grove in Florida. A 1921 pro-spectus for Gulf Ridge Groves, Inc., of Lakeland begins: "It is an undisputed fact and it has been proved conclusively that a FLORIDA orange or grape-fruit grove, when given perfect care, will produce highest quality fruit and will positively make big money for the owner."[35] A 1922 prospectus for the "Pitts-burgh–Florida Orange and Grapefruit Groves" of Avon Park promises a life-time of profits "without the necessity of moving to Florida or even of giving up your present work." The company also offered a limited number of home-building sites reserved for investors who may want winter homes or perma-nent homes near the groves. "Here you can live as you have long wanted to live," say the authors. The Florida Land and Mortgage Company, for example, offered a pamphlet entitled *Florida, The Italy of America* (London, 1883) and the Silver Springs Park Florida Land Company published a prospectus entitled *Florida, Land of Oranges, Tropical Scenery, Health and Sunshine* (New York, 1885).[36]

The railroads produced their own booster literature. The Seaboard Air Line Railway Company's 1924 pamphlet, *Florida: Our Last Frontier,* invited the "sons and daughters" of the Western pioneers to be twentieth-century pio-neers in "America's last great frontier." "The task of the twentieth century pioneer is less arduous," promised the pamphlet, "and he will be more gener-ously rewarded than the pioneer of the West. . . . He will escape the rigors of the Northwestern winters and the fierce heat of the Southwestern summers. While he comes to wrest a home from the virgin forests, or the hammock growth, he has real work to perform, but once his land is ready for the crop there is no place in America where nature is more generous in rewards for intelligent industry." The Development Department of the Seaboard Air Line Railway Company also published informational pamphlets aimed at inform-ing growers along the line of new products and processes in orange culture.[37]

Harriet Beecher Stowe, of all people, was one of the most famous boosters for the virtues of owning a Florida orange grove. She and her husband moved to northern Florida in 1868 and wrote a piece for the *Atlantic Monthly* in 1879 describing their orange plantation.[38] The Stowes' fruit became highly prized in the North.[39]

The booster literature for Florida emphasized the contrast between the cold, dark, snowy winter of northern climes with the warm, light, sunny environment represented by oranges. An illustrated advertisement for the Florida East Coast Railroad pictured a couple bundled against the cold and preparing to board a train in the midst of a sleet storm. The same couple smiles amid sunshine and graceful palm trees in the lower part of the ad, which begins: "Out of Winter's Bleakness into the Golden Glow. . . ." Even the names of some of the orange products emphasized the paradox of a winter fruit. Snow Crop was the name of a major frozen orange juice company.

This contrast also became a visual commonplace on postcards and other souvenirs of Florida. Typically, such a postcard appealed to the vacationing tourist spending January on sandy beaches or enjoying tropical flowers instead of shoveling snow in the North. "Snowbirds" is Florida slang for winter tourists. In every way, then, the paradox of the winter symbolism of the orange created a powerful draw to warmth, fragrance, and romance.

## California

The orange entered California by way of the gardens and orchards planted by the Franciscan clergy who built the twenty-one missions beginning in 1769. Historians of California agriculture point to the extensive orchard set out in 1804 by Father Thomas Sanches at the San Gabriel Mission as the beginning of the story of the orange in the state.[40] Although there were small

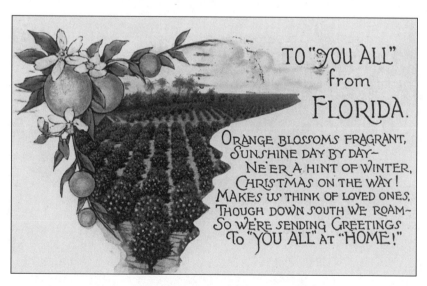

Fig. 6.1. Postcard, "To 'You All' from Florida."

groves in Los Angeles for personal use in the 1830s, the first commercial grove was one set out by William Wolfskill in 1841.[41] As in Florida, the real impetus for commercial growing came with the railroads. The completion of the Southern Pacific in 1873 made it possible to market California oranges outside the state. The opening of the Atchinson, Topeka & Santa Fe Lines into Southern California in 1885 created the greatest boom in orange planting, land sales, and irrigation company development.[42] The Valencia orange became a standard for the industry, and the Washington Navel—dubbed the "King of Oranges"—made a great reputation for Riverside.

California had its own booster literature on the orange, and we find in the California literature all the commonplaces invoked by the Florida boosters. Thomas A. Garvey, for example, began his 1882 handbook on *Orange Culture in California* with a chapter of "Introductory Remarks on Orange Raising," and the remarks were as romantic a reverie as Moore's on Florida. "An individual or an audience," wrote Garvey,

> never tires of listening to the history of our peerless groves of golden apples—the handsome, symmetrical, electrifying Golden Glory of the Pacific slope.
>
> How grand, how beautiful is an orange orchard in full bearing! When planted artistically their ever-enduring dark-green foliage, studded with beautiful gems of golden spheres, give renewed life and health to all that behold the orchards or partake of the fruit. Those who are so fortunate as to tread the soil in the shade of the majestic trees, and breathe their fragrant exhalations, look upward, and from their most interior selfhood they thank the Great Author of the grand, useful, and beautiful in nature for so sublime a manifestation of His works, and His good gifts to mortals. There is inspiration, as well as beauty and princely profits, in an orange orchard.[43]

A few years later, still another booster for the profits to be made growing oranges in Southern California took as his epigram Milton's lines from *Paradise Lost:*

> Groves whose rich trees wept odorous gum and balm,
> Others whose fruit, burnished with golden rind,
> Hung amiable, Hesperian fables true,
> If true here only, and of *delicious taste.*

Completing the cycle of European commonplaces, A. C. Smith had this to say on the back cover of his pamphlet: "The golden apples Earth gave Hera at her marriage with Zeus, guarded of old by the watchful Dragon, which required a Hercules to kill, she now offers to all for the talismanic touch of intelligent toil with Water on the Desert." "When the Orange Belt of Southern California is planted with skill and cultivated with care, the dreams of the Orient will become realities at the Occident and the fables of Mythology be made the facts of History."[44]

As in the Florida booster literature, the California literature warns that the orange business takes men of unusual intelligence and character. A pamphlet on orange culture in California published by the Los Angeles Chamber of Commerce claimed that "It has taken brains and hard work, as well as climate and soil, to produce the California orange of commerce." The authors continue with this theme:

Southern California, the modern Garden of Eden, minus the serpent and blossoming as the rose, was once thought arid and useless desert—was, in fact, part of what was known as the Great American desert. The transformation has not been wrought through a miracle, but by the thought and hard work of California citizens. They have experimented with localities, brought water upon dry land, studied the soil that they might enrich it, worked and watched and waited and prayed—possibly some of them have cursed; and now that their sheaves, i.e., their full orange crops, are in, their success is attributed to God Almighty. It is due to Him . . . for God created not only the California country and climate, but the California citizen.[45]

Citrus production is "brainy work," explained another pamphlet promoting the industry, so "citrus fruit growers will be generally marked by refinement and culture. Indeed, the successful citrus orchardist must be a student and must possess rare intelligence."[46] Citrus fruits, wrote another booster, "become then the token, not alone of superior natural endowments, but of the type of manhood which can use them to the best advantage."[47]

Also mirroring Florida, the railroads in California produced some of the most attractive booster literature. The Santa Fe Line's 1938 pamphlet, *California and Arizona Citrus Fruits: An Epic Story*, for example, is illustrated with beautiful color photographs and nearly as colorful descriptions of "The Citrus Empire." "To peel an orange and munch its luscious segments," write the railroad's public relations wordsmiths, "or to extract or drink its sparkling juice, is to sit at the table of the Olympian Gods."

*Sunset* magazine of March 1911 featured a cover story, "In the Orange Country," that brought the formula success narrative to the telling of the story of the orange in California. "Where an Orchard is a Mine," crowed the subtitle.[48] The author, Walter V. Woehlke, promised to tell the story of "The Human Factor Among the Gold-bearing trees of California." Woehlke's is a reporter's piece, very much like McPhee's, actually, telling the story of his visits and interviews with some the major growers in Southern California. The author quotes liberally from his informants, shows color pictures of their homes, and in between recounts some of the history of the orange-growing industry in the state. The following example of Woehlke's prose gives the reader some idea of the tone of the entire article:

> Through the wide busy streets of beautiful Pomona, set in a sea of orange-groves, past the campus of Claremont College, at the foot of the snowy San Gabriel Range, the motor-car hurried, following the reddish slash of a road smooth as asphalt through the endless succession of well-kept orchards. Stately palms, the soft green of red-berried pepper trees, lined the avenue. On either side streams of sparkling water gurgled through concrete ditches. Like golden globes illumined from within, the oranges glowed in the deep shadows of the dark foliage, every vista between the hurrying ranks of uniform trees revealing the white and purple background of the silent range.

Woehlke meets the rancher and his wife and begins a conversation about the profit to be made growing oranges. Then he invokes a theme common in the California literature. "It was midwinter," he begins:

> In February, March, and early April, months of sleet and slush every-where, the wax-white blossoms open their petals and send wave after wave of sweet, heavy odor through the orange belt. The groves are filled with the languorous scent. . . . It is at this time when the end of one orange cycle overlaps the beginning of the next, when golden fruit and silvery blossoms gleam side by side on the trees, when long trains are thundering over the mountains hurrying the harvest to the East, that the citrus belt is garnering the by-product of the orange groves—the tourist crop. For every departing orange train the railroads bring in two trainloads of refugees seeking to escape from the tyranny of snow shov-els, frosted window-panes and frozen water pipes. By the ten thousand they come from the outer darkness of cold purgatory into the sunny antechamber of paradise, but only nine thousand go back again.[49]

So Woehlke, among others, sees the orange as a symbol of the light, warmth, and health that contrasts with the dark, cold, and (by implication) sickness from which the tourists are fleeing, and it is the railroad that carries both crops—the oranges and the tourists. Woehlke's passages sound much like those in the Florida booster literature, but there is one important difference, a difference signaled by his reference to the "snowy" San Gabriel Range. In the California discourse the contrast is all the more paradoxical because the snows of winter and the oranges of sunshine appear within the same visual compass.

This paradox became a major commonplace, both verbal and visual, in the presentation of California to tourists and to potential investors in land and in orange groves. Characteristic is the imagery conjured by A. C. Fish. "Of all the fruits of earth," wrote Fish, "the Orange is Queen. Its history is full of poetry and its culture, in Southern California, is full of profit." This, explained Fish, is the poetic side of the orange, the side inherited from European culture. But Fish then went on to weave a narrative that is distinctly New World, distinctly late-nineteenth-century American in its language and theme. "Recall or imagine the transformation scene," he wrote,

> seemingly magical, which actually occurs to the traveller as he passes from the drifting snows and biting cold of the North, in a Pullman or Tourist car, down among the beautiful orange-groves and into the perpetual Summer of the Great San Bernadino and San Gabriel valleys. Standing in an orange-grove at Riverside, Ontario, Pomona or Pasadena in February, let the stranger, while meditating on the story he may hear of the profits of a ten acre orchard, look over the landscape and take in, with the perfume of orange blossoms, the grandeur of the scenery, the beautiful valley dotted with homes, the green hills, the mighty range of mountains which acts as a barrier against the north winds of Winter, and in Summer a reservoir to store up the melting snows and send them down to him to grow these apples of gold in living green! Amid such surroundings, it is a pleasant thing for the eye to rest upon the "beautiful snow"—at a distance, and to see Winter a perpetual prisoner of the mountaintops.[50]

Fish was painting with words a portrait of Southern California that was quickly becoming a visual commonplace on postcards, travel books, and even orange-crate labels.[51] Some of the formula postcards resembled those from Florida, with a split image of northerners coping with snow and Californians basking in sunshine. Some of these split-image postcards bear the caption: "You may throw snowballs for me . . . And I'll eat oranges for you." Most common, however, was the postcard that fused the snow/oranges, cold/warm, winter/spring iconography in the same view. These photographs featured variations of the same theme: in the background are snow-capped mountains, and in the foreground are orange groves or flower gardens. The cards bear captions emphasizing the "California Paradox," captions such as "From Oranges to Snow—A California Anomaly," "From Orange Groves to Snow Mountains," "Midwinter in California, Old Baldy from the Orange Trees," and "Flower Beds and Snowbanks, Beautiful Winter Scene in California."

Symbolic of the way in which California boosters exploited the contrast between northern and California winters was the California Midwinter Fair, which opened officially on January 1, 1894, in San Francisco's Golden Gate Park. Newspaper publisher and San Francisco civic leader M. H. de Young was a director of the California exhibits at the Columbian Exposition in Chicago, and he observed the beneficial effects the fair had on business in Chicago. The success of that fair and the developing financial crisis of 1893 gave de Young

*Fig. 6.2. Postcard, "A California Paradox."*

the idea to move many of the Columbian exhibits to San Francisco once the Chicago fair closed. De Young managed to create the organization and raise the money that would make possible what was called the California Midwinter Fair. Hurriedly assembled on two hundred acres of Golden Gate Park, the fair faced problems and local resistance from the start. The plan was to open the exposition on January 1, 1894, and close the fair July 4. "The object," notes one historian, "was to hold the fair in the middle of winter to demonstrate to the world that such an exhibit could be held in mid-winter in California, while the East was suffering from cold and snow. . . ."[52] Ironically, heavy snowstorms in the Sierra Nevada forced the rerouting of the trains carrying the Chicago exhibits to San Francisco, so the fair's grand opening was delayed until January 27. The Southern Pacific Railroad Company, of course, helped promote the fair, publishing an attractive pamphlet, *California for Health, Pleasure and Profit: Why you Should Go There* (1894).

## Juicy, Sexy

Although Florida and California both experienced brief resurgences of land booms in the prosperous 1920s, the Golden Age of the marriage between railroads, land sales, and orange production was pretty well over by that decade. In the 1930s the marketing focus changed toward tourism and citrus commodities, especially orange juice.

California orange growers began advertising in 1908, when it became clear that the cooperative organization for production and distribution had to be matched by equally aggressive, cooperative organization in marketing the fruit. Sunkist, the label of the California Fruit Growers Exchange, the largest cooperative in Southern California, launched a $10,000 advertising campaign in Iowa in 1908 and increased the orange consumption of that state by 31 percent. The 1909 campaign invested $25,000 in advertising aimed at Iowa, and the proportionate success led Sunkist to double the amount spent in 1910 and again in 1911, expanding the campaign throughout the snow belt.[53] As the advertising manager of the California Fruit Growers Exchange explained it, the Sunkist campaign made two basic appeals—to appetite and to health. But there was a definite change of strategy from the earlier boosterism. "In our more recent Sunkist orange advertising," he explained in 1920, "only 'still life' illustrations have been employed; that is, pictures simply of the fruit itself, so that the reader's attention is focused upon the product. Pictures of orange groves which add romance and atmosphere, but which cause readers to think about a trip to California or the purchase of a grove instead of eating oranges are also generally omitted. Our advertisements must sell fruit—not land or railroad tickets."[54]

The perfection of concentrating and freezing orange juice just after the Second World War sent the industry into its second great phase of advertising. In 1945–46, 35 percent of the Florida crop became frozen concentrate, but by 1954 the proportion was 60 percent.[55] New York City is known in the industry as the "citrus bowl" because New Yorkers consume 40 percent of the juice marketed in the country.[56]

The California and Florida tourist industries picked up where the railroads and land companies had left off, using the orange in their promotions of both states. Oranges continued to dominate the iconography of Florida and California postcards, advertisements, and souvenirs. As automobile touring replaced railroad travel, orange juice stands greeted the carloads of northern tourists as they crossed the state line into Florida. Similar stands offering freshly squeezed juice, souvenirs, and the occasional alligator farm lined the main highways running down the state. At these stands, tourists could arrange to have boxes of citrus fruit mailed to friends and family back home, a more extravagant equivalent of mailing split-image postcards to folks back in the snowbound North. The Orange Blossom Trail Association, Inc., was a cooperative tourist promotion organization bringing together owners of restaurants, motels, and tourist attractions. The association identified U.S. Routes 441 and 27 as the "Orange Blossom Trail, Central Florida's Most Scenic Route" and produced attractive marketing brochures and maps describing the route.

California created its own ways of using the orange to help promote tourism. One chain of orange juice stands, Giant Orange, created a signature commercial architecture of giant oranges along California highways. Florida also had some of this architecture, but California excels in popular architecture of the sort Robert Venturi dubbed "the painted duck."[57]

In 1935 south Florida promoters and University of Miami football boosters created the Orange Bowl as one of the first post-season "bowl games" in college football. Almost as important as the game itself is the lavish King Orange Jamboree Parade, instituted the next year and for decades held on New Year's Eve, the night before the New Year's Day game. The parade features elaborate floats covered with flowers, oranges, and shapely women in bathing suits. The parade was broadcast on CBS radio in 1936, and in the 1950s began to be televised nationally.[58] All of the imagery of the parade served to tell the same story as the older postcards—you throw the snowballs and I'll eat the oranges. Come on down!

The scantily clad young women on the floats of the King Orange Parade remind us of the ways in which sex has been used to market both Florida and California tourism. Oranges plus sunshine plus beaches equals women in bikinis, or less. A recent formulaic postcard pictures women wearing bikini bottoms and wet T-shirts with pictures of oranges and the caption, "Squeeze Me!" emblazoned across the women's breasts. But this formula is older than one might suppose, as fruit labels and photography from the 1940s and 1950s clearly establish a connection between women's breasts and juicy citrus fruit.

These racy images may be versions of some very old customary and visual commonplaces in Western culture. Recall the classical mythology and widespread folk customs linking oranges with marriage and romance. A recent magazine advertisement for Grand Marnier liqueur literalizes this association by portraying an orange as the bride to a bottle of Grand Marnier as the groom, against

*Fig. 6.3. Postcard, "Orange Picking Time in Florida."*

the background of a grove of orange trees. "Love is Grand," announces the only text in the ad. For oranges to be linked to sex is not much of a transformation from the love and marriage association. Women in the French court of the seventeenth century would bite into oranges for the reddening of their lips caused by the peel oil,[59] and some Victorian era etiquette manuals advised women to hold a handkerchief or napkin in front of their mouths while eating an orange, so as to mask the potentially provocative and seductive sight of juice running out of the mouth.[60] Some oranges themselves literalize the metaphor of the orange as fertile bride. The Navel orange bears within its body a fetal orange (as McPhee calls it), and one wonders whether there is an equally powerful feminine meaning in the blood orange, a variety popular in Europe but one that, as McPhee puts it, "frightens" American women.[61]

## What the Orange Hides

The early booster discourse on orange production occasionally sought to define orange culture not as agriculture but as a form of manufacture, a form requiring intelligence and special knowledge. The Los Angeles Chamber of Commerce pamphlet quoted earlier, for example, argues that, with the "brains and brawn" it takes to produce the commercial orange, "it may almost be classed as a manufactured product."[62] Woehlke's piece in *Sunset* goes even further. What he sees on his visits to the homes and groves of modern orange growers "leads to the suspicion that the orange-grower is not a farmer. He isn't. He is a specialist in citrus fruits, a manufacturer whose raw material, soil, water and sunshine, is transformed into the finished product by living trees instead of machinery. He is a business man whose mode of living, whose pleasures, recreations and intellectual pursuits are identical with those of other business and professional men living in suburban homes."[63]

Why was there this effort to redefine the orange grower as a manufacturer, as a businessman, rather than as a farmer? In part, certainly, the aim was to attract as investors businessmen who considered themselves sophisticated urbanites and suburbanites, not rural folk.[64] As Woehlke assured his readers, the "country store with a whittling, chewing crowd of hayseeds is unknown in the orange belt, but there are dozens of country clubs with cozy buildings of their own, whose tennis-courts and golf links are ever in demand."[65] But something else is happening in this redefinition, something more than merely making orange culture seem more businesslike and, no small matter, clean. The redefinition of orange culture made invisible two important developments in the industry—the rise of agribusiness to replace the entrepreneurial farmer and the widespread use of migratory labor to harvest California's and Florida's winter crops, especially oranges.

We can see in the citrus industry the trend toward consolidation and specialization that marked other agricultural enterprises in the twentieth century. Despite America's ongoing narratives about, first, the entrepreneurial farmer, and then about the democratic virtues of farmers' cooperatives, the reality in Florida and California agriculture was that a few large companies were taking over the production of oranges. And in California the growth of agribusiness was tied to the politics of water. Agribusiness was becoming the central feature of Florida and California citrus raising at just the time the literature was imagining an agrarian utopia of small holdings.

The second thing masked or ignored by all the discourse on oranges is the matter of migratory labor and the working conditions of those who picked the sunshine crops in Florida and California. The reader searches the orange literature in vain for references to who is actually picking the oranges, though the old postcard imagery suggests that both black and white men were the pickers. McPhee describes briefly an interesting picker, but this portrait is nowhere near as complete as those of the more important men in the hierarchy of the orange industry. Moreover, the picker McPhee chooses is white, despite McPhee's knowledge that three-fourths of the pickers in the mid-1960s were black.[66]

In truth, since the first decades of the century the pickers have been poor migratory laborers who move around with the crops and seasons. In the 1960s CBS news did a documentary entitled "Harvest of Shame" about the living and working conditions of migratory laborers in south Florida, and there have been televised documentaries periodically ever since that first exposé. Child psychiatrist Robert Coles's second volume in his *Children of Crisis* series of studies is devoted to *Migrants, Sharecroppers, Mountaineers*, and Coles obtained some of the materials for the book by interviewing children who travel the migrant farmwork route from summers in the Northeast to winters in Florida.[67] The most recent attention in Florida has been to the plight of sugarcane workers, but much the same could be written for those who harvest the citrus crop.[68]

American commonplaces about the orange, many inherited directly from traditional European beliefs and customs, belong to a metaphoric cluster that sees the orange as representing the feminine, especially the bride of romance, of marriage, and of fertility. This metaphoric bride stands for sunshine and light, warmth and health. She contrasts with the cold and dark. She is alive while her opposite is dead; she stands for the sunbelt's "clean" to the industrial belt's "dirty." The ultimate paradox of the orange is that it represents healthy, sunny, clean, while the migratory labor that picks the orange lives a life that is sickly, dark, dirty. So the American commonplaces of the orange not only made it possible for the marketers of land and of railroad tickets and of oranges to bring to their commodities all the benefits of these metaphoric clusters. The same commonplaces helped disguise major transformations in the systems that brought food to the tables of twentieth-century Americans.

# Notes

1. Richard Wright, *Black Boy* (New York: Harper and Row, 1945), 87.
2. Tangerines, in fact, must be harvested by cutting the stems, rather than by twisting and pulling the fruit from the stem, as most oranges can be picked.
3. Part of the lore connecting the orange with Christmas centers on Saint Nicholas, bishop of Lycia (now in Turkey) in the fourth century. Legend has it that, as part of giving away his inheritance, the bishop tossed three bags of gold into the house of a family too poor to provide a wedding dowry for its three daughters. These three bags of gold became St. Nicholas's (Santa Claus, as the Dutch called him) bags of presents for children, but they also became symbolized as three orbs of gold (the same symbol marking pawnshops). The orange symbolizes an orb of gold and memorializes St. Nicholas's generosity. See Maria Leach and Jerome Fried, eds., *Funk and Wagnall's Standard Dictionary of Folklore, Mythology, and Legend* (San Francisco, Calif.: Harper and Row, 1972), 967.
4. Walter J. Ong, *Orality and Literacy: The Technologizing of the Word* (London: Routledge, 1982), esp. 110–11.
5. I mean "shared" here in the special sense that public culture may be a mechanism for the organization of diversity rather than the replication of uniformity. This usage assumes a distinction between public cultures and private cultures. See Anthony F. C. Wallace, *Culture and Personality*, 2d ed. (New York: Random House, 1970).
6. John McPhee, *Oranges* (New York: Farrar, Straus and Giroux, 1967).
7. R. A. Divine, "A History of Citrus Culture in Florida, 1565–1895" (senior thesis in history, Yale Univ., 1952), 1.
8. *Women's Day Encyclopedia of Cookery* (New York: Fawcett, 1966), 8: 1266; McPhee, *Oranges*, 64.
9. McPhee, *Oranges*, 64; "Gallesio on the Orange," reprinted as an appendix to T. W. Moore, *Treatise and Hand-Book of Orange Culture in Florida, Louisiana and California*, 4th ed. (New York: E. R. Pelton and Co., 1892), 178.
10. McPhee, *Oranges*, 70.
11. "Gallesio on the Orange," 179.
12. McPhee, *Oranges*, 66–67.
13. "Gallesio on the Orange," 182–85.
14. McPhee, *Oranges*, 23.
15. "Gallesio on the Orange," 189.
16. McPhee, *Oranges*, 66. Here and elsewhere in his discussion of the orange in European art and literature, McPhee relies upon S. Tolkowsky, *Hesperides: A History of the Culture and Use of Citrus Fruits* (London, 1938).

17. *Encyclopedia of Cookery,* 8: 1266; McPhee, *Oranges,* 72–73.
18. *Encyclopedia of Cookery,* 8: 1266.
19. McPhee, *Oranges,* 73–75.
20. Ibid., 79. Here McPhee relies on Tolkowsky's discussion of oranges in art.
21. Ibid., 80.
22. Much early American alligator lore is based on the Nile crocodile. See Jay Mechling, "Alligator," in *American Wildlife in Symbol and Story,* ed. Angus K. Gillespie and Jay Mechling (Knoxville: Univ. of Tennessee Press, 1987), 73–98.
23. McPhee, *Oranges,* 76–77.
24. T. Frederick Davis, "History of the Orange in Florida, 1575 to 1900," typescript, Yonge Library of Florida History, Univ. of Florida, 1937(?), 1.
25. Ibid., 2–6.
26. McPhee writes about this, explaining that oranges grown on the Ridge are sweet orange buds grafted onto rough lemon root stock. The different root stock, sort of soil, and climate of the Indian River fruit results, somehow, in a markedly sweeter, juicier product.
27. Frank R. Ficarrotta Jr., "The Citrus Industry of West Central Florida" (M.A. thesis, Univ. of Florida, 1955), 12.
28. Davis, "History of the Orange in Florida," 13–15; Divine, "A History of Citrus Culture," 52. For more general histories of the Florida railroads, see Howard D. Dozier, *A History of the Atlantic Coast Railroad* (New York: A. M. Kelley, 1971), and Richard E. Prince, *Seaboard Air Line Railway: Steam Boats, Locomotives, and History* (Green River, Wyo., 1969).
29. Davis, "History of the Orange in Florida," 21.
30. Moore, *Treatise and Hand-Book,* viii–ix.
31. Ibid.
32. Ibid., 14.
33. For a popular printed edition of the lecture, see Russell H. Conwell, *Acres of Diamonds* (New York: Harper and Brothers, 1915).
34. Moore, *Treatise and Hand-Book,* 16.
35. This prospectus and others mentioned here are held by the F. K. Yonge Library of Florida History at the Univ. of Florida.
36. Described by Divine, "A History of Citrus Culture," 40–43.
37. The Seaboard Air Line Railway Company Development Department published, for example, a pamphlet promoting *The Satsuma Orange* (1927), one of the varieties of the so-called "kid-glove" or loose-skinned orange, *Citrus nobilis.*
38. Harriet Beecher Stowe, "Our Florida Plantation," *Atlantic Monthly* (May 1879).
39. McPhee, *Oranges,* 95–96.
40. B. M. Lelong, *Culture of the Citrus in California* (Sacramento: State Printing Office, 1900), 17.

41. *From Seed to Consumer: Orange Culture in Southern California* (Los Angeles, Calif.: Los Angeles Chamber of Commerce, 1909), 4.
42. Lelong, *Culture of the Citrus*, 19.
43. Thomas A. Garvey, *Orange Culture in California* (San Francisco: Pacific Rural Press, 1882), 7–8.
44. A. C. Fish, *The Profits of Orange Culture in Southern California* (Los Angeles, 1890), text from back cover.
45. *From Seed to Consumer*, 4.
46. A. J. Cook, *California Citrus Culture* (Sacramento: State Commission of Horticulture, n.d.), 5.
47. E. J. Wickson, *The Orange in Northern and Central California* (San Francisco: California State Board of Trade, 1903), 6.
48. Walter V. Woehlke, "In the Orange Country," *Sunset* 26 (Mar. 1911): 251.
49. Ibid., 262–63.
50. Fish, *The Profits of Orange Culture*, 3, 5.
51. For an excellent analysis of the sort of imagery mentioned here, see Paul F. Starrs, "The Navel of California and Other Oranges: Images of California and the Orange Crate," *California Geographer* 28(1988): 1–41. For an illustrated history of the orange in visual materials, see Helen L. Koben, "Perfume, Postcards, and Promises: The Orange in Art and Industry," *Journal of Decorative and Propaganda Arts*, 23 (1998): 32–47. This entire issue is a theme issue on Florida.
52. Raymond H. Clary, *The Making of Golden Gate Park: The Early Years, 1865–1906* (San Francisco: California Living Book, 1980), 114, 116. For a larger perspective on fairs as an American cultural text, see Robert W. Rydell, *All the World's a Fair: Visions of Empire at American International Expositions, 1876–1916* (Chicago: Univ. of Chicago Press, 1984).
53. Woehlke, "In the Orange Country," 258.
54. Don Francisco, "The Plans Behind Sunkist Advertising," *California Citrograph* (Jan. 1920): 9. Literary critic Leo Spitzer, in offering a critical "experiment" to demonstrate his critical method, chose to analyze a picture-with-text Sunkist poster prominent in drugstores in the late 1930s. This analysis of the symbolism of the orange and how the ad suggests California still makes interesting reading. See Leo Spitzer, *A Method of Interpreting Literature* (Northampton, Mass.: Smith College, 1949), 102–49.
55. Ficarrotta, "The Citrus Industry," 81.
56. Florence Fabricant, "Chilled Orange Juice: Demand and Prices Continue to Grow," *New York Times*, Apr. 25, 1990.
57. Robert Venturi, Denise Scott Brown, and Steve Izenour, *Learning from Las Vegas* (Cambridge, Mass.: MIT Press, 1972).
58. Loran Smith, *Fifty Years on the Fifty: The Orange Bowl Story* (Charlotte, N.C.: East Woods Press, Fas and MacMillan Publishing Co., 1983).
59. McPhee, *Oranges*, 131.

60. Joan Brumberg, *Fasting Girls: The Emergence of Anorexia Nervosa as a Medical Disease* (Cambridge, Mass.: Harvard Univ. Press, 1988).
61. McPhee, *Oranges*, 11, 4.
62. *From Seed to Consumer*, 3.
63. Woehlke, "In the Orange Country," 263. *Sunset* repeats this point with a caption beneath a photograph of a neat, attractive home: "The orange-grower is not a farmer. His home in a citrus-belt city, his recreations and intellectual pursuits, are identical with those of business and professional men" (252).
64. As Starrs, "The Navel of California," notes (17), most of the booster literature and imagery for California stressed that this was a middle-class agrarian lifestyle.
65. Woehlke, "In the Orange Country," 263.
66. McPhee, *Oranges*, 54–57.
67. Robert Coles, *Migrants, Sharecroppers, Mountaineers* (Boston: Little, Brown, 1971).
68. Alec Wilkinson, *Big Sugar: Seasons in the Cane Fields of Florida* (New York: Alfred A. Knopf, 1989).

# Tad Tuleja

Among the more amusing materials recorded by the Federal Writers' Project in Vermont was a story from one Arthur Carlton about a giant pumpkin discovered by his grandfather. According to Carlton, his "Grandsir," a farmer, used to let his pigs forage along the Connecticut River, and one day, when a pregnant sow failed to return to the farm for dinner, he and some friends went to find her. What they found instead was a "goralmighty big" pumpkin vine that had sent two sturdy, thick trailers across the water "clear over to the New Hampshire side." Following the sow's tracks up to this prodigy, they realized that she had crossed the river on it, and set out in a canoe to bring her back. Sure enough, on the New Hampshire side, the sow's tracks took up again. They led to the biggest pumpkin any of them had ever seen—one with a hole in the side. Peeking in, they discovered not only the lost sow but, sleeping soundly beside her, a just-born litter of her offspring.[1]

On the surface, this is standard stuff: broadly an American tall tale, more narrowly an offering from the Yankee liar's bench, and more specifically still an example of the "fast-growing vine" motif that makes appearances from New England to Arizona.[2] But for two reasons the story is both unusual and provocative. First, the prodigious vine is a jumper, not just a runner. No respecter of boundaries, it hurdles the region's major waterway in a single leap, thus violating simultaneously both a natural and a cultural margin. Second, its fruit is not only phenomenal, but phenomenally nurturing. Pumpkins are not uncommonly fed to swine, but this pumpkin provides more than food. Spacious enough to contain the sow and her litter, it serves as a sheltering incubator, that is, as a home. Once it settles down into a domestic role, it is as protective of boundaries as it had previously been disdainful. The tale thus embodies a conflict between transgression and docility, between the intemperate energy of a wild thing and the comforting strength of the nested fruit as a kind of nonce nursery.

If this conflict were peculiar to Mr. Carlton's tale, we might dismiss it as culturally insignificant. But in fact it is anything but peculiar. Whether he was drawing from his own family repertoire or had tapped into some Jungian motif bank, Mr. Carlton's Vermont anecdote reflects a traditional ambivalence about the pumpkin that may be observed in visual, oral, and written sources from colonial times to the present day. In this essay, I examine that ambivalence and try to show that the pumpkin as symbol reflects a duality in cultural consciousness touching not just how we look at plants or food, but how we view domestication itself.

Interestingly, the symbolic duality I will be discussing—the contrast between the "wild" and the "civilized" pumpkin—was preceded, by several decades, by a simpler ambivalence. In the eighteenth century, the term "pumpkin" meant a dolt or a simpleton—a reference, probably, to the fact that the gourd is about head-sized and hollow. It retained this negative meaning into the beginning of this century: L. Frank Baum's genial but foolish Jack Pumpkinhead is one representative of the tradition. Almost concurrently, however, the plural "pumpkins" acquired the *opposite* connotation. By the 1840s, to be "pumpkins"—or even better, "some pumpkins"—was to be "a person of consequence or importance."[3]

In this initial duality of connotation, we may be seeing merely a vestige of the human propensity to confuse loaded terms with their opposites—that rhetorically subtle capacity for confounding Aristotle that we see in endearments like "How are you, you old son-of-a-bitch?" and "Jim, you're a bad motherfucker." But the duality I will be addressing indicates more than mere banter. It is a duality, I will try to show, which reflects the contradictions not only of a single symbol, but of symbol-making itself.[4]

## Pumpkins as Presence and Promise

In 1615, writing his promotional *True Discourse of the Present State of Virginia*, settler Ralph Hamor compared the American "Pumpion" favorably with the squashes then known in England. "Of the West Indies kind in great abundance," he wrote, "of one seed I have seen a hundred, much better than ours and lasting all the year." He was not alone in remarking on the vegetable's abundance. John Rolfe and Thomas Hariot both mentioned it as a staple of the colonists' diet, and John Smith enumerated it among the native fare that made even fainthearted "Tuftaffaty humorists" think twice about returning home.[5]

The situation was similar in the North. Alice Morse Earle, commenting on eating customs in "Old New England," suggests that the colonists "never turned very readily" to pumpkins, but their disaffection, it seems, owed less to distaste than to satiety. So common were pumpkins in seventeenth-century Massachusetts that they came under attack by ascetic churchmen, who observed that Thanksgiving had been so transformed by the groaning board that it ought to be called "St. Pompion's Day." Edward Johnson, in his *Wonder-Working Providence,* mocked the mockers, noting that pumpkins had been a Godsend in time of need: "With this fruit the Lord was pleased to feed his people to their good content, till Corne and Cattell were increased." The rich, if tedious, abundance of pumpkins is also observed in a popular rhyme: "We have pumpkins at morning and pumpkins at noon./If it were not for pumpkins we should be undone." Thus the fruit which had served Native American populations for centuries became, very early in settlement history, both a staple food and an emblem of New World bounty.[6]

The Indians had used the pumpkin, and squashes in general, in baked, boiled, roasted, and dried forms. The colonists, quick to appreciate the fruit's versatility, soon employed it not only in puddings and stews, but also in breads, johnnycakes, porridges, butter, syrups, and pies. Sarah Knight, on her 1704 journey from Boston to New York, was served a bread made of pumpkin and corn meal, and John Josselyn, in his *New England Rarities Discovered* (1672), gives a recipe for a kind of pumpkin relish—stewed "pompions" spiced with vinegar and ginger—which he calls "The ancient New-England standing Dish."[7]

But of all the gifts bequeathed to the colonists by "St. Pompion," none added more to American folklore, and none so distinctively came to represent American plenty, than the Thanksgiving favorite, pumpkin pie. Johnson spoke of this dish as already old in 1654, and although he likely meant the crustless variety favored by colonists short of flour, it's clear that the idea of pumpkin pie, if not the modern reality, was "traditional" well before the American Revolution. A Maine housewife's kitchen book from 1763 contains a "receipt" for the dish, as does the first published American cookbook, Amelia Simmon's *American Cookery* (1796). So traditional was the item in colonial Connecticut that, in 1705, a temporary shortage of molasses forced the town of Colchester to postpone its Thanksgiving from the first to the second week in November, until that essential ingredient was obtained.[8]

Popular literature of the nineteenth century gives ample evidence that pumpkin pie was considered, in many circles, an indispensable feature of

Thanksgiving. Women's magazines carried recipes for it, and numerous memoirs also attest to an association with the supposedly New England holiday. Sarah Josepha Hale, whose tireless promotion of the feast day led to its nationalization by President Lincoln, noted in her 1827 novel *Northwood* that pumpkin pies were "an indispensable part of a good and true Yankee Thanksgiving." The author of the most celebrated piece of Thanksgiving doggerel, Lydia Child, included a recipe for the pie in her 1829 homemaker's guide, *The Frugal Housewife*. The editors of the *Yale Literary Magazine*, in an 1838 holiday paean, described a "constellation of pies" in which the "huge pumpkin" shone majestically, like a "Sirius among the lesser lights." And a New England–born Louisiana resident, writing to relatives in 1846, promised to "try to have a real Yankee dinner, pumpkin pies and everything to match." Without exaggeration, a recent historian of the holiday claims that, turkey and cranberry sauce notwithstanding, pumpkin pies constituted "the first culinary Thanksgiving tradition."[9]

But the association of the pie with Thanksgiving is indistinguishable from its association with the American home, and with the annual reunion of family, so often viewed through a nostalgic mist, which Thanksgiving represents. In the last century, as Americans became geographically more venturesome, and as the extended family fell victim to the lure of cities and upward mobility, Thanksgiving was linked more and more to pictures of an idealized rural past; pumpkin pie, as a symbol of the holiday, began to evoke not just any family meal, but a sentimentalized *cena illo tempore*, where the realities of separation were forgotten and Grandmother's redolent country kitchen was magically, if only temporarily, restored.

Probably the most famous example of this "nostalgizing" trend was John Greenleaf Whittier's poem "The Pumpkin," written in 1846. The central stanza of that lyric, evoking a Thanksgiving Day with "the old broken links of affection restored," ends with this rhetorical question:

> What moistens the lip and what brightens the eye?
> What calls back the past like the rich Pumpkin pie?

The wan, almost elegiac mood is heightened by an apostrophe, in the final stanza, to an unnamed baker, presumably the poet's mother:

> Fairer hands never wrought at a pastry more fine,
> Brighter eyes never watched o'er its baking than thine!

And it is clinched in the lyric's final prayer that the baker's

> . . . life be as sweet and its last sunset sky
> Golden-tinted and fair as thy own Pumpkin pie![10]

The stodginess of the verse may have been peculiar to Whittier, but the saccharine sentiments were not. In the same decade, Lydia Maria Child's lyric "Thanksgiving Day" also linked the ancient New England standing dish to a rural past and an aproned materfamilias:

> Over the river and through the wood–
> Now grandmother's cap I spy!
> Hurrah for the fun!
> Is the pudding done?
> Hurrah for the pumpkin pie![11]

Later in the century, even Josh Billings, whom no one could accuse of stodginess, also adopted a nostalgic tone in describing the dish he called "the sass ov Nu England": "I would like to be a boy again, just for sixty minnits, and eat miself phull ov the blessed old mixtur. . . . Punkin pi iz the oldest American beverage I kno ov, and ought to go down to posterity with the trade mark ov our grandmothers on it; but i am afrade it wont, for it iz tuff even now to find one that tastes in the mouth at all az they did 40 years ago."[12]

The entropic home truth embodied in this last observation—that nothing is as good as it was when we were six—will sound cogent to anyone who has recently tasted a ballpark hot dog, a "draft" root beer, or a candy bar and remembers how they tasted in 1950. Coming from Billings, it may be marked up to poetic hyperbole, but hyperbole does not explain the continued popularity of the notion into the new century. As waves of immigrants passed through Ellis Island and the frontier was officially closed, popular writers with none of Billings's humor lamented frequently that "genuine" pumpkin pie had become a thing of the gloried past. What has happened, cried Kate Stiles in 1908, to "the lost art of making, of spicing, and baking/The pumpkin pie famed in the good days of yore?" In his youth, wrote Walter Prichard Eaton in 1912, "pung-kins" were "much larger than they are now and made a more delicious pie." The search for a "treasured" pie recipe is the pretext for a domestic mystery in Adele Thompson's 1902 story "Ye Pumpion Pye," while the modern pie, claimed the editors of *The Independent* in 1906, is a mere "mathematical production"; the intuitive skill of transforming what they call the "gourd glorious" into an "old New England pumpkin pie" has become "a lost art."[13]

That skill, as turn-of-the-century encomiums stressed, was a maternal one. If one theme runs through all panegyrics to the gourd glorious in the gaslight age, it is that of motherhood (sometimes grandmotherhood) as the inspiriting presence of a bygone Harvest Home. The *Independent*, evoking an era "when the steam whistle had not yet shrieked through the valley," exhorted the homemakers, with martial exuberance, to revive the dignity of ancient labors: "Throw back your cap strings once more, little mother! March up to the rolling pin broad-shelf, with that fine confidence that belongs to real art! Pour together the constituents by the instincts of a born home-maker! Shove the pies into an oven heated with hickory wood! And we will stand about you in silent reverence; for what else in all the world is so wonderful, so beautiful, so much to be loved and trusted as a good homekeeper?"[14]

As if that were not enough to drive every Gibson Girl in the country straight back into a corset, E. P. Powell reiterated the theme in the same paper seven years later, when he cautioned that only milk from the "home cow" be used in the preparation of pumpkin pie, and observed that the true secret to its appeal was in having "the right woman to mix and cook it." As late as the 1930s, Dorothy Kirk Sinker, writing in the *Literary Digest* on "pumpkin pie, an American institution," praised the "closer family relationship" that was to be expected from women resuming such "discarded domestic activities" as canning, fruit drying, and baking. A letter to the editor of that weekly offered a "true Down East receipt" for the national dessert, signed "Yours respectfully, Gramma."[15]

By the late nineteenth and early twentieth centuries, then, many Americans had come to view the nation's most common pumpkin dish as something more than a culinary delight. New Englanders especially took pride in its traditional nature, and as modernity continued to erode traditional folkways, pumpkin pie increasingly came to symbolize not simply the warmth of Thanksgiving Day reunions, but an entire cluster of domestic memories, richly nostalgic, that centered on Mother cheerfully running the kitchen of a perfectly happy, because perfectly static, childhood home.

One interesting tangent to this domestic symbolism is the supposed connection, in both New and Old World belief, between pumpkins and pregnancy. Alan Dundes once tweaked his quondam allies, the psychoanalysts, for failing to provide even "minimal evidence" for this connection; yet folk sources do suggest a link.[16]

Consider the childhood fiction that babies grow, like vegetables, in a garden. The vegetable most commonly linked with this idea is the cabbage, but the Cannon collection does cite a belief that "babies come from the pumpkin patch," and it may not be accidental that the popular Cabbage Patch dolls bear a family resemblance to gourds. The tradition appears with a peculiar twist in a 1906 story by Kate Wiggin, where the heroine, Rebecca, finds an infant in a clump of goldenrod and, because of his yellow face, names him Jack-o'-Lantern.[17]

There are other examples of this "pregnant garden" motif. One is the motif of the classic numskull who mistakes a garden rabbit for a foal, just "hatched" from a supposedly egg-like pumpkin. Another is Arthur Carlton's tall tale regarding the sow who farrows in a pumpkin. The womblike pumpkin, used as shelter, also appears in a North Carolina story, where a huge gourd houses two hogs and is later turned into a hotel. Cinderella's carriage, while not very convincing as isolated evidence for the "pregnant pumpkin," does acquire a certain cogency as yet another example of this "gourd as shelter" motif.[18]

One should also mention the traditional nursery rhyme in which Peter the pumpkin eater, unable to "keep" his wife, puts her in a pumpkin shell and thereby keeps her "very well." One does not need recourse to Freudian symbol indices to read the shell here as a code for "family way," or to realize that the pumpkin eater's achievement is to contain his wife in the realm of *Küche und Kinder*. This symbolism is made explicit in Penelope Mortimer's novel *The Pumpkin Eater*, whose heroine is virtually addicted to pregnancy. It is twisted oddly in Sarah Addington's 1923 story "The Discontent of Mrs. Pumpkin-Eater," where Peter's wife *asks* to be placed in a shell; and in Margaret Sangster's 1933 story "Pumpkin Shell," where a husband tames his flighty (and sexually unresponsive) wife by showing that a good marriage is like a "nice, tight, friendly box" to which the husband, like the pumpkin eater, holds the key.[19]

Why folk belief should have established a connection between the pumpkin and pregnancy is not clear, although the answer may lie with visual resemblance. The pregnant woman's swelling midriff, protuberant and roughly globular, may suggest concealment of a large fruit, such as a watermelon or pumpkin, and there may be point here to the juvenile joke that, if you swallow too many pumpkin or watermelon seeds, the plant will grow inside you. Consider also the use of "pumpkin" as a term of affection for young children—a usage facilitated by the built-in diminutive *kin* and reflecting, perhaps, the initial idiomatic ambivalence of the word as indicating both importance and stupidity. Whatever the explanation, however, the connection clearly reinforces the social value of the pumpkin as a symbolic member of a protected, rather than wild, realm. Whether the "gourd glorious" appears as the ancient New England standing dish, as a nonce nursery for piglets, or as the most traditional dessert from "Gramma's" oven, one consistent symbolic strain in pumpkin imagery has been its association to domestic warmth, to hearth and home.

Let me turn now to a second consistent strain—one which not only does not support these domestic resonances, but quite dramatically seeks to undermine them.

## The "Worked" Pumpkin

In becoming a holiday dessert, the pumpkin undergoes a transformation. To use a term that Jack Santino has adapted from Lévi-Strauss, it is "worked" out of its natural, free-growing state into a cultural creation.[20]

The working involves several steps. First, the shell is cut open and the edible flesh is scooped out. Then this flesh is mixed with spices (typically ginger and nutmeg), boiled, mashed, and placed into a second, manufactured shell of pastry dough. Finally, this filled shell is placed in an oven and baked—so that the masterpiece that eventually sits on a windowsill to cool has actually been cooked two times. To appropriately characterize the pie, therefore, we must emend Lévi-Strauss's observation about the distinction between roasted and boiled food. "Boiled food," he says, "is doubly mediated, by the water in which it is immersed,

*Fig. 7.1. One well-known association of pumpkins with pregnancy occurs in the nursery rhyme "Peter, Peter, Pumpkin Eater." This illustration by Blanche Fisher Wright appeared in* The Real Mother Goose, *copyright c. 1916 Checkerboard Press. Inc. Used by permission.*

and by the receptacle that holds both water and food."[21] Since the double-cooked pie is prepared in two different receptacles, it may be said to be *triply* mediated—a kind of supersocialized product of kitchen labor.

Domesticity here leaves nothing to chance. By virtue of the double working, the "gourd glorious" is transformed into a generic puree, more closely resembling other purees than it does the plant from which it was extracted. The obligatory spices, like the double cooking, further "denature" the fruit, while at the same time placing an idiosyncratic cultural signature—the "instincts" of each "little mother"—on a plant that, "in the raw," has little taste.[22] One impulse of cultural transformation, in this case, is to invest nature with "personality."

The elaboration here described, however, is only one that can be performed. The pumpkin may also be worked into quite a different cultural icon, the American jack-o'-lantern. This second version of the transformed plant, every bit as symbolically resonant as the pie, stands, however, not for Thanksgiving but for a quite different, indeed contradictory, harvest festival: the playful threat to domestic order called Halloween.

The celebratory distinction is absolute. One may eat a pumpkin pie "around Halloween," and one finds an occasional jack-o'-lantern straggler still gracing a porch in November, but these are incidental exceptions. Commercial advertising and popular idiom agree that the carved head belongs to witching night, and the pie to the gathering of the clan. The wholly natural, "uncultured" pumpkin, it is true, may stand equally well for either holiday; like other harvest emblems (apples, Indian corn), "the unworked vegetable carries the general seasonal symbolism."[23] But once human agents step in, the symbolism becomes bifurcated and "dedicated."

The bifurcation occurs, I would suggest, as a way of maintaining a conceptual distinction between two proximate harvest celebrations that serve entirely different cultural functions. Thanksgiving celebrates reunion, harmony, security; its pumpkin is comfortingly edgeless, warm, temperature-controlled—so successfully worked away from its wild origins that its very identity as a plant is concealed. Halloween celebrates disjunction, disharmony, uncertainty; it dares to play (in a highly managed fashion, to be sure) with the most ancient of all metaphors for loss of security, the imagined gateway between the living and the dead. Thus its pumpkin, reasonably enough, is still half wild. *Cucurbita pepo* as severed head, the jack-o'-lantern is clearly still a plant, although manipulated by a grotesque imagination. Each holiday gets the pumpkin it deserves, while the symbolic distinction between them derives not from the fact of transformation (for both pie and jack-o'-lantern are transformations), but from the degree and the type of the working involved. Whatever symbolic resonances attach to the two objects are invested in them by that working.

Today, as Jack Santino helpfully implies, the differences between making a pie and making a jack-o'-lantern begin even before the pumpkin is brought home.

Faced with the pressures of double careers and the more insidious pressures of convenience foods, the homemaker today, even if she doesn't surrender completely to Mrs. Smith, at least bypasses the scooping-out, mashing, and boiling stages by using seasoned pie filling from a can. For a jack-o'-lantern, on the other hand, the raw fruit itself must be manipulated, and this often involves a symbolically charged journey "from an urban or suburban environment to a rural or semirural environment" from which the wild icons may be retrieved.[24]

The relative wildness of the jack-o'-lantern is further reflected in the working itself. Generally, the top of the shell is removed, the pulp and seeds are taken out, with perhaps a little of the edible flesh as well; removal of this food is not critical, however, because the lantern is fundamentally a raw item, meant to be seen, not eaten. Once the pumpkin is thus hollowed out, it is carved into the semblance of a head, or metonymically speaking a face; a candle is placed behind this face for illumination, and the lantern is set on a porch or in a window, to be observed by trick-or-treaters and other revelers. This finished product, with its cold single light, is traditionally the product of a male, not a female, hand, and it is as evocative of imagined terrors *beyond* the domestic circle as the pumpkin pie is of the hearth.[25]

The same dichotomy persists with regard to function. The "mother's pumpkin," fully wrested from its savage state, is designed to provide communal nourishment at a ceremony specifically dedicated to communitas. The "man's" (or "boy's") pumpkin remains only half-civilized, the elaboration it has undergone heightening rather than muting its otherness. Far from being a potential comestible, its function is to be seen and then discarded—returned to the realm of the unincorporable after it has reminded the community (the community of pie eaters) of the fragility of domestic control.

To a generation that has grown up on "funny face" carving contests, my emphasis on the horrific, alien nature of the jack-o'-lantern may seem like structuralist ax grinding. Certainly contemporary Halloween customs suffer (some would say benefit) from "Disneyfication." The jack-o'-lantern's traditional connotations, however, belie its recent adoption as a cheery "Mr. Pumpkin": those connotations are plainly terrifying. A brief history of the term's usage will make this point.

In contemporary usage, the term "jack-o'-lantern" refers almost exclusively to the hollowed-out, illuminated pumpkin. But this meaning is fairly recent. In the seventeenth century, when a "jack" was a man, a jack-o'-lantern was simply a man with a lantern, that is, a night watchman. This British usage, now obsolete, gave way gradually to a second meaning: Jack-o'-Lantern as an eponymous representative of the *ignis fatuus*, or will o' the wisp. Belief in this creature—typically depicted as a wandering ghost whose flickering lantern leads travelers astray—has been recorded widely among American blacks and has numerous European antecedents. There is symbolic as well as etymological sense in seeing a link between this dangerous fugitive and the flickering lights we place on our porches. Let me highlight four features of the wandering Jack-o'-Lantern tradition to provide a context for establishing that link.[26]

First, the figure inhabits a region that is physically beyond domestication. Science commonly explains the "flickering light" phenomenon by identifying it with combustible marsh gas, and folk belief confirms this hypothesis. Although occasional sightings have been reported in scrubland and woods, the typical haunt of the *ignis fatuus* is a bog or swamp—terrain that resists cultivation. A creature of the wild, Jack-o'-Lantern lures travelers not abstractly into "danger," but specifically into terra incognita, into an uncharted, uncultivated wasteland.[27]

Second, the figure also inhabits a *spiritual* wasteland: a region beyond mortal ken that is associated variously with the Devil and with Death. In a common tale about the superstition's origin, a man named Jack, having cheated the Devil of his soul and being too wicked to get into Heaven, is condemned to pace the earth forever, a new Cain. In other versions, a mocked Death takes revenge; it is worth noting in this regard that a flickering candle, often seen as a harbinger of death, is linked by some informants to the wandering soul: the Cannon archive has Jack, also known as Will o' the Wisp, as "a corpse candle carried by ghosts." The common denominator here is demonic: whether in medieval Europe or rural Maryland, *ignis fatuus* is a supernatural presence.[28]

Third, the wanderer goes not from town to town or farm to farm, but through a dwellingless void, the tractless "wild." Like Norfolk's "hytersprites" or German *Wassergeister*, Jack may function as a kind of "warning fiction." But while they are geographically stable—the Nixies of Magdeburg, the River Tee's Peg Powler—he is not. Like Cain a "fugitive and vagabond," he inhabits a domain where *domus* is unknown.[29]

Finally, he is doomed as a result of transgression—and a very particular type of transgression. Unlike Cain or his medieval fellow traveler Ahasuerus, who are condemned for offenses against charity, the *ignis fatuus* is doomed for breaking man's law—for violating or ignoring a church sacrament. Dying unbaptized, dying without absolution, being buried in unconsecrated ground—any of these could lead to his Cain-like fate. The structural pattern is clear. Whether as guilty as the Devil cheater Jack or as innocent as a newborn child, one becomes a wandering ghost, a jack of the lantern, for *failing to negotiate a prescribed boundary*. William Wells Newell confirms this point in identifying one "especially abhorred" crime—the unauthorized removal of landowners' boundary stones. In a fitting, Dantesque kind of penance, the one who subverts domestic propriety, who obliterates property, must drift forever in a realm where neither exists.[30]

Is there more than mere nomenclature to suggest a link between the wasteland ghost and our ghostly pumpkinheads? The answer is uncertain, because the *ignis fatuus* is not peculiar to Halloween, because the American jack-o'-lantern generally sits on a porch rather than wandering, and because in England, where turnips are the favored vegetable for carved lanterns, "jack-o'-lantern" usually means *ignis fatuus;* most turnip lanterns are called "punkies."

Nonetheless, one may argue for a connection. English punkies, from which our pumpkin lanterns most likely evolved, do "wander" about the streets at Halloween: youthful "guisers" use them both to light their way and, suspended on poles, to frighten householders. In Devon, children carry them in procession, both on Halloween and on Guy Fawkes Day. At Stoke Pero Church in Somerset, *ignis fatuus* is known as a "spunkie," and spunkies come "from all around" on Halloween to "guide this year's ghosts to their funeral." And at Hinton St. George, also in Somerset, villagers celebrate a "Punky Night" just before Halloween. Tradition has it originating in the Middle Ages, when wives had to lead

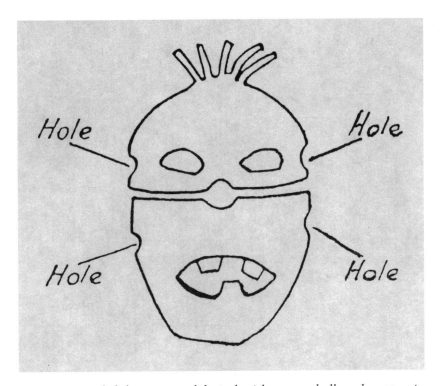

*Fig. 7.2. An English forerunner of the jack-o'-lantern: a hollowed-out turnip or swede containing a candle. As one Monmouthshire teenager explained, "You light the candle and go out into the street and if anyone comes along pop out from around a corner and frighten them." From Peter and Iona Opie,* Lore and Language of Schoolchildren *(1959). Used by permission of Oxford University Press.*

their drunken husbands home with the help of carved-out beetroot lanterns. Today the celebration involves a procession around the perimeter of the village—marking the boundary lines disdained by the wandering ghost.[31]

But the best evidence for a link is perceived function. British punky carriers vary in their opinions, but many believe their turnip lanterns to be apotropaic. They provide protection against "witches and other mischief"; they "keep aways the evil things that are about" on Halloween; they act as a bane for "evil spirits."[32] American informants tell the same story. No matter how harmless looking they may be today, the American Halloween's major icons—witches, ghosts, and jack-o'-lanterns—are still idiomatically understood to be "scary." Walter Prichard Eaton, writing in 1912, claimed that "pungkins existed primarily to be converted into jack-o-lanterns, and jack-o-lanterns, in turn, existed to scare the life out of Old Lady Jones." Modern versions of Washington Irving's "Legend of Sleepy Hollow" depict Ichabod Crane being terrified by the ghostly horseman who bears a jack-o'-lantern in place of his head. The Cannon archive reports a belief that Halloween porch pumpkins are designed specifically "to scare away evil spirits and goblins." Similar beliefs appear in western Massachusetts. In 1972 Carole Bakos, a folklore student at the University of Massachusetts, interviewed householders who had adorned their front stoops with pumpkinhead scarecrows or "dummies." They sat there, she was told, to "ward off evil spirits," to "scare away the devils and demons."[33] Whether they sit on fences and gateposts, as in England, or on porches and windowsills, as in the United States, the lanterns' root purpose is clear: on the night that the dead walk and goblins prowl, they keep the house protected from unseen terrors.

If that were all there was to it, we could comfortably view the porch lantern as a kind of border guard for domestic security: the external defender of that inner warmth that its own "insides" both supply and represent. But it is not that simple. The carved pumpkin displays an irony that is not invested in the "triple worked" pie. Closer to its natural state and thus closer to the realm of the intractable, the jack-o'-lantern effectively repels the terrible only, and precisely, by adopting its visage. Christina Hole's concept of "impersonation as protection," Santino's notion that Halloween decorations "incorporate" and thus vitiate "death and randomness," Anna Freud's definition of "identification with the terrifying object" as a defense mechanism against unconscious fears—all of these insights are relevant to an understanding of the glowing porch pumpkin that at once represent, attracts, and repels evil.[34] That it performs this mediating function at a liminal moment and in a liminal space demonstrates further how it twists symbolic polarities, creating, as it were, within a single "golden orb," an ambivalence within an ambivalence.

There is a second irony, too. As clearly as the jack-o'-lantern stands for "otherness," it has also become invested with a certain homey, almost avuncular quality. Without ever surrendering its horrific aspect, it serves as a beacon to wandering children, a nontraditionally *reliable* will-o'-the-wisp. "The dying glow of a jack o'lantern," wrote Martha Williams in 1906, sinks "into the watcher's soul, there to shine through all the years a lamp unto his feet, guiding his heart homeward wherever his feet may stray." Gushy, but not inaccurate. For what really, rather than symbolically, happens on Halloween? Costumed children, who are theatrically rather than truly frightened by the pumpkins, are able to identify the neighborhood soft touches—the folks who are "in the spirit of the season"—by the presence of these flickering "terrors." Juanita Browne has called them "ghoul greeters"—a good phrase that highlights quite accurately how their dramaturgic "scariness" actually reassures.[35]

The ghouls referred to here are the costumed children, and this suggests to what extent the ironies I am addressing inhere in the holiday itself. As the descendant of an ancient feast of the dead, Halloween necessarily celebrates the transitional, the uncategorizable, the liminal. It should not be surprising, perhaps, that the porch pumpkin both welcomes and warns; the children who are welcomed and warned by it embody an identical ambivalence—one which serves to mediate dichotomies not only between the inner and outer spheres of family life, but between nature and culture, good and evil, life and death. Both the children and the pumpkin have been "worked"—we might say that both have been "dressed"—to represent forces beyond the realm of common control. By that very representation, those forces *are* controlled—if not empirically, then symbolically. And the final irony of the porch lantern may consist in just this fact: that the honor paid to evil saps its strength, that by embodying a threat to domestic order, glowing Jack—like the gargoyles on medieval cathedrals—actually makes that order more secure.

This fact is not lost on neighborhood teenagers, who are drawn to the flickering emblems not as moths to flame, but as rivals in the art of boundary testing. As irritating as it may be to property owners, there is cultural propriety in the practice of smashing porch pumpkins after Halloween. By this act of eccentric "harvesting," adolescents—themselves liminal creatures—ritually endorse the ironies of the season. In smashing Old Lady Jones's jack-o'-lantern, do they, like Jack himself, violate boundaries? Or do they invigorate the domestic realm by obliterating its opposite? The answer is "Both." Whatever the individual motivation of pumpkin trashers (sociopathic? Oedipal?), their action closes a circle. Just as the destiny of uneaten food is to become spoiled *(corrompu)*, the destiny of a liminal artifact is to be broken *(rompu)*; for this reason, when neighborhood boys do not fulfill their ceremonially vandalistic function, householders themselves see to the job: "If they last too long," one Massachusetts resident told Carole Bakos of his pumpkinhead dummies, "then we junk them ourselves."[36]

Thus, with regard to their cultural dynamics—their life cycles in the community—the pumpkin pie and the jack-o'-lantern share a common, and quite "natural," destiny. In the words of songwriter Paul Simon, "Everything put together falls apart," a statement that is true of both "elaborated" objects. Composed by different makers and for ostensibly different ends, they decompose to the same end. No more secure from the logic of decay than any natural object, they too become refuse in their time.

Which leaves the communitas they have both served open, once again, to the threat of entropy. The "pumpkinness" of the fruit—its conceptual fragility, its emptiness—overcomes all attempts to "secure" it. And the dual meaning of the pumpkin, perhaps, reflects the American's uneasiness within walls. If the "gourd glorious" began symbolically as God's bulwark against starvation, and if it broadened to become a sentinel against demons, then perhaps the pie and the lantern together suggest an underlying ambivalence about security. Perhaps the fission of valences itself—our investing the plant with a split personality—symbolically registers an old confusion: our uncertainty as a settled people about the wisdom and virtue of settlement. Might the unspoken secret of this heavily ensymboled fruit be that the productive and the prodigal are one vine?

## The Signifying Pumpkin

To suggest that the two major valences of "pumpkin" share a source and a destiny, however, does not obliterate the perceived distinction between a pie and a lantern. Nor does it suggest that, in their dynamic presence in culture, the two objects "mean" the same thing. Objects, to paraphrase Robbe-Grillet, do not mean anything in themselves; they acquire significance—they come to signify—because human beings *invest* them with meanings. In the case of cultural, "worked" objects, those meanings reflect not only the conceptual categories that inform all human perception, but also the psychic and physical energy of the working itself. A whittled stick signifies something quite different to its maker and his community than a mere stick *trouvé*, because his investment of time and effort both personalizes and "cultivates"; likewise, Mom's or Dad's work on the pumpkin invests it with cultural evocations that modify its natural status.

But Mom and Dad do not perform identical labor on the fruit. On the contrary, the pumpkin's two iconic forms are the result of quite different processes, and the difference influences meaning. It ensures, in fact, the ambivalence that has informed understanding of the fruit for three hundred years. We may visualize that ambivalence schematically in a structuralist paradigm, presented in the following comparison of conceptual categories:

| | |
|---|---|
| *Pumpkin Pie* | *Jack-o'-lantern* |
| Culture | Nature |
| Inner (Core, Hearth) | Outer (Shell, Border) |
| Home (Domesticity, Family, Communitas, Safety) | "Other" (Wildness, Solitude Exile, Danger) |

| Female (Mom, Mrs. Smith) | Male (Dad, Mr. Pumpkin) |
|---|---|
| Cooked | Raw |
| Thanksgiving | Halloween |
| Life | Death |

Insofar as the American pumpkin is what Americans perceive it to be, it is appropriate to adopt this kind of stereoscope: in gross terms, it fairly charts the basic contrasts. Fine-tuning, however, is in order. The staunchest acolyte of the Parisian school will be compelled to admit that, with regard to the "nature" side of this balance sheet, the divorce from "culture" is not final. For one thing, the raw jack-o'-lantern, while clearly resembling a wild plant, is also undeniably worked: it is, if you will, half-processed, half-brought over to the cultured side. For another thing, it is *physically* brought over: it sits not in terra incognita, but in a transitional zone, a porch or window. Finally, it is not completely raw: to define the culinary status of a vegetable that surrounds an open flame, one is tempted, not entirely facetiously, to use the mediating category of "partially cooked" or "roasted." And while the roasted bears an "affinity" to the raw, it is, strictly speaking, not the same.[37]

Such ameliorations of dichotomy have been implicit in the symbolism of the pumpkin since the first "ghoul greeter" graced a porch. In this century—in the age of Disneyfication and "packaged marginality"—a further amelioration has been at work, fostered by the marketing needs of an increasingly youth-centered economy and abetted by a peculiarly modern tendency to bleed the venom out of celebration. A few historical examples will indicate how insistent has been this process of turning the pumpkin into a "friendly fruit."[38]

Martha Williams described a "jocose" jack-o'-lantern as early as 1906, and merely "decorative" versions appeared in shop windows at the same time. By the 1920s, the once "scary" emblem was serving as a welcoming card for dinner guests: the *Ladies Home Journal* in October of 1923 recommended using orange placecards whose "quaint inked features" might reveal the name of each guest. The utility of the "not really scary" jack-o'-lantern as a holiday emblem has continued throughout the century, as thousands of greeting cards and painted store windows attest. In one typically cute card from the Hallmark Company, the reassuring message behind a pumpkin face reads:

Mr. Pumpkin sits in place
And makes a spooky, scary face,
But he's not trying to be mean,
He just says, "Happy Halloween!"

In addition, the carving itself has become etiolated, sapped out, as indicated by the prevalence of "funny face" carving contests, roadstands full of "happy horrors," and—most telling of all—the substitution of painting for carving as a less intrusive method of "decorating" a pumpkin. *Sunset* magazine reflected the dominant tone in October of 1977 when it gave directions for making "cheerful pumpkins to greet your Halloween visitors." It is largely painted pumpkins that are featured in the annual Sycamore, Illinois, Pumpkin Festival, devoted to turning Halloween into "a time of fun and creativity." Even California artist Sam Gendusa, "King of the Pumpkin Carvers," produces grinning gourds that are, while undeniably imaginative, evocative more of fun than of fright: Gendusa himself makes the observation that the modern Halloween is about "fantasy and humor."[39]

Children's literature has also played a role in the devolution of fearsome Jack into a "friendly fruit." In the 1961 schoolchildren's play *The Pumpkin Giant,* for example, a pumpkinheaded ogre who boasts of being able to consume "many fat little boys" gets his comeuppance at the hands of young Peter Popover, who, after knocking off his head with a potato, exclaims, "Why, it's only a vegetable. . . . Weren't we silly to be afraid of a pumpkin!" In the 1973 play *Who's Afraid of the Big Bad Pumpkin?* the paper tiger nature of the pumpkin threat is made even more explicit, as the Pumpkin is brought to trial in a "courtroom of spooks" for having "lost his power to terrify." He's acquitted of the charge because, in the words of the defense attorney Skeleton, "This Pumpkin is perfect for Halloween 1973 because Halloween itself has *changed.*" Changed how? The other characters explain:

> All Hallow's Eve, in modern times,
> Is much more treat than trick.
> There are prizes, games, and costumes,
> Much more fun than fear.

And, of course, there is Charles Schulz's ingenuous Linus, who equates his fantasy Great Pumpkin with Santa Claus, waiting patiently in a pumpkin patch each October for his sincerity to be repaid with gourd-borne toys. The president of the International Pumpkin Association, Terry Pimsleur, attributes an American "pumpkin fetish" to the popularity of the *Peanuts* strip, and it's certainly true that, for some children, the "good" gourd has overcome the old images. In 1985, for example, a young reader joined Linus in a *folie à deux,* sending off a letter to the Great Pumpkin requesting money, a new doll, and world peace. Enough to put even wandering Jack in his grave.[40]

Finally, a particularly blatant example of how a rationalized economy has flattened out the nature-culture dialectic with regard to the symbolic pumpkin. In a 1983 issue of *Mother Earth News,* pumpkin decorator Kathy Kellogg advises readers to make the best of both possible worlds by first painting and then cooking the fruit: "Who said you *have* to cut into that pumpkin? True, there won't be any winking candles or firelit expressions on your Halloween ghoul. But I'll bet your young goblins will think that small 'sacrifice' is well rewarded when they bite into a delicious, moist, custardy piece of pie." The goal here is rationalized mediation: to internalize the symbol in both its guises, so that the horrific aspect of the fruit is repressed and "gourmet good-ies" drive out the goblins. It is hardly surprising that, in this cozy atmosphere, novelty makers are able to further defang the former terror by transform-ing it into a plastic candy satchel—or that children carry that container, full of treats, into a realm it was once meant to protect. We have reached a mer-cantile and psychological la-la land, where "fears are formalized, somewhat playfully" and fully "incorporated into daily life."[41]

This flattening out of the lantern's horrific affect, this chummification of the deadly, reflects a cultural process of demystification that touches more than sentinel pumpkins. In a secular age, when the terrors of the night are more likely to be kooks than spooks, all of the traditional Halloween fright figures now sit around the hearth like eccentric cousins. Our witches are giggly youngsters like *Dell Comics'* Wendy. Our ghosts are cutely friendly, like Casper, or at least grotesquely friendly, like the *Ghostbusters'* ectoplasmic buddy, Slimer. Even Beelzebub, once identified with the Archfiend himself, was transformed in the 1988 film *Beetlejuice* into a merely irritating practical joker. And as the symbols go, so goes the holiday: Catherine Ainsworth was not far off the mark when, in a 1973 essay, she called the modern Halloween the most "child-directed"—that is, innocuous—of our major holidays.[42]

Yet there are limits to this taming of evil Jack, and they are the limits not so much of public sentiment as of bicameral consciousness itself. If Americans for one hundred years have seen the pumpkin as an ambivalent symbol, it is not because ambivalence emanates from the plant, but because the perceivers of the fruit are themselves ambivalent. If the meanings of the pumpkin contradict each other, it is reasonable to suppose that those who have invented those meanings are themselves conceptually in conflict—and that they have used the pumpkin as an objective correlate for their own felt contradictions.

The conceptual conflict that I am suggesting underlies our ambivalence about the pumpkin is one between domesticity and "the wild," between the cooked fruit as fully mediated "Mother's pie" and the carved fruit as partially mediated witch bane. But this conflict is not typically, and certainly not exclusively, American. It resonates vibrantly here because of the frontier experience.[43] But it is also fundamental to human consciousness; the tug-and-pull between security and insecurity lies at the heart of everyone's earliest experiences. Therefore, if the pumpkin has taken on this basic conflict as part of its symbolic apparatus, we should expect that, no matter how vigorously the Dewey-eyed may deny it, the darker half of ambivalence will reassert itself, and the rage for prettification that now characterizes American celebrations will be met, in a nonrationalized fash-ion, by the resurrection of a gruesome grinner.

This is exactly what has happened. Driven underground by Hallmark and

Disney, evil Jack has resurfaced in the most predictable of places: our generation's version of Grand Guignol: low-budget slasher films. Three examples will make the point.

First, John Carpenter's successful *Halloween* (1983), in which a psychotic slasher, the "unkillable" bogeyman Michael Murphy, obsessively relives a childhood trauma by "remurdering," again and again, his long-dead sister. To the student of urban legend, this film is interesting principally as a potpourri of modern threat motifs, especially those involving young, vulnerable women.[44] For the "pumpkinologist," three elements stand out. One, the killer wanders, permanently masked, condemned to immortality like the undead *ignis fatuus*. Two, his weapon, a kitchen carver, is perfectly suited to transform pumpkins into jack-o'-lanterns, and, in fact, a promotional shot for the video version displays the lethal blade as *part* of the fruit. Three, after the most gruesome of many death scenes, a victim's body is laid out between candles with a grinning jack-o'-lantern near her head. In this film, though the word "pumpkin" is never mentioned, the lantern's affinity to dark forces is perfectly clear.

Two years after making *Halloween*, Carpenter followed it with the first of many sequels. In *Halloween II*, with the bogeyman again on the prowl, the "horrific pumpkin" imagery is more blatant. The credits still feature a glowing, pulsing lantern, but here the lantern opens to reveal a grinning skull. (The continuing malleability of the pumpkin symbol is suggested by the fact that, some years later, the rock band the Grateful Dead used the same skull-and-pumpkin motif as advertisement for a "fun" Halloween concert.)

As a final example of the return of the repressed in pumpkin symbolism, consider Stan Winston's 1988 exploration of demonic revenge, the "folkloric" thriller *Pumpkinhead*. In this oddly moving pastiche of "hillbilly" cliches and special effects technology, a father who has lost his son in an accident wreaks vengeance on those responsible by summoning the demon Pumpkinhead—a kind of Ozark version of the *Alien* monster who, when it is not "settling on bad," slumbers in a graveyard pumpkin patch that is about as far from Linus country as you can get. The conjunction here between pumpkins and corpses grotesquely refracts the traditional pregnancy associations, while the mourning father's most horrifying discovery is that the monster he there gives birth to is not a creature of the "wild," but himself. There could hardly be a more vivid confirmation of a truth expressed by the doctor in *Halloween II*. Referring to the ancient Celtic festival that is the progenitor of our Halloween, he observes, "Samhain isn't evil spirits. It isn't goblins or ghosts or witches. It's the unconscious mind. We're all afraid of the dark inside ourselves."

What I have called the flattening out of the dialectic is a cultural attempt to bury that truth. Its violent resurrection in shlock movies testifies to the impossibility of the endeavor. Weakly resonant symbols, perhaps, may be redefined rather quickly by partisan or commercial impulses: the blue jean as the uniform of youthful rebellion has been effectively remarketed for yuppie bankers, and the scientific symbol for "female" has been politicized by radical feminists. Stronger symbols resist such "co-option." Because it was supercharged with significance in the 1930s, the ancient swastika is unlikely for generations to lose its basic public meaning as a Nazi symbol. The bald eagle will not suddenly come to signify anti-Americanism. Nor will the pumpkin, with its long history of dual resonance, easily be reduced to a single valence. As long as Americans remain ambivalent about their communal taming of the wild, as long as "domestic" has a checkered connotation—indeed, as long as "harvest" itself means both death and life—then errant Jack will not be puréed.

# Notes

1. The tale is cited in B. A. Botkin's *Treasury of New England Folklore* (New York: Crown, 1947), 267.
2. For the fast-growing vine lie, see Motif X1402.1 in Ernest W. Baughman, "A Comparative Study of Folktales of England and North America" (Ph.D. diss., Indiana Univ., 1953).
3. See Mitford Mathews, ed., *A Dictionary of Americanisms on Historical Principles* (Chicago: Univ. of Chicago Press, 1951). Jack Pumpkinhead appears in L. Frank Baum, *Little Wizard Stories of Oz* (Chicago: Reilly and Brinton, 1914). Other European languages also equate "pumpkinness" with stupidity: the Italian *zucca*, the German *Kurbiskopf*, and the Greek *kolokythas* all mean, roughly, "pumpkinhead." In addition, as far back as the first century, Seneca-made gourds in general symbolize simple-mindedness. His satire on the dimwitted Claudius, *Apocolocyntosis Divi Claudii*, has the emperor becoming "gourdlike." Apostolos Athanassakis translates the piece cleverly, if anachronistically, as *The Pumpkinification of Claudius* (Lawrence, Kans.: Coronado Press, 1973).
4. Roger Abrahams discusses the contradictory connotations of "motherfucker" in *Deep Down in the Jungle* (Chicago: Aldine, 1970). See also Freud's classic essay on such contradictions, "The Antithetical Meaning of Primary Words," in *Complete Works* (London: Hogarth Press, 1957), 11: 153–61.
5. Ralph Hamor, *A True Discourse of the Present State of Virginia* (1615; reprint, Richmond: Virginia State Library, 1957), 22. John Rolfe, *A True Relation of the State of Virginia in 1616* (Charlottesville: Univ. of Virginia Press, 1971). Thomas Hariot, *A Brief and True Report of the New Found Land of Virginia* (1588; fasc. ed. Ann Arbor: Clements Library Associates, 1951), C. Smith's snap at the fainthearted, dating from 1612, appears in his *Complete Works*, ed. Philip Barbour (Chapel Hill: Univ. of North Carolina Press, 1986), 1: 212.
6. Alice Morse Earle, *Customs and Fashions in Old New England* (New York: Scribner's, 1894), 150. For clerical antipathy to "St. Pompion," see Mary

Caroline Crawford, *Social Life in Old New England* (Boston: Little, Brown, 1914), 472. Edward Johnson, *Johnson's Wonder-Working Providence*, ed. J. Franklin Jameson (New York: Scribner's, 1910), 85. The frequently quoted pumpkin couplet appears, e.g., in Earle, *Customs and Fashions*, 151.

7. Sarah Knight, *The Journal of Madame Knight* (1825; New York: Peter Smith, 1935), 46. For the "standing Dish" recipe, see Edward Tuckerman's edition of Josselyn's *Rarities* in *Transactions and Collections of the American Antiquarian Society* 4 (1860): 121.

8. Johnson, *Wonder-Working Providence*, 174. For a description of the crustless pie, see U. P. Hedrick, *A History of Horticulture in America to 1860* (New York: Oxford Univ. Press, 1950), 46. The Maine housewife was Anne Gibbons Gardiner; *Mrs. Gardiner's Receipts from 1763* appeared in a private printing (Hallowell, Maine: White and Horne, 1938). The Simmons volume has been reprinted as *American Cookery 1796*, ed. Iris Frey (Green Farms, Conn.: Silverleaf Press, 1984). The Colchester molasses-shortage anecdote appears in Crawford, *Social Life in Old New England*, 479.

9. For magazine recipes, see, e.g., *The Lady's Book* 3 (Aug. 1831): 120; *Godey's Lady's Book* 119 (Dec. 1889): 539; and *Godey's Lady's Book* 121 (Nov. 1890): 426. Child's *Housewife* was published at Boston (Mar. 1829). "Thanksgiving" appeared in the *Yale Literary Magazine* 4 (Dec. 1838): 102. For the Louisiana refugee's lament and the identification of the "first culinary tradition," see Diana Karter Appelbaum, *Thanksgiving: An American Holiday, An American History* (New York: Facts on File, 1984), 111 and 226. Pumpkin pie is, of course, still thought indispensable to Thanksgiving. In a more recent feature recommending variety in the use of pumpkin, Lisa Furgatch still asks rhetorically, "What would a traditional Thanksgiving be without pumpkin pie?" See her "Pumpkin Dishes," *Country Journal* 14 (October 1987), 49.

10. Now known as "The Pumpkin," the poem first appeared in the Boston *Chronotype* in 1846 under the title "Song of the Pumpkin." Whittier included it in his 1849 *Poems*.

11. Child first published "A Boy's Thanksgiving Song" in her "Flowers for Children" series (1844–46). See William S. Osborne, *Lydia Maria Child* (Boston: Twayne, 1980), 117.

12. "Josh Billings," *Old Probability: Perhaps Rain, Perhaps Not* (New York: G. W. Carleton and Co., 1879), 12.

13. Kate R. Stiles, "An Ode to the Pumpkin," *New England Magazine* 39 (Nov. 1908): 299. Walter Prichard Eaton, "Pung-kins," *Outing* 61 (Oct. 1912): 33. Adele Thompson, "Ye Pumpion Pye," *New England Magazine* n.s. 27, no. 3 (Nov. 1902). "The Pumpkin," *Independent* 61 (Nov. 15, 1906), 1183.

14. "The Pumpkin," 1183.

15. E. P. Powell, "Pumpkin Pie," *Independent* 76 (Dec. 4, 1913), 451. Dorothy

Kirk Sinker, "Pumpkin Pie, An American Institution," *Literary Digest* 116 (November 11, 1933), 28. The letter to the editor appears under the heading "Down East Punkin Pie," *Literary Digest* 116 (Dec. 30, 1933), 35.

16. Alan Dundes, ed., *A Cinderella Casebook* (New York and London: Garland, 1982), 220.

17. Number 3 in Anthon Cannon's collection *Popular Beliefs and Superstitions from Utah*, ed. Wayland Hand and Jeannine Talley (Salt Lake City: Utah: Univ. of Utah Press, 1984). Kate Wiggin, "Jack-o'-Lantern," *Scribners Magazine* 40 (July 1906): 138.

18. For the numskull and the "ass's egg," see Type 1319, Motif J1772.1 in Stith Thompson, *Motif-Index of Folk Literature* (Bloomington: Indiana Univ. Press, 1957). The pumpkin-turned-hotel is mentioned in Elsie Clews Parson, "Tales from Guilford County, North Carolina," *Journal of American Folklore* 30 (1917): 190–91.

19. "Peter, Peter, pumpkin eater" is no. 405 in *The Oxford Dictionary of Nursery Rhymes*, ed. Peter and Iona Opie (Oxford: Clarendon, 1952). Addington's story appeared in the *Ladies Home Journal* 40 (11) (Nov. 1923). Mortimer's 1962 novel became a 1964 film, scripted by Harold Pinter. Sangster's "Pumpkin Shell" appeared in *Good Housekeeping* 97 (Nov. 1933).

20. Lévi-Strauss's term is *elaborée*, typically translated "elaborated" or "transformed." Santino uses "worked" and "unworked" in his essay "Halloween in America: Contemporary Customs and Performances," *Western Folklore* 42 (1983): 1–20.

21. Claude Lévi-Strauss, "The Culinary Triangle," *Partisan Review* 33 (Fall 1966): 588.

22. For a different slant on American spicing, see Octavio Paz, "Gastronomy and Eroticism," *Daedalus* 101 (4) (Fall 1972).

23. Santino, "Halloween in America," 14.

24. Ibid., 14–15.

25. The progress of recent years notwithstanding, it is still largely women, wielding pots and pans, who bake the pies, and men, wielding knives, who carve the pumpkin. For an interesting example of lantern carving as a "real boy's" occupation, see Martha McCulloch Williams, "An Orb of Joy," *Country Life in America* 11 (Nov. 1906).

26. For the etymology of "jack-o'-lantern," see Mathews, *Dictionary of Americanisms*. An early, and still definitive, study of the *ignis fatuus* is William Wells Newell's "The Ignis Fatuus: Its Character and Legendary Origin," *Journal of American Folklore* 17 (Jan.–Mar. 1904): 39–60. American versions of the belief are found also in C. V. Jamison, "A Louisiana Legend Concerning Will o' the Wisp," *Journal of American Folklore* 18 (Jan.–Mar. 1905), 250–51; Langston Hughes and Arna Bontemps, *The Book of Negro Folklore* (New York: Dodd, Mead, 1958), 166–67; Harry M. Hyatt, *Hoodoo, Conju-*

*ration, Witchcraft, Rootwork* (Memoirs of the Alma Egan Hyatt Foundation, 1970), 45; and *The Frank C. Brown Collection of North Carolina Folklore* (Durham, N.C.: Duke Univ. Press, 1970), 7: nos. 5764–67.

27. The Brown Collection, no. 5765, states that jack-o'-lanterns lead people "off into the woods." Among the Pennsylvania Germans, as in Europe, the favored haunts are marshes and moors. See, e.g., W. F. Hoffman, "Folklore of the Pennsylvania Germans," *Journal of American Folklore* 2 (1889): 23–35; Doris Jones-Baker, *The Folklore of Hertfordshire* (London: B. T. Batsford, 1977), 53; Kingsley Palmer, "Punkies," *Folklore* 83 (Autumn 1977): 244; Jon Raven, *The Folklore of Staffordshire* (Totowa, N.J.: Rowan and Littlefield, 1978). Raven cites a common Staffordshire jingle, "Jack o' the Lantern, Jack o' the Light, Jack in the quagmire every night" (16).

28. Jack against Death and the Devil is mentioned passim in Newell, "Ignis Fatuus." The Cannon "corpse candle" citations are nos. 10346–48

29. For "hytersprites," see Daniel Allen Rabuzzi, "In Pursuit of Norfolk's Hytersprites," *Folklore* 95 (1) (1984): 74–89. For German spirits, see "Wassergeister" in *Handbuch des deutschen Aberglaubes,* ed. E. Hoffman-Krayer and H. Bachtold-Staubli (Berlin: de Gruyter, 1934/35). Also relevant here is Katherine Brigg's identification of such figures as "nursery bogeys." See her *Encyclopedia of Fairies* (New York: Pantheon, 1981), and the essay "Some Unpleasant Characters among British Fairies," in *Folklore Studies in the Twentieth Century,* ed. Venetia Newall (Woodbridge, Suffolk: Brewer, 1980).

30. For a classic study of Ahasuerus, see George K. Anderson, *The Legend of the Wandering Jew* (Providence, R.I.: Brown Univ. Press, 1965). Transgressions for which one might be doomed to wander are cited in Newell, "Ignis Fatuus," 48.

31. For punkies and Punky Night, see Palmer, "Punkies," 40–44; Kingsley Palmer, *The Folklore of Somerset* (London: B. T. Batsford, 1976), 105–7; Ralph Whitlock, *The Folklore of Devon* (Totowa, N.J.: Rowman and Littlefield, 1977), 153; Peter and Iona Opie, *The Language and Lore of Schoolchildren* (Oxford: Clarendon Press, 1959), 267–68; and Homer Sykes, *Once a Year: Some Traditional British Customs* (London: Gordon Fraser, 1977), 127.

32. Palmer, *Folklore of Somerset,* 105; Palmer, "Punkies," 243; Opie and Opie, *Language and Lore of Schoolchildren,* 269.

33. Eaton, "Pung-kins," 33. For examples of the pumpkinheaded horseman, see the Disney version of the tale and David Levine's illustrations to Washington Irving, *Rip Van Winkle and the Legend of Sleepy Hollow* (New York: Macmillan, 1963). The Cannon citation is no. 10283. Carole Bakos's report, "Halloween Scarecrows," is no. 73–23X in Professor George Carey's folklore files at the University of Massachusetts, Amherst.

34. Christina Hole, *British Folk Customs* (London: Hutchinson, 1976), 91; Santino, "Halloween," 15–18. Anna Freud's treatment of defense mecha-

nisms is discussed in Victor Turner, *The Ritual Process* (Chicago: Aldine, 1969), 174.

35. Williams, "Orb of Joy," 20; Juanita Browne, "Pumpkin People," *Mother Earth News* 71 (Sept./Oct. 1981): 141.

36. For Lévi-Strauss's identification of the rotten *(corrompu)* with the boiled, see his "Culinary Triangle," 588–89. Bakos, "Halloween Scarecrows," n.p.

37. Lévi-Strauss, "Culinary Triangle," 588.

38. The phrase "packaging of marginality" was first used, I believe, by Marcus Raskin, referring to the "co-option" of political dissidence in the 1960s. For encomiums to the "friendly fruit," see Terry Pimsleur and Mary Bettencourt, *The New Pumpkin Book* (San Francisco: International Pumpkin Association, 1981).

39. Williams, "Orb of Joy," 20; *Ladies Home Journal* 40 (10) (Oct. 1923): 130. For "happy horrors," see, e.g., "Illinois Pumpkin Patch Gargoyles," *Life* 33, Oct. 27, 1952, 67; "Cheerful Pumpkins," *Sunset* 159 (Oct. 1977): 160; and "Bewitching Pumpkins," *McCall's* 111 (Oct. 1983): 126–29. For information on the Sycamore funfest, I am indebted to its chamber of commerce. Sam Gendusa's book *Carving Jack O'Lanterns* is distributed by SG Productions, Dayton, Oregon.

40. Mary E. Wilkins, "The Pumpkin Giant," *Plays* 21 (Oct. 1961): 61–66; Claire Boiko, "Who's Afraid of the Big Bad Pumpkin?" *Plays* 33 (Oct. 1973): 61–66. Terry Pimsleur is quoted in Lamar B. Graham, "Pumpkin Fever," *Boston Phoenix*, Nov. 10, 1989. For the child's letter—sent to Punkin Center, Arizona—see Terri Fields, "Letter to the Great Pumpkin," *McCall's* 113, Oct. 1985, 67–68.

41. Kathy Kellogg, "Make a Jack o'Lantern . . . and Eat Pumpkin Pie, Too!" *Mother Earth News* 83 (Sept./Oct. 1983): 28. For the formalization and incorporation of fears, see Santino, "Halloween," 15.

42. Catherine Harris Ainsworth, "Hallowe'en," *New York Folklore Quarterly* 39 (3) (Sept. 1973): 163.

43. For related perspectives on the American "bad faith" with settlement, see my essay "The Turkey" in *American Wildlife in Symbol and Story*, ed. Angus Gillespie and Jay Mechling (Knoxville: Univ. of Tennessee Press, 1987); and my thesis, "Heroism and Deviancy in the Hollywood Western" (Univ. of Sussex, 1971).

44. For the urban legend motifs "Killer in the Backseat" and "Babysitter and the Man Upstairs"—both of which figure in *Halloween*—see Jan Harold Brunvand, *The Vanishing Hitchhiker* (New York: Norton, 1981), 52–57.

# C. W. Sullivan III

Even if it were banned tomorrow as a certified health risk, tobacco and its uses would have achieved a kind of mass cultural immortality. The cigarette dangling insolently from Marlon Brando's lips or sensually from Humphrey Bogart's, the jaunty cigar raised by Groucho Marx or the defiant one brandished by Sir Winston Churchill, and the pipe over which Sherlock Holmes meditated or the one that creates the wreathed smoke encircling Santa Claus's head all have their places in the popular imagination, an imagination continually refreshed and renewed by history books and novels, television and movie screens, and holiday advertisements for everything from Coca-Cola to Hallmark cards.

Tobacco's place is secure in folk culture as well. The tale of Sir Walter Raleigh's servant dousing him with beer, thinking Raleigh was on fire when he was only enjoying an after-dinner smoke, or the legend of cigar smoker Rodrigo de Jerez, a crew member with Columbus who was later arrested as a devil worshipper in his native Spain (the evidence: the smoke coming out of his mouth and nose), are still well known in oral tradition, as are superstitions about three on a match, referring to the use of one match to light multiple cigarettes (which is considered bad luck), references to cigarettes as "coffin nails," and the traditional ways to use tobacco as an herbal medicine.

Tobacco's popularity and reputation are such that, perhaps more than any other plant, it is as well known among its nonusers as it is among its users. It may well be that, except for the automobile, no other single item has become ingrained into the social and economic fabric of Western culture as rapidly or as completely as tobacco; in the space of only five hundred years, we have come to represent ourselves, characterize others, and to some extent structure and interpret our society according to tobacco and its uses.

## The Plant

Smoking as a ritual activity, practiced for sacred reasons as well as for physical well-being, is as old in the nontobacco-producing regions of Europe, Asia, and Africa as it is among the tobacco-smoking Indians of North and South America. Egyptian records include accounts of Assyrians and Jews burning incense and inhaling the smoke, and Hippocrates prescribed the inhalation of smoke for therapeutic purposes.[1] Herodotus and Plutarch described smoking rituals by which the Scythians and the Thracians and Babylonians, respectively, purified themselves after a funeral.[2] Dioscorides, Pliny, and Galen prescribed "the inhalation of smoke for the treatment of asthma and some other ailments. The substances which supplied the medicinal fume were coltsfoot, dried cow dung, and others."[3] "All over the Old World, men smoked mixtures of dried grasses, leaves, and flowering herbs that produced an aromatic, non-narcotic smoke, the effect of which was pleasantly soporific like that of tobacco."[4] Whatever they smoked, and in some cases it may have been the hemp product we call marijuana, it was not tobacco. Tobacco came from the Americas.

Tobacco use in the Americas has been documented to within five hundred years of the birth of Christ: "The earliest documented evidence of the use of tobacco is a bas-relief from a temple at Palenque in the State of Chiapas, Mexico, dated A.D. 432, showing a Mayan priest blowing smoke through a tubular pipe during a ceremony. . . . Another find consisted of loose tobacco and pipe dottle left by the cave-dwelling Pueblo Indians of northern Arizona. These remains, dating from approximately A.D. 650, have been shown by chromatographic and spectrophotometric analyses to contain nicotine."[5] Of these two finds, among the only evidences of the early use of tobacco, only the second is indisputably tobacco; the assumption that the Mayan priest was smoking tobacco is based on analyses of the geography of cultivated tobacco, which seems to have spread from South America to North America before the time of Columbus.[6]

"Tobacco belongs to the Solanaceae family, also known as the potato or nightshade family, and to the genus *Nicotiana*, which was established by Linneaus in 1753."[7] The specific plant we call tobacco (fig. 8.1) and make into commercial tobacco products is the species *tabacum* of the genus *Nicotiana*. This species, which exists in several varieties, provides virtually all of the commercial tobacco. A second species of the sixty-three or more listed under *Nicotiana, N. rustica,* a smaller and hardier plant, is also grown commercially, but in very small quantities, primarily in some parts of Eastern Europe and Asia. The tobacco seed itself is very small, three hundred thousand to four hundred thousand to the ounce, but it produces a plant that may be six feet in height with broad, green leaves and a flowering top. Although tobacco is occasionally used as a decorative plant, virtually all of its cultivation is for private use or commercial sales.

The earliest Western eyewitness accounts of tobacco use appear in the journals of the first European explorers of the New World and show that all of the recreational uses to which we put tobacco today were known by the Indians. On October 15, 1492, Columbus was very probably referring to tobacco when he recorded meeting "a man alone in a canoe who was going from the Island of Santa

*Fig. 8.1. Young tobacco plant.*

Maria to Fernandia. [He had food and water] and some dry leaves which must be a thing very much appreciated among them, because they had already brought me some of them as a present at San Salvador."[8] In that area and in Central and South America, explorers found Indians smoking cigars and cigarettes (or at least a prototype of the cigarette), chewing dried tobacco, dipping snuff, and smoking pipes of tobacco. The explorers of North America also found tobacco use widespread, but focused on the pipe and the rituals during which the pipe was smoked. Although Cabral (1500), Ponce de Leon (1512), and Verrazano (1523) all must have observed pipe smoking and perhaps pipe-smoking rituals, their accounts of this strange practice were not as clear as they might have been; the French explorer Jacques Cartier was the first to accurately describe pipe smoking in the record of his second Canadian expedition (1535–36). What the Europeans learned of tobacco during the first half of the sixteenth century had been known to the Indians for generations.[9] Since that time, tobacco use has changed very little as it has become a multibillion-dollar business and a bitterly debated health and social issue; for a while, however, it was a very popular medicine.

## An Herbal Cure

It is possible that the Europeans were introduced to some medicinal uses of tobacco by the American Indians, but it seems that the Native Americans were relatively temperate in their use of tobacco as a cure.

> Indians west of the Mississippi used tobacco in three ways. Combined with chips of water oak as a discutient, it was applied to abscesses, "gatherings," and other local inflammations. The leaves were laid warm over the afflicted part and kept moist by continual addition of the infusion to them. The dried leaf was applied to old ulcers, and the leaves were also steeped in bear's grease for use as an embrocation on swellings and cutaneous and eruptive diseases. This method was frequently used externally for dropsy, and an application to the abdomen was thought to act as a vermifuge.[10]

Other Indians blew smoke into the ear for earache, drank a brew made from tobacco for stomach cramps, blew smoke on snake bites, or used tobacco in magical rituals to ward off illness. The Mayans are recorded as having had a least a dozen different ailments for which a tobacco remedy was prescribed. Among the Indians, of course, tobacco was also used in various sacred rituals and ceremonies.[11]

When the western Europeans began to use tobacco as a medicine, they expanded its areas of application tremendously. In 1560 Jean Nicot, after whom nicotine takes its name, wrote "to a friend, the Grand Prior, Cardinal of Lorraine, that he had acquired an Indian herb of marvellous curative powers." And by the early 1600s, tobacco, alone and in various compounds, was being used to cure everything from bad breath to gonorrhea.[12] People at all levels of society found it beneficial: "Catherine de Medici took as snuff the leaves presented her by Nicot. For the headaches of her son Charles IX, snuff was prescribed, and thus patronized by royalty, its use speedily became a practice of the beau-monde."[13] Physicians on the Continent and in Britain lauded the powers of tobacco, and medicated snuffs were largely sold as "cure-all-ills."[14] "Monardes in Seville and many other physicians became famous for their cures for bites, headaches, colds, rheumatism, and the rest . . . in England, the distinguished doctor William Barclay called the plant 'one of the best and surest remedies in the world' for apoplexy and giddiness."[15] And Samuel Pepys comments that he took to tobacco, as did many of his contemporaries, to ward off the ills of the Great Plague of the 1660s.[16]

As Europeans came to settle in the Americas in ever-increasing numbers, they brought their tobacco remedies with them. John Josselyn, a seventeenth-century writer who published an entire volume on New England medicine, enumerated the virtues of tobacco as follows:

> It helps digestion, the gout, the toothache, prevents infection by scents; it heats the cold, and cools them that sweat, feedeth the hungry, spent spirits restoreth, purgeth the stomach, killeth nits and lice; the juice of the green leaf healeth green wounds, although poisoned; the syrup for many diseases, the smoke for the phthisic, cough of the lungs, distillations of rheum, and all the diseases of a cold and moist cause; good for all bodies cold and moist taken upon an empty stomach; taken upon a full stomach, it precipitates digestion.[17]

Josselyn does admit, however, that taken to excess tobacco can "dry out the body, inflame the blood, hurt the brain, and weaken the eyes and the sinews."[18]

The colonial period was the high-water mark for the use of tobacco as a medicine; thereafter, it began to fall from favor. It has not, however, died out completely as a folk remedy. A perfect example of *gesunkenes Kulturgut,* an item whose currency moves from professional learning to folk belief, tobacco remedies are no longer a part of the medical establishment's sanctioned procedures, but some do continue to exist among the folk and are handed down traditionally.

The most popular medicinal use of tobacco, according to a 1978 collection made in eastern North Carolina, is on a wasp or bee sting. An application of wet, cured tobacco, alone or in combination with another substance, is said to relieve pain and, sometimes, to reduce the swelling caused by a bee or wasp sting. Occasionally, it is reported that the tobacco will "draw out the poison" and/or "draw out the stinger." The tobacco must be cured tobacco; the raw leaf does not work. Any cured tobacco—chewing tobacco, snuff, cigar, pipe, or cigarette tobacco—seems to work. Some remedies just call for tobacco, while others specify one or two of the above named varieties. Moreover, most of the cures call for the tobacco to be wet; and although some remedies call for "chewing" or "chewed" tobacco, others merely say to put the tobacco on the sting and then wet the tobacco. Some remedies call for the tobacco to be mixed with meat tenderizer or tomato juice, but mixtures of tobacco with other substances as a remedy for stings are very rare. Perhaps the immediate attention a bee sting requires excludes all but the simplest concoctions.[19]

There are but four other medicinal uses of tobacco currently popular in eastern North Carolina. These include using tobacco to stop the itch of insect bites, combining tobacco with various other substances (lard, kerosene, turpentine, and/or mustard plaster) for external application in the case of pneumonia, spitting tobacco into a snake bite, and blowing tobacco smoke into the ear of a person complaining of an earache. Earlier collections in North Carolina and other areas of the United States found many more widespread uses of tobacco as an herbal medicine—including the use of a tobacco compound as a love potion.[20] But existing tobacco remedies seem to be narrowing in scope, and those that continue to survive are among the oldest cures, cures dating back to American Indian medical practices.[21] Today, it would seem, tobacco belongs instead to the world of big business.

## Cash Crop

In spite of the almost immediate opposition of England's James I, in his famous *A Counterblaste to Tobacco* (1604), and America's Puritan minister, Cotton Mather, in his *Manuductio ad Ministerium* (1726), tobacco soon became a staple of colonial commerce. James I placed his initial tax on tobacco in an effort to restrict the amount imported and sold in England, but the revenues he gained from that tax soon became more important to him than his dislike for the plant. And when Charles I came to the throne, he continued to allow tobacco to add to the government's income. The granting of tobacco monopolies by James I and Charles I paved the way for similar activities on the Continent, activities that helped tobacco spread as a business as well as a habit. In the first decades of the seventeenth century, tobacco use spread throughout Europe, the Near East, and the Orient.[22] By 1630 London was receiving 1,400,000 pounds of tobacco annually; by the end of that century, the Chesapeake region of the colonies was curing 40,000,000 pounds annually; and by the 1770s, just before the American Revolution, Britain's yearly imports were averaging 100,000,000 pounds.[23]

The popularity of tobacco, primarily smoked in pipes but also smoked as cigars and increasingly inhaled as snuff, was reflected almost immediately in the literature of the late sixteenth and early seventeenth centuries. Although Shakespeare did not mention tobacco, Raleigh referred to it only a few times, and Milton, a pipe smoker, wrote nothing about tobacco during his early years, others were quick to find literary uses for the new substance and the social styles it encouraged. Ben Jonson and the other dramatists of the period—Dekker, Marston, Chapman, Beaumont, and Fletcher—all featured smokers in their writings, often making the London fop and his smoking style a subject of broad satire.[24] And although Samuel Johnson made his usual satiric remarks about smokers and snuff takers, many of his eminent eighteenth-century contemporaries, among them Joseph Addison and Jonathan Swift, were unapologetic snuffers.[25]

Between the Revolutionary War and the Civil War, tobacco became an enormous cash crop in the United States. There were three major tobacco-growing districts: Maryland and the adjacent Chesapeake region, Virginia and North Carolina, and the West (parts of Kentucky, Tennessee, Illinois, Indiana, Ohio, and Missouri). Some tobacco was also raised in parts of Pennsylvania and Connecticut. In charge of its own commerce now, the United States developed manufacturing centers from the Connecticut Valley to New Orleans with a commercial capital in Richmond, Virginia. The cigar began to rival the pipe in popularity, snuff continued to be popular, and a new form of recreational tobacco, the plug, began to take its own place. The plug, otherwise known as chewing tobacco, became the "chief method of tobacco consumption during the first half of the nineteenth century" and was "the only one of [America's] tobacco customs which did not originate in a conscious imitation of European manners."[26]

Halfway through the century, however, a new development in pipe smoking helped reinvigorate that component of the tobacco business. Before the middle of the nineteenth century, most pipes were made of clay, but a few were made of stone and other make-do materials.[27] In 1720 a Hungarian carver and shoemaker was given some small blocks of meerschaum out of which he carved meerschaum pipe bowls and provided, perhaps, the first cool smoke. Meerschaum pipes—expensive, fragile, and fairly rare—became popular only among the nobility, who could afford the material and the expense of hiring a famous artist to carve it. Around 1820 the briar was discovered by a traveler on the way to visit Napoleon's tomb. He had broken his meerschaum and accepted a local farmer's offer to carve a pipe for him out of an unusual material—wood. The briar, made from the underground burl of the heath tree or *"bruyere,"* soon became and still remains the pipe of choice. The briar is porous, like the meerschaum, and so it provides a cool smoke; but the close-grained wood is much stronger than meerschaum and can be packed along easily in pocket or pouch.[28] In America, the need for an inexpensive pipe was filled, in part, in another way. After about 1850, the corncob pipe became popular. The corncob pipe may have been first smoked among those Indians who cultivated maize, and Daniel Boone, known to have smoked a corncob pipe, may have given it the popular name "Missouri Meerschaum," by which it is still known.[29] Perhaps the most famous smoker of corncob pipes was Gen. Douglas MacArthur who seems to have one in his mouth in almost every photograph.

Although the four basic types—clay, meerschaum, briar, and corncob—do not exactly represent a proliferation of pipes, they are enough to divide roughly among social classes. The meerschaum, because of its relative scarcity, its price, and the carving of the bowl that characterizes the final product, is the aristocrat of the pipe family. The briar, because of its durability as well as its good looks—both polished and worn—comprises the large middle class of pipes. The lowly clay pipe was inexpensive and hot to smoke, but a man might have several of them, enough so that he could offer one to a friend who dropped by. A bit of the clay stem would be broken off so that each new smoker might have a clean bite. As the twentieth century progressed, the clay and the corncob became the poor relations in the pipe family. Still, the class lines among pipes are not final, and a smoker who has numerous briars might also have a meerschaum or two and pick up a corncob or a clay pipe from time to time—as my father did.

Unlike the corncob and the clay pipe, the cigarette was able to overcome its lowly origins. The accelerated industrialization of America after the Civil War had its effects on tobacco as mechanized, large-scale production, and mass-media advertising created what we today call the tobacco industry. The major change in the tobacco industry involved neither pipes, plugs, and cigars, which have continued to be popular, nor snuff, which is still manufactured, though in smaller quantities, but rather cigarettes, which went from being a much-scorned smoke to the most popular in the space of only a couple of generations. In 1880, according to government statistics gleaned from production and tax records, "Americans consumed 2.5 billion cigars and another 150 million pounds of pipe tobacco, snuff, and plug."[30]

Cigarette smoking, however, was on the rise. In 1880 half a billion manufactured cigarettes were sold, and perhaps another billion roll-your-owns were smoked. The British had "discovered" the cigarette in the Crimea, and when the troops came home, they brought their new habit with them. Shortly thereafter, Americans traveling abroad brought this "delectable curiosity" to the United States.[31] But the cigarette smokers of the late nineteenth century were specific small groups: Eastern and European dandies, immigrants, the poor, bums, children, and occasionally women. "Should a middle-aged, middle-class man light up a cigarette in New York or Boston, he would attract glances and run the risk of being considered effeminate or un-American."[32] The cigar and pipe remained the primary indulgences as the century wound toward its close, awaiting only Buck Duke's mechanized production and R. J. Reynolds's advertising campaign to make the cigarette available to and acceptable for all smokers.

James Buchanan "Buck" Duke of Durham, North Carolina, took over the Bull Durham Tobacco Company in the mid-1880s, just about the time he turned thirty, and by popularizing the use of cigarette-rolling machines and hooking them up to airtight containers, he became, within just a few years, the nation's largest cigarette manufacturer. The machine, the invention of James Bonsack of Virginia, could produce 120,000 cigarettes per day, operat-

Fig. 8.2. Duke Homestead, c. 1902. Courtesy of the Duke Homestead State Historical Site.

ing at roughly fifty times the rate of hand rollers, and required only three people to run it. By 1890 Duke's monopoly, the American Tobacco Company, had been founded, and Duke then moved to take over all aspects of the tobacco business. By 1904 he had driven just about everyone else out of business or had bought them up, and he was the tobacco business in cigarettes, snuff, and plugs—and he almost made it in cigars, too. Although he personally survived the threats of the anti-tobacco groups and the antitrust movement, they had their effect on his business. Duke remained a wealthy man, founded the Duke Power and Light Company, and contributed enough money to Trinity College to get the name changed to Duke University.[33] Today, the Duke Homestead is a living tobacco museum that not only houses permanent and rotating exhibits but also re-creates various aspects of farm life as they were in the eighteenth and nineteenth centuries.

If Buck Duke showed the tobacco industry how to make cigarettes, R. J. Reynolds showed it how to sell them. The R. J. Reynolds Company was not in the cigarette business when an antitrust decision in 1911 distributed the old American Tobacco Company's cigarette business among the new American Tobacco Company, Liggett & Meyers, and P. Lorillard. But in 1913, the Reynolds company created a cigarette blend, called it the Camel, and set out to sell it. "The Camels are coming!" and "Tomorrow there will be more Camels in this town than in all Asia and Africa combined!" caught the public's attention. In 1914, the first year Camels were on the market nationally, fewer than half a billion were sold, but over 1.5 million dollars—an unheard-of sum—was spent on advertising. By the end of 1915, the Camel cigarette was the first national brand and boasted sales of 2.4 billion (which accounted for 13 percent of the American production), and the R. J. Reynolds Tobacco Company reported earnings of 4.7 million dollars.[34] The recent popularity of "Joe Camel," the cartoon figure recognized most readily by children, illustrates the effectiveness of advertising even among those who do not or cannot yet smoke.

Buck Duke and R. J. Reynolds had revolutionized the production and sale of tobacco products, and the rest of the twentieth century has seen the more-or-less predictable evolution of an industry that continues to earn high profits in spite of antitrust suits by the government, competition at home and from overseas, and attacks by antismoking groups that believe tobacco to be hazardous to one's moral and/or physical well-being. The tobacco economy is multileveled, earning money for the people who grow, process, and sell tobacco as well as for the local, state, and federal governments, who tax tobacco products and the incomes of people who work in tobacco. It is unlikely that government fiat, even in a badly mixed metaphor, will kill the golden leaf that lays the golden egg, and so the tobacco products and their uses will continue to inform our cultural worldview.

## From Cure to Curse

The success of tobacco as a source of revenue, both personal and governmental, has not gone unchallenged. Since the time of James I and Cotton Mather, there have been those who have spoken out against tobacco's use—usually with but few and temporary results. Smoking was just too popular an activity to be legislated or preached out of existence—even though the preachers and the legislators continued to try.

In the eighteenth and nineteenth centuries, as tobacco's popularity and acceptance as a recreation and medicine increased in western Europe and America, tobacco became more than just a part of the literature of the age; it became, on occasion, the focus of that literature, some of which was written by authors made famous by "more serious" works. In his *Pipe and Pouch* (1897) and *A Smoker's Reveries* (1909), Joseph Knight collected poems in praise of tobacco by such famous figures as Rudyard Kipling, Charles Lamb, Daniel Webster, Charles Baudelaire, and Lord Byron. Kipling's "The Betrothed" is a long poem in praise of the Cuban cigars which his fiancée, Maggie, demands he give up. The poem ends:

> A million surplus Maggies
> 　　are willing to bear the yoke;
> And a woman is only a woman,
> 　　but a good cigar is a smoke.
> Light me another Cuba:
> 　　I hold to my first-sworn vows,
> If Maggie will have no rival,
> 　　I'll have no Maggie for spouse![35]

Most of the poems in these two books, however, are anonymous or have been culled from popular magazines or newspapers that did not provide an author's name. One such proclaims:

> Sir Walter Raleigh! name of worth,
> How sweet for thee to know
> King James, who never smoked on earth,
> Is smoking down below.[36]

Quite a few of the smokers extol the bachelor life of witty conversation, stout comrades, strong drink (often ale), and good cigars or pipes. A number of pieces celebrate the pipe (meerschaum, briar, clay, or corncob) or the cigar (almost always a Havana). A few poems consider the woman as smoker, but such portraits are always negative, asserting that women should not smoke or that they cannot (without getting violently ill). And one poem, "My Husband's Pipe," a wife's loving portrait of her husband smoking his pipe, concludes:

> Yet naught in my horizon do I scan
> That promises the comfort and the cheer
> Such as he finds when twilight settles drear
> And husband lights his pipe.[37]

One can but wonder what Freud might have made of a woman praising her husband's pipe. A more recent collection, Sylvestre Watkins's *The Pleasures of Smoking* (1948), contains, in addition to poetry, passages from fiction, short essays of philosophy or instruction, anecdotes (usually about famous smokers such as Mark Twain and Thomas Edison), and humor.[38]

The nineteenth-century anti-tobacco forces had their books, too, books that tried to convince the reader of tobacco's moral and, to a lesser extent, physical danger. One of the more delightful of these is *Thoughts and Stories on Tobacco for American Lads* (1852) by "Simeon Toby." If the pro-tobacco poems overstated the benefits of tobacco, books like this are wonderfully exaggerated arguments against tobacco and could have been the models for the anti-marijuana movie *Reefer Madness*. In the preface, Toby admits to both a specific and a general guilt regarding tobacco: "That was a sad hour when polished Europeans, caught its use of naked savages on our Continent, for the hand on the dial plate of civilization turned backward a great way. I am no stranger to the power of this weed on myself. I shall write, rather, as a Washingtonian, or as one redeemed from this vile Monster."[39] Most of the chapters that make up the bulk of this book are in the form of letters from Uncle Toby to Billy, and each letter tells the story of some poor wretch doomed and damned because he used tobacco. The best title of the lot has to be "James Dixey, the Boy who was made a Maniac by using Tobacco; or Tobacco and Insanity."

The book also contains letters and testimonies from Horace Mann, P. T. Barnum, John Quincy Adams, and a number of other (less well-known) figures arguing against the use of tobacco, for, as Barnum says, "The boy who loves Tobacco, will, ten chances to one, make a tippler; he cannot indulge a taste so unnatural without being led into other unnatural habits. He only wants the peculiar coat and cravat to make him a dandy."[40] The last page of the book contains an anti-tobacco pledge: "We, the Subscribers, believing the use of Tobacco, whether in the form of Smoking, Snuffing, or Chewing, to be uncleanly, unhealthy, and expensive, hereby pledge to abstain from its use totally and forever."[41] And there are extra copies of the pledge which the reader is encouraged to cut out, attach to blank pieces of paper, and circulate for signatures.

The popular literature of the time, the penny dreadfuls and dime novels that provided fiction "for the masses," were decidedly followers of the temperance philosophy, arguing by example against both drinking and smoking. According to Mary Noel, "the imperfect hero was altogether an extinct species in the story-paper world."[42] In these popular stories, she further states, the hero was dutifully required to refuse the smokes and drinks that would be ritually offered to him in the course of the story. The villains, on the other hand, were fond of both drinking and smoking, activities that (as Barnum had suggested above) masked or were the indicators of much worse tendencies, from gambling and stealing to rape and murder.[43] Smoking thus joined the beard and the black hat as symbols of villainy in the popular imagination of the first part of the twentieth century.

After the demise of the story-papers, the penny dreadfuls, and the dime novels, these heroes and villains continued their careers in pulp fiction (westerns, detective stories, and science fiction); but as the twentieth century moved along, it became harder and harder to tell the heroes from the villains on the basis of tobacco and alcohol use. Like publications of James I and Cotton Mather, however, the early fictional *exempla* against tobacco use were largely based on moral and ethical philosophies and, in the face of other (primarily economic) forces, they were not successful in changing the habits of most Americans.

Recently, however, smoking and not smoking have taken on overtones involving something more serious than image and of more immediate concern, perhaps, than moral or ethical attitudes; since the 1950s, the federal government and various independent agencies have been attempting to convince people to stop smoking for reasons of health. In addition, nonsmokers have begun to insist that they, too, are at risk and want to be protected from the smoke of those who still indulge. But the contest is not just a struggle between those who wish to smoke unhindered by rules and regulations and those who wish to be smoke-free; it is a debate one side of which is funded by the enormous and profitable tobacco industry, an organization almost as powerful at thwarting anti-tobacco legislation as the NRA is at blocking proposed gun regulations.

The recognition of tobacco as a physically dangerous substance is not new. "As early as 1665 [Samuel] Pepys witnessed a Royal Society experiment in which a cat was promptly dispatched when 'a drop of distilled oil of tobacco' was introduced into its body."[44] Later study by Posselt and Reimann, culminating in 1809, isolated what is now called nicotine as the active constituent in tobacco,[45] and scientists in the second half of this century have linked tobacco use and nicotine ingestion with various types of cancer, especially lung cancer, throat cancer, and lip or mouth cancer. Moreover, recent studies have shown that nonsmokers who inhale the smoke from someone else's pipe, cigar, or cigarette are also in danger.

The debate over smoking has, thus, taken on broader ramifications in recent years. No longer is the smoker a danger only to himself or herself; now the smoker is a danger to whoever might breathe the smoke he or she creates. As a result, more and more places where smokers and nonsmokers must encounter each other, such as airplanes and elevators, are being regulated to protect the nonsmokers, as are those places, such as restaurants and grocery stores, where smokers and nonsmokers might come into proximity. In some places, such as New Orleans, smoking is forbidden in taxi cabs; in other places, most notably in eastern North Carolina (the major tobacco-growing region in the United States), there are relatively few restaurants with sections for nonsmokers, and many cars and trucks sport bumper stickers that proclaim "Pride in Tobacco."

Fig. 8.3. Traditional tobacco barn.

As concerns about health in general gain momentum (witness the increased awareness of the benefits of exercise, weight loss, lower cholesterol levels, lower levels of pesticides on crops and additives in food, and the like), concern over tobacco use, both public and private, will increase and should result in more restrictions on who can smoke and where. The tobacco industry is fighting such regulations, of course, and has much more capital behind it than do the various health organizations. Like many other concerns with national/ social ramifications (pollution, recycling, consumption of natural resources, and others), the concern over nonsmokers' rights (and health) will not be decided until a significant portion of the population believes that it should not have to breathe smoke-filled air. Until then, the debate will continue.

Ironically, the very barns in which tobacco has been cured or stored have become a center of controversy in tobacco-growing states. Many of the traditional log barns (fig. 8.3) have been replaced by newer, bulk-curing barns, which look like small mobile homes without windows, and although the barns are picturesque, many of them have fallen into disrepair. Their neglected state has caused a segment of the population in eastern North Carolina to call for their complete destruction, while at the same time, people who want to preserve such elements of material culture gather together in outdoor museums like Greenville's Village of Yesteryear.

## Cultural Images

Like a number of other products that come in a variety of styles, makes, and price ranges (most notably, perhaps, liquor, automobiles, and clothing), certain tobacco brands and products have become interwoven with numerous social and cultural concepts so that the buying of a certain item, whether it involves a choice among cigarette brands or a choice between cigarettes and the other available tobacco products, is an act that may identify the chooser—to himself, herself, or others—according to cultural attitudes involving gender, age, class, and/or status. Moreover, this kind of cultural awareness is not new; there is considerable evidence in historical studies of tobacco's use as well as in the literature of the eighteenth and nineteenth centuries that, for much of tobacco's history, what one smoked might be an important indicator of that person's character.

Tobacco certainly separated the men from the boys and the men from the women in the late nineteenth century. Tobacco has always been an adult privilege and a pleasure forbidden to the young. One of the reasons Tom Sawyer is attracted to that archetypal bad influence, Huck Finn, is that Huck smokes. But in his own book, Huck himself notes the somewhat hypocritical attitude of society here: "Pretty soon I wanted to smoke, and asked the widow to let me. But she wouldn't. She said it was a mean practice and wasn't clean, and I must try not to do it anymore. . . . And she took snuff too; of course that was all right, because she done it herself."[46] Adult tobacco users have always, it seems, attempted to dissuade the young on the basis of age, asserting that the use of to-bacco—like the use of alcohol—should be an adult privilege. In the folklore of many families is the story of the father who, finding out that his son smokes, allows or forces the boy to smoke a whole cigar in hopes that it will make him so sick that he will not smoke, at least not for a long time. Of course, there are some versions in which the boy enjoys the cigar and the father's plan backfires.

Although our society continues to try to discourage the young from smok-ing, women as smokers have been courted by the tobacco companies as they have become major consumers in their own right. The Virginia Slims slogan, "You've come a long way, baby!" is usually accompanied by two different pictures of women. One shows a woman in turn-of-the-century costume ei-ther sneaking a cigarette or being caught (by her husband, one supposes) smoking a cigarette; the other shows a woman in contemporary dress proudly and freely smoking a cigarette—another right won! In fact, Virginia Slims cigarettes, with their women dressed for the professions rather than for house-work, seem to be directed toward the professional and perhaps single, up-wardly mobile woman. There are other female groups, of course, and accord-ing to the news media, R. J. Reynolds has recently come under fire for aiming its Dakota cigarettes at blue-collar women, especially young women who have no education beyond high school and who enjoy, these ads presume, going to tractor-pulling contests with their boyfriends.

This active courting of women by the tobacco companies reflects the dramatic changes that have taken place over the last century in our culture's attitudes toward women. In the late nineteenth century, smoking was largely the prov-ince of men in America; it was not thought proper nor, perhaps, possible for women to enjoy smoking. One late-nineteenth-century poem describes the re-sults of a young woman's trying her brother's cigarettes as follows:

> Her eyes with briney tears were wet,
> Her bang grew limp beneath its net,
> Her brow was gemmed with beaded sweat,
> And to her bed she went, you bet.[47]

Although this and other such descriptions maintained that women couldn't smoke, American women were beginning to learn, as their European sisters already had, that the "pleasures of smoking" could be theirs.

Occasionally, the law or institutional regulation joined literature in forbid-ding women the right to smoke. In 1908, for example, a New York City ordi-nance made it illegal for women to use tobacco in public, and although the law was generally ignored by the authorities, few women risked their reputations by smoking in public, and few men "were willing to appear on the street with a female companion smoking the disreputable 'thing.'"[48] Moreover, there were "frequent cases, in the 1920's, of women dismissed from employment, expelled from institutions of learning or otherwise penalized for daring to smoke."[49]

In the middle 1920s, however, advertisements began to show women and cigarettes in the same picture, each suggesting that if a woman did smoke she would smoke that particular brand. And in the late 1920s, a campaign suggesting that women could stay slim (and healthy) by smoking instead of eating candy— "Reach for a Lucky Instead of a Sweet"—made smoking a legitimate and defensible practice for American women.[50] In smokers' rights as in suffrage, American women were catching up to their western European counterparts.

There are other cultural distinctions marked by the use of tobacco and tobacco products, and some are related to gender. It is almost always men who light women's cigarettes, seldom the other way around. We also recognize a difference between male and female smoking styles, so that men and women hold their cigarettes differently while speaking, eating, or drinking, as well as when inhaling or exhaling. As a result, a man whose smoking style resembles that of a woman may be suspected of being homosexual. Conversely, a woman who smokes anything but a cigarette may be thought to have lesbian tendencies. Anyone smoking a cigarette in a cigarette holder these days may be considered a snob or, if male, be judged effeminate. However, a woman smoking a cigar or pipe might be making a political or social statement, asserting her right, as a woman, to smoke whatever she wishes. Generally, though, women seem to continue to be culturally restricted to the cigarette; as it has been for hundreds of years, it is still unusual to see a woman smoking a cigar or pipe and even more unusual to see a woman chewing and spitting—except in areas of rural poverty, where cigarettes, even hand-rolled, would have been and might still be prohibitively expensive, while pipes are reusable and "chews" require no external paraphernalia.

In addition to marking gender, certain tobacco products mark the user's socioeconomic class. Camels and Luckies are "tough" cigarettes, often found rolled up in the shirt sleeves of teen-aged boys or in the shirt pockets of construction workers. Cigarettes with names like Benson & Hedges or Dunhill are clearly for people in the upper classes. The "class" distinction among pipes has already been mentioned, but in addition to that class distinction, pipes are stereotypically considered the smoke of professional men, especially male university professors, and suggest their users to be deep or perceptive "thinkers"—as was Sherlock Holmes. (A car salesman once told me that he knew he would have a hard time making a profit from a customer who came in smoking a pipe.) Chewing tobacco and snuff are for outdoorsmen (or men who think that they fit that image) and are often advertised by men who are (or are supposed to be) cowboys, railroadmen, or loggers. Chewing tobacco and snuff have also long been considered the tobacco of the lower classes, even though dipping has recently been advertised by sports figures and has become quite popular among boys of high school age.

The way a cigarette is advertised and the places in which it is advertised can be a key to the particular culture group at which it is aimed. Ads that appear occasionally in the *New York Times Magazine* feature stylishly dressed, obviously professional women enjoying True cigarettes. The ads in *Car & Driver* often include "mod" young men smoking Kools, show Salem and Pall Mall cigarettes in outdoor scenes, or feature Marlboro or Winston cigarettes, two sponsors of auto racing. The pages of *Bon Appétit* show a young woman dressed in white smoking a low-tar cigarette called, appropriately, More White Lights. *Newsweek* and *Consumer's Digest* contain low-tar Merit and Carlton cigarette ads for their "thinking" readers. *Ski* includes ads for Marlboro, a sponsor of ski races, and upscale ads for Benson & Hedges cigarettes. Benson & Hedges ads also appear in *Ebony, Tennis World,* and *Vogue,* all magazines that direct advertising at consumers in the upper socioeconomic levels. Such advertising suggests that you should smoke and insists that you smoke a cigarette appropriate to your image.

Class is one aspect of cigarette advertising; sex is another. Certainly the recent ads for Lucky Strike cigarettes, featuring an attractive young woman looking provocatively into the camera and saying "Light my Lucky" had sexual overtones. Among single people, "getting lucky" is a euphemism for finding an acceptable sexual partner—if only for one night. An earlier Lucky Strike slogan, "L.S./M.F.T." (Lucky Strike Means Fine Tobacco), had no sensual presentation or obvious sexual overtones, and yet adolescent boys of the fifties and sixties told each other that the letters stood for "Loose Sweaters Mean Floppy (or Flabby) Tits." The "Show Us Your Lark Pack" campaign for Lark cigarettes was presented without sensuality, but the slogan was assumed to be an exhibitionist metaphor with the Lark pack symbolic of genitals. And if there is no sensuality in smoking, why did the dancing Old Gold pack have such shapely legs?

This association of tobacco with sex may be due, at least in part, to the age restrictions placed by our culture on the "adult" pleasures and privileges: smoking tobacco, drinking alcoholic beverages, driving a car, and having sexual relationships. These are activities that separate children (or adolescents) from adults, and engaging in them is thought to be engaging in adult behavior. Thus smoking, like driving a car or drinking beer and alcohol or bragging about sexual exploits, is considered a sign of adulthood. Smoking is for grownups. In a contest of fairly recent origin, which comes not from the farm, the factory, or the store, adolescent boys crush out cigarette butts on their own hands or arms to show how tough—grownup?—they are as they hang out behind the school, at the diner, or at a local gas station. Inhaling cigarette smoke, too, is the sign of an experienced smoker, as is the ability to blow a smoke ring. Tobacco's association with image, and perhaps especially self-image, begins, thus, when its consumers or potential consumers are very young.

## Customary Practices

Even when the risks to health are accepted, tobacco will not easily be disentangled from the fabric of our culture; it is woven in too tightly and in too many ways. It is not only through the images from the popular culture media—the insolent cigarette of Marlon Brando and the friendly pipe of Santa Claus, or the images from folktales and legends, the dousing of Sir Walter Raleigh and the arrest of Rodrigo de Jerez as a devil worshipper—that tobacco is kept alive in our culture; there are the everyday rituals and usages that are less obvious and therefore, perhaps, more powerful in keeping tobacco an accepted (and, thus, acceptable) part of everyday life.

Folklorists, psychologists, and sociologists have commented on some of the most obvious rituals and practices involving tobacco and tobacco products. Fathers give out cigars to mark the birth of a child; men retire to brandy and cigars after dinner; fraternities (and now sororities) hold "smokers" to attract new members; criminals are given a last cigarette before being hanged or shot; deals (especially political) are made in smoke-filled rooms; smokers feel free to borrow cigarettes from one another (unless it is a person's last cigarette); some people will not light three cigarettes on one match; others will carefully avoid breaking the tax stamp when opening a pack of cigarettes; and cigarettes can be used as a medium of exchange in prisons, reform schools, and other institutions in which the supply is much less than the demand.

Many of these rituals involve sharing a cigarette or sharing the smoking experience. This sharing can be a feature of many "first-time" smoking experiences in which the new smoker is introduced to the practice by an experienced smoker. Sharing is also a part of some male-female smoking rituals: the man always lights the woman's cigarette, sometimes putting two cigarettes in his mouth and lighting one for each of them; men and women smoke together at specific times—after meals, on coffee breaks, with drinks, and after sex; and a man always offers a woman a cigarette if he is going to smoke.

More and more, those who do smoke are being required to share the activity (even if each brings his or her own cigarettes) in a specific place: the smoking room or area at school, the smoking lounge in the office building, the smoking section of the restaurant, the smokers' rooms in a hotel or motel, and the smoking cars on the train or subway. Such sharing is mutually supportive, and in places where smokers are restricted to certain areas or rooms, the sharing communally reinforces the right and, perhaps, necessity to smoke.

In parts of the country where tobacco farming is the primary way of making a living, the events that make up the raising and selling of tobacco have insinuated themselves into leisure as well as work activities. The crop-related festival is a traditional local celebration in America, whether it celebrates apples, strawberries, seafood, maple syrup, or any other crop that most of the people of the region raise to sell. In the tobacco areas, there are tobacco festivals that include displays of some of the newest and some of the oldest machinery used to work tobacco, architectural exhibits of preserved buildings, historical re-creations of farming methodology, and various competitions: pipe-smoking contests, tobacco-tying contests, and tobacco-spitting contests. In addition, there is usually a parade with local school bands, farm machinery, floats, etc., and a Tobacco Festival Queen. For the people of the area, then, tobacco is not just their work, it is a part of their play as well.

Tobacco has woven itself into our culture in less obvious ways as well. In our folk speech or slang, we refer to cigarettes as "coffin nails," "fags," "cancer sticks," and "butts." A cheap cigar is called a "rope" or a "Manila rope." A pipe is a "pot" or a "nose warmer." Plug tobacco is a "cut." A person does not ask to borrow a cigarette, he asks to "bum" one. To excessively wet the end of a cigarette or cigar while smoking is to "Bogart" or "nigger-lip" the smoke. To have cigarette papers and loose tobacco is to "have the makin's," and to roll one's own cigarette is to "fix makin's."[51]

There are also folk sayings, proverbs, bits of folk wisdom, and folk beliefs about tobacco passed along in oral tradition. About someone who is constantly "bumming" a smoke: "He hasn't stopped smoking; he's just stopped buying." Smokers are advised, "Every cigarette is a minute off your life." Famous people are quoted, "What this country needs is a good five-cent cigar," and misquoted, "A woman is just a woman, but a cigar is a good smoke." Someone might be described as "Dumb as a cigar store Indian." And every so often the belief that collecting enough empty cigarette packs will enable the local hospital to get a free kidney machine sweeps the community, and smokers and nonsmokers alike collect cigarette packs until they discover that there is no place to turn them in.

Because tobacco has influenced and added to American culture on so many levels (a number of which, such as slang and crafts, have been largely ignored by sociologists, psychologists, and folklorists), it will be difficult to make a case strong enough that tobacco can be legislated out of existence. The presence of various references to tobacco in our speech, customs, and rituals creates an implicit tolerance for or, perhaps, a benign acceptance of the topic, a tolerance or acceptance that underlies and solidifies the continued existence of the "noxious weed" as a commercial product.

## Collectibles and Conclusions

A final aspect of the cultural immortality I suggested for tobacco at the beginning of this piece comes not only from tobacco and smoking, but also from the paraphernalia that has been created along the way. The tobacco companies themselves have intentionally created much of it through advertising gimmicks such as free lighters, or other merchandise, emblazoned with the

company's logo, for every so many packs or cartons bought. Other paraphernalia was created indirectly; cigar boxes and tobacco cans, once merely the
containers for the materials, are now collectable items in their own right. And
original pieces of advertising, or, better still, the lithographs and engravings
from which those advertisements were printed, are now the subject of museum shows and catalogues.[52]

Materials developed to aid the smoker have also become collectable. Snuff
boxes, tobacco pouches, matchboxes, lighters, ashtrays, pipe tools, cigar cutters, plug cutters, and humidors can bring more than their original prices at
flea market sales and, if old or rare enough, can command quite high prices.
In 1986 a late-nineteenth-century cigar store Indian was auctioned off for
forty-four thousand dollars. Archeological finds containing Indian pipes, pipe
bowls, or pipe stems are handled with extreme care and are often then put on
display in museums of art or natural history.

Thus completely surrounded now by the images and artifacts of tobacco,
if not by smokers themselves, the debate that began with James I's
*Counterblaste* rages on. The antismoking forces have made significant gains
in recent years, the tobacco lobbyists seem to have less effect in Washington
than in the past, and smokers complain that they are an oppressed group being deprived of their rights; but the federal government's price supports are
still in place, and the farmers and the governments are still making a great
deal of money from the growth, manufacture, and sale of tobacco and tobacco-
related products. Tobacco is now a significant part of American culture and
will continue to be so for quite some time.

## Notes

Special thanks to Melody Hedges, a graduate assistant in the East Carolina University English Department, for helping with the research and
to A. Dale Coats, Duke Homestead State Historic Site, for providing the
historical photograph of Duke Homestead.

1. Raymond Schnitzer, *Leaves from a Tobaccoman's Log* (New York: Van-
tage, 1970), 83.
2. Jerome E. Brooks, *The Mighty Leaf: Tobacco Through the Centuries* (Boston: Little, Brown, 1952), 13.
3. Ibid., 7–8.
4. Schnitzer, *Tobaccoman's Log,* 87.
5. D. U. Gerstel, "Tobacco," in *Evolution of Crop Plants,* ed. N. W. Simmons
(New York, Longman, 1976), 275.
6. T. H. Goodspeed, *The Genus Nicotiana* (Waltham, Mass.: Chronica
Botanica, 1954).
7. T. C. Tso, *Physiology and Biochemistry of Tobacco Plants* (Stroudsburg,
Pa.: Dowden, 1972), 3.

8. Brooks, *The Mighty Leaf,* 11.
9. Ibid.,11–20.
10. Virgil Vogel, *American Indian Medicine* (Norman: Univ. of Oklahoma Press, 1970), 384.
11. Ibid., 381–84.
12. Brooks, *The Mighty Leaf,* 37–44.
13. W. A. Penn, *The Soverane Herbe* (New York: Dutton, 1902), 259.
14. Penn, *Soverane Herbe,* 270.
15. Alfred Dunhill, *The Gentle Art of Smoking* (London: Max Reinhardt, 1954), 7.
16. Brooks, *The Mighty Leaf,* 39–40.
17. Richard Dorson, *American Folklore* (Chicago: Univ. of Chicago Press, 1959), 10–11.
18. Ibid., 11.
19. C. W. Sullivan III, "Tobacco Medicine," *North Carolina Folklore Journal* 27 (1) (1979): 26–31.
20. Katherine T. Kell, "Tobacco in Folk Cures," *Journal of American Folklore* 78 (1965): 112.
21. Wayland Hand, ed., *Popular Beliefs and Superstitions from North Carolina,* vol. 4, *The Frank C. Brown Collection of North Carolina Folklore* (Durham, N.C.: Duke Univ. Press, 1961), 116–357; Vance Randolph, *Ozark Superstitions* (1947; reprint, New York: Dover, 1964), 98–99; Sullivan, "Tobacco Medicine," 26–30.
22. Brooks, *The Mighty Leaf,* 75.
23. Joseph C. Roberts, *The Story of Tobacco in America* (New York, Knopf, 1949), 10–40.
24. Brooks, *The Mighty Leaf,* 72–75.
25. Ibid., 141–42.
26. Roberts, *Story of Tobacco,* 43–102.
27. Brooks, *The Mighty Leaf,* 211.
28. Schnitzer, *Tobaccoman's Log,* 72–78.
29. Brooks, *The Mighty Leaf,* 211–12.
30. Robert Sobel, *They Satisfy: The Cigarette in American Life* (New York: Anchor, 1978), 6–7.
31. Brooks, *The Mighty Leaf,* 233–34.
32. Sobel, *They Satisfy,* 7.
33. Roberts, *Story of Tobacco,* 138–53; Sobel, *They Satisfy,* 23–73.
34. Roberts, *Story of Tobacco,* 230–33; Sobel, *They Satisfy,* 77–78.
35. Joseph Knight, *Pipe and Pouch* (Boston: Page, 1897), 112.
36. Ibid., 158.
37. Joseph Knight, *A Smoker's Reverie* (New York: Caldwell, 1909), 43.
38. Sylvestre C. Watkins, *The Pleasures of Smoking* (New York: Schuman, 1948).

39. Simeon Toby, *Thoughts and Stories on Tobacco for American Lads: or Uncle Toby's Anti-Smoking Advice to His Nephew Billy Bruce* (Boston: Rand, 1852), 6.
40. Ibid., 149.
41. Ibid., 179.
42. Mary Noel, *Villains Galore* . . . (New York: Macmillan, 1954), 41.
43. Noel, *Villains Galore,* 242–49.
44. Brooks, *The Mighty Leaf,* 281.
45. Ibid., 281–82.
46. Mark Twain, *Adventures of Huckleberry Finn* (1885; reprint, Boston: Houghton, 1958), 4.
47. Knight, *Pipe and Pouch,* 80.
48. Brooks, *The Mighty Leaf,* 271.
49. Ibid., 272n.
50. Sobel, *They Satisfy,* 98–101.
51. Raymond Jahn, *Tobacco Dictionary* (New York: Philosophical Library, 1954).
52. James B. Byrnes, *Tobacco Smoking in Art* (Raleigh, N.C.: Museum of Art, 1960).

# David Scofield Wilson

"For me, the real garden season starts at tomato time," John McDowell confessed in *National Gardening*; "They're my favorite vegetable, but though I plant them in mid-May, the main crop doesn't come in until mid-August."[1] "That's a long time for a tomato lover to wait," he continues, and then ticks off the list of hybrids he has tried over the years to shorten the wait, getting it down to as early as July 22. While the date may vary by region—my neighbor in Davis, California, admires a friend who brings in the first ripe tomato by Mother's Day each year—McDowell speaks for the American tomato-gardening public in his commitment to tomato culture and in his passion for this symbol of home-grown succulence. And yet this passion for the tomato and its culture is a relatively new theme in American colloquial culture.

The tomato has also served as a symbol of female succulence in American popular culture. One thinks of the tough guys of 1940s movies calling women "tomatoes." This metaphorical usage and backyard gardening came together in an old "VIP" cartoon showing a man bending over to peer at a scraggly plant on which miniature naked women hang as fruit. A second man, presumably the grower, enlightens the visitor, declaring, "Tomato vine."[2]

FREE Gifts!
See p. 20A

Fourth of July Tomato

Fig. 9.1. Burpee "Fourth of July Tomato" on an American flag-patterned fabric, from the cover of a Burpee 1998 seed catalogue. Photograph by David Scofield Wilson.

Collectors of folklore regularly retrieve superstitions about the tomato's poisonousness, its vulnerability to tobacco smoke, its reputation as an aphrodisiac ("love apple," "*poma amoris*"), its use as an epithet for women, or their breasts, and its symbolic, bloody "fleshiness": "Three tomatoes were taking a walk and the baby tomatoe [*sic*] was getting behind his two parents. He started to get further and further behind so his father told him to walk faster, but the baby didn't do anything about it. So, the daddy tomatoe got real mad and walked up to his son and stomped on him, saying, 'Catch up (ketchup)!!'"[3]

Sex, blood, beauty, and bounty—a complex significance for such a passive fruit. Its botanical kin the *Capsicum annuums* (chile peppers, cayenne peppers, jalapeños, and the like) incarnate a kind of gustatory assertiveness that invites interpretation as masculine, but there is little in the texture or taste or smell of a common garden tomato to justify such a rich complex of cultural significations. One plausible source for some of the darker symbolic tenor of the tomato may lie in European superstitions clustered around belladonna and mandrake and witchcraft, on one hand, and in the recognition by herbalists and apothecaries, on the other, of the tomato's evident kinship to native nightshades, many of which were known as poisonous.

Behind these surface significations lies another, a meta-signification perhaps, for the tomato (like the rattlesnake and poison-ivy and Venus's-flytrap) was native to North America but unknown in Europe before 1500. Explorers and settlers had to "make sense" of a sometimes ambiguous New World nature as best they could, drawing on traditional learning and habits of use, but inventing appropriate new recipe knowledge and narratives of telling resonance in order finally to own their new land and its products: "The land was ours before we were the land's," Robert Frost declared in a somewhat different context, but one which is nevertheless to the point.[4]

Old World herbalists and botanists and cooks needed also to adopt this import and to adapt their cuisine and custom to it (or not) as these somewhat familiar-seeming but still quite alien plants entered their markets and gardens. The Italians' *pomi d'oro* takes the tomato as a variation on the apple model (poma). Later, botanists would bestow a Latinate name on the new arrival and link it thereby to ancient European lore, calling it *lycopersicon*. That name's inner tension (*lyco-* means "wolf"; *persicon*, "peach") neatly compresses the mixed promise and danger awaiting Europeans there. Whatever the pre-Columbian Mexicans may have made of the *tamatl* they domesticated from an earlier, wild Andean stock, Euro-Americans perceived an ambiguity in much of the New World nature they encountered. The tomato may serve us as a kind of synecdoche, an instance of the whole, for an exploration of the significance of nature in American expressive culture. It never becomes wholly familiar and comfortable; it promises wealth and health and pleasure; it may yield to exploitation or development; but it may strike back in unanticipated ways the moment we drop our guard.

The Old World foiled farmers too, of course, when they attempted to manage nature or exploit it, but the recipe knowledge and superstitions Americans have attached to poison-ivy and to rattlesnakes and to peppers and tomatoes suggest that nature here had an impish edge at least and a lethally sinister one at worst.[5] People died from bites they took of it (e.g., of Death-Camas) or it took of them (rattlesnakes). Cautionary lore warns one not to get complacent or the tables may turn. To coax luscious tomatoes up out of the cold earth, then, acquires for the grower a kind of extra aura of mastery and wisdom. Congruently, to develop new tomato cultivars that take mechanical handling and to build machines that can harvest them earns the scientists and engineers who do it considerable fame, and earns those who make a new agribusiness out of capitalizing on such innovation millions, as a recent piece in the *Sacramento Bee* reports that Jack Anderson of Davis, one of the earliest to make use of this University of California at Davis achievement, did.

Just as one can enter on a study of the webs of value and meaning at the core of American culture through the study of dense novels like *Moby-Dick* or of eloquent constructions such as the Empire State Building and Brooklyn Bridge, so may one begin with the more matter-of-fact furnishings of our woods and gardens and of the epithets and recipes of everyday life in our search for the patterns of belief and affect by which we make sense of life here. Just as study of the military-industrial complex yields telling insights into the dynamics of American society and government, an explication of the canning-agribusiness-university complex admits us to regions of culture where the utilitarian, the symbolic, and the affective converge.

## The Tomato as a Nightshade

Botanically the tomato belongs among the Nightshade family *(Solanaceae)*. Those paradoxical plants have fascinated natural historians, horticulturists, pharmacognicists, agriculturists, and taxonomists since the earliest times. The family resemblance of petunias, tobacco, eggplant, datura, henbane, and belladonna to tomatoes and potatoes and peppers was evident to attentive lay naturalists long before the connection had been diagrammed systematically. Linnaeus named the tomato *Solanum lycopersicon*. As Charles B. Heiser explains, "Some of the pre-Linnaean 'botanists' attempted to associate all plants with earlier classical writings and the tomato was thus identified with Galen's *Lycopersicon* although the American tomato, of course, was unknown to Galen, who lived in Pergamum in the second Century before Christ."[6] The interesting thing here for students of symbolic culture is that moderns like Linnaeus espied in the tomato an ambiguous compound of wild (*lyco*, "wolf") and sweet (*persicon*, "pear") congruent to Galen's herb.

Later botanists split the tomato off from *Solanum* and put it into its own genus, *Lycopersicum*, retaining thereby the Galenic-Linnaean denomination.

All our domestic cultivars but one derive from *Lycopersicum esculentum*, though wild *cerasiforme* and *pimpinellifolium* varieties and species are "grown to a limited extent,"[7] and some wild species from Peru and the Galapagos have been utilized to create domestic cultivars tolerant of salt *(L. cheesmanii)*, of drought *(L. pennellii)*, and of tropical humidity. This sort of naming matters; it not only locates the species but relates them to other more or less similar ones.

To call tomatoes *Solanum lycopersicon*, as Linnaeus did, affiliates them with a cluster of other plants, including the benign potato *(S. tuberosum)*, the edible Black Nightshade, or Wonderberry *(S. nigrum)*, the beautiful Jerusalem Cherry *(S. pseudo-capsicum)*, and the decorative Bittersweet *(S. dulcamara)*. Linnaeus described only species and genera, but did not place genera in families as bota- nists do today. Casting *Lycopersicum* and *Solanum* species as members of a larger family, *Solanaceae*, adds kin, as it were, to the family tree. It becomes akin to tobacco *(Nicotiana)*, Mandrake *(Mandragora)*, Belladonna *(Atropa)*, Jimsonweed *(Datura)*, hot peppers *(Capsicum)*, and Black Henbane *(Hyoscyamus)*. No won- der knowledgeable Europeans approached tomatoes and potatoes with suspicion at first—they saw what later taxonomy ratified; namely, that these imports bore striking likenesses in their flower shape and foliage coloration to herbs they knew well and knew were often toxic or narcotic.

While all this naming spun out patterns of kinship to both benign and dan- gerous plants from the New World and Old, the naming also "tamed" them in the sense that anything named belonged now to a world of words and to a sys- tem of (verbal) meaning making that allows us at least to speak of them famil- iarly. The perfect rage for Linnaean classification in the New World during the eighteenth century may be seen, in part at least, as a kind of taming of the world beyond Europe by European words—the entire plant (and animal) kingdom lay ready to be given binomial epithets in a Latin-based language, and by standard- ized procedures (counting sexual parts, etc.) Some names encoded the economic or gustatory virtues of the plants described (hence *L. esculentum*, "edible"); oth- ers honored botanists (hence *Gardenia*, for Dr. Garden of Charlestown) or other figures of honor *(Sequoia*, for example). Plants known for their apothecary uses were often given *officialis* as a specific epithet. But sometimes the names encap- sulated a sort of drama, a kind of internal tension, as in the *pseudo-capsicum* above, or as in the almost oxymoronic vibrancy of *lycopersicon*, "wolf + peach." Here the nomenclature recognizes and preserves the symbolic ambiguity the populace also sensed in the plant.

Symbolic anthropologists often note that cultures commonly divide up the world categorically (earth, air, and water; animal, vegetable, and mineral; wild- life and livestock; front and back, etc.). And then they are left with certain items that cannot be catalogued that way, or that shift their qualities. Such anoma- lies must be dealt with, explained, or explained away—they must be called "exceptions that prove the rule," at the very least. These anomalies may be dangerous exceptions or exciting ones or both at once, but objects, creatures, or plants that partake of categorically antagonistic natures are frequently treated as dangerous or powerful and needing to be explained or tamed or fixed. The mermaid or the unicorn incarnate that sort of intriguing monstrosity. And just as the rattlesnake fascinates by its union of lethal venom on one end and apparently beneficent warning "bell" on the other, or as the strikingly beautiful "poison-oak" unfairly "bites" or "poisons" the unwary (it is named *Toxicodendron,* "poison" + "plant"), many nightshades, and the tomato in particular, seem to present a kind of mixed heritage. And in this case that categorical ambiguity has been deposited in its scientific name. To appreciate the poetic impact of the wedding of wolf and peach, of wild and domestic, of animal and fruit, of sharp and sweet, perhaps we need only recall the importance to the savants of the eighteenth century of the aphorism borrowed from the ancients, *dulce et utile,* "sweet and useful," or "sweetness and Light" in Jonathan Swift's 1710 satire, *The Battle of the Books,* and in Matthew Arnold's late-nineteenth-century criticism of modern culture.[8]

One might add that such naming is not, of course, in itself science. It does furnish the international community of scientists with a lexicon in terms of which to carry on the discourse that is so vital to that elite, or learned, culture, and which gives shape and meaning to their many experiments and field studies. Further, this naming and description of New World plants in Latin carries a cultural baggage with it and amounts to a form of "universe maintenance"[9] as it absorbs into European consciousness and gardens and larders such exotic stuff. Whatever symbolic dramas or aesthetic tensions appear to be invoked in European and Euro-American consciousness by the tomato descend at least in part from a heritage of values and expectations developed in cultures whose members never met a tomato. Once the tomato is introduced, lay and scientific growers may begin to learn from the tomato and generate novel meanings for it and uses of it.

One might speak in this regard, half-seriously, of the culture of tomatoes, meaning both the technical wisdom clustered around the actual planting and hybridizing and harvesting of the fruit, on the one hand, and the popular fascination, superstition, legends, jokes, art, history, and hobbies that humans have developed as they attended to tomato matters, on the other. Farmers' almanacs, gardening magazines, Saturday supplements to newspapers, seed catalogs, personal advice, and simple talk about tomato matters overflow with intriguing instances of a culture's making sense of the tomato. And in this regard, one of the delights of reading technical works and talking to tomato experts is the discovery of all the nonscientific fun and fascination these fully informed experts also feel about the tomato. Liberty Hyde Bailey's little classic *How Plants Get Their Names* (1933), for example, makes several nightshade species the heart of his engaging compound of botanical history, scientific biography, taxonomical chronicle, and confessional essay on plants and their names and their uses.[10] That this author of *Hortus* and the many-volumed *Standard Cyclopedia of Horticulture* (1914), who could have selected any of the thousands of species people around the world have cultivated, should make the nightshades the occasion of his excursion into this history suggest both that he himself was taken by their ambiguities and little puzzles and that he knew his American readers would be too.

Anyone sufficiently intrigued by the convergence of scientific, historical, and popular understanding and uses of the nightshades will find in Charles Heiser's *Nightshades* an entertaining, accessible, and authoritative essay on the tomato and its relatives. And even within the scientific and technical treatments of tomatoes by Charles Rick, called "Mr. Tomato" on his campus, non-technical history and interesting misunderstandings enliven the accounts otherwise stuffed with detailed cytotaxonomic, genetic, morphological, and historical information.[11] In it Rick allows right at the beginning that the tomato is "a fruit that is almost universally treated as a vegetable and a perennial plant that is almost universally treated as an annual."[12]

Agricultural, scientific, and popular understandings and uses are not entirely congruent. Science seeks a general clarity as well as particular understandings, and it is a system of knowledge generally conceded great authority in American culture, but as Rick's parenthetical admission signifies, there is more meaning and are more uses of plants in American culture than can be digested by science.

## Vegetable or Fruit

The *esculentum* of the scientific name means "good to eat"; *Lycopersicum*, as we have already seen, means "pear," in part, but is this plant that is good to eat a vegetable or fruit? The question makes no sense to the scientist as scientist. Of course it is a fruit, the "fruit of the vine."

And tomatoes are surely vegetables, not animals or minerals. In the culture of the learned laboratory or herbaria, no confusion between vegetable and fruit need exist; in fact they are words of difference logical types, the first denoting the seed-bearing ovary of the flowering plant, and the second distinguishing the one kingdom the organism belongs to instead of the other. And yet to the people who ask scientists over and over again to their despair, "Is the tomato really a fruit?" or say, "I've heard it is really a vegetable." The dilemma feels genuine. And it retains a touch of the uneasiness over an alien plant the first Europeans felt, for though the tomato is a New World native, we in the North acquired it by way of Europe in a kind of reverse "Columbian Exchange."[13]

The taxonomy of the market or table need not—and will not, of course—match. But the gastronomic categories "fruit" and "vegetable" are alive with affect and associations in our everyday experience and so are hard to shake or to bracket off. "Fruit" connotes sweetness as well as succulence and suggests a climactic position in a meal; "vegetable" implies an earlier position, perhaps as a side dish with the entree, or as a first-course salad. And entailed, at least for some eaters, is the matter of whether to salt it or sugar it—either may be done to tomatoes by Americans. But as Rick rightly reports, American eaters class the tomato most commonly as a vegetable.

The matter was settled once, if not once and for all, back in 1893 when an importer of tomatoes challenged the Port of New York's collector of customs' classification of tomatoes as "vegetable in their natural state" and so subject to tariff. The importer argued instead that they fell under the classification of "fruits, green, ripe, or dried" and should be allowed to enter free. Associate Justice Horace Gray, like a good folklorist, credited the "performance," as it were, and "delivered the unanimous opinion of the court" that "botanically speaking, tomatoes are the fruit of a vine, just as are cucumbers, squashes, beans, and peas. But in the common language of the people, whether sellers or consumers of provisions, all these are vegetables which are grown in kitchen gardens, and which, whether eaten cooked or raw, are, like potatoes, carrots, parsnips, turnips, beets, cauliflower, cabbage, celery, and lettuce, usually served at dinner in, with, or after the soup, fish, or meats which constitute the principal part of the repast, and not, like fruits generally, as dessert."[14]

If settling on the tomato's status within a meal were all that remained, Judge Gray's appeal to common practice might be sufficient to lay aside the symbolic ambiguity. And, after all, one family might treat tomatoes one way and another the other way. The evidence that the ambiguity remains unresolved and still within American culture is suggested by the public response to the inclusion of "tomato ice cream" in the Davis Food Co-op's Tomato Festival:

> At our First Annual Tomato Festival in 1982, the confection was mostly greeted with cries of "EEeuuww!" and "Yukk" from the younger Co-op members and a more tactful "Hmm, very interesting!" from the older. Perhaps this had something to do with the Ketchup in the recipe . . . this ingredient has since been omitted, with very much improved results. After all, the tomato *is* a fruit!
>
> Recipe for a gallon:
> 2 quarts half & half
> 1 + 2/3 cups sugar
> small pinch of salt
> 1 teaspoon vanilla
> 8 oz. tomato paste

Dissolve salt and sugar in 2 cups of the half & half. Then add the tomato paste. Stir till there are no lumps, and add the rest of the half & half and the vanilla and freeze.[15]

The ice cream went fast and was one of the chief attractions, but what is clear is that the play around the putative fruit/vegetable dilemma seemed funny to the co-op and proved amusing to the patrons.

Evidently Americans have a stake less in resolving the categorical ambiguity than they have in keeping it alive. The headline for the Old Sacramento Tomato Festival (July 1986) announced "Favorite fruit (or vegetable?) is feted in Tomato Festival."[16] In popular imagination the tomato has become an object of humor, not wariness. Americans have by now come to value it as food and can afford to take its ontological ambiguity as funny and fun. The Co-op Festival featured tomato juggling, contests for the ugliest as well as biggest and smallest and most grotesque tomatoes. The Old Sacramento Festival promised tomato croquet, cherry tomato spitting, green tomato pie-eating contests, a tomato toss (across the Sacramento River), bobbing for tomatoes, a cherry tomato dart board, and a race for waiters carrying ketchup and tomato juice drinks.

Several of these mock events reveal their origin in older pie-eating and apple-bobbing and watermelon-seed-spitting contests, but these also all feature fruits. Tomatoes may be "vegetable" at table, but are taken as "fruit" in these festivals. Perhaps the *mis*taking of tomato vegetables and fruits functions as the kind of reversal common to festive celebrations, as in Mardi Gras, where men dress as women and the reverse, and where blacks go as Indians, and the powerless go as kings and queens for a day. The number of events that feature splitting or spitting or tossing the food about suggest also that the festivals are where one can "play with your food" at last without being brought up for it.

Tomato wine was advertised for the 1986 First Annual Woodland Tomato Festival but failed to materialize. Nevertheless, the mind which thought that up grasped the comical fruitiness of the vegetable, or the inappropriate vegetableness of the fruit. Other dishes featured in the "Gourmato" stalls were "blackened tomatoes" (Cajun) and "red beer" made of beer and tomato juice.

While one must not make too much of these contrived events, which after all constitute a minor genre of public boosterism and have their equivalents in garlic festivals (Gilroy, California), Onion Days (Vacaville), and the like, the two bits of lore dredged up for every journalistic treatment is 1) that people used to think it was poison and it is not, and 2) that its nature (fruit or vegetable) is moot. A third is that tomatoes and bodies and blood go together somehow.

## The Iconic Tomato

Sarah Tomato, the Bay Area woman who "incarnates" tomato-ness by dressing in a poofy red satin outfit with a green collar, appeared at the tomato festivals in Woodland and Old Sacramento, California (1986). She has a "storehouse of tomato lore," we are told by a puff piece for the Old Sacramento affair,[17] and she so identifies with the tomato that she even wore her costume to her own wedding. In appearing *as a tomato* she turned herself into a virtual icon, both standing for the fruit in her red and green outfit, on the one hand, and "looking like it," on the other.

Robert Plant Armstrong explains in *The Powers of Presence* that things, such as costumes, statues, and pictures, may *mean* in two modes: digitally (i.e., arbitrarily) and analogically—a black hat, for example, may connote evil, but there is nothing inevitable about black's evil anymore than about white's purity, as Melville demonstrates at such great length in his chapter on the whiteness of the whale in *Moby-Dick*; an *X* at a railroad crossing, however, displays a kind of analogue of crossing in its signification.[18] When these two semiotic modes of meaning converge, the upshot is an icon, says Armstrong, a sign of especially persuasive power, for it enlists our linguistic heritage of symbolic meanings and culturally arbitrary narratives, while at the same time drawing on a kind of self-evident presence as well.

While Sarah Tomato's incarnation amounts finally to a kind of lighthearted impersonation, one that ultimately undercuts the convention of typing women as tomatoes in America, either entire or in part, her parody points out the iconic intuition underlying even the most demeaning objectivations of "dames" as tomatoes, or as beings whose breasts are metaphorically so rendered. The argument, if one were made, would admit a convention of casting others as animals (stud, goat, bitch, cat, etc.) or their parts as vegetables (cucumbers, bananas, melons, etc.) but add that tomatoes also possess a degree of corporeal, juicy redness that is like that of a human body and that their fullness mimics the plumpness of women's breasts and buttocks. One need not consent to this analogy to credit its persuasive power amongst those who do, and to recognize that the "aptness" of the characterization of women as tomatoes rests on the apparent iconicity of the sign.

Such an aptness has a history. In the twentieth century the "poetry of the people," as slang is sometimes called, had made the identification of the tomato with women explicit. Richard A. Spears, in *Slang and Euphemisms* (1981), lists *tomato* as a term for an attractive girl, and in U.S. underworld argot, as a term for a prostitute. Partridge cites Damon Runyon's *Guys and Dolls* (1930) as his source for *tomato* as "a girl, a young woman."[19] By the 1940s, *tomato* had become slangy, he-man talk in Hollywood gangster and World War II films. By 1968 the "tomatoes" had begun to turn, as an item from Alan Dundes's folklore archives at the University of California at Berkeley reveals; the use of "tomato" as an epithet is recorded in this "Folk Speech" item:

David first heard this expression when in Amador-Valley-High School in Pleasanton, California. It is a four year high school populated mainly with Caucasians and "a few" Mexicans. David started to use the expression a lot while living for the Winter in Squaw Valley, California. It is used, he says in reference to a girl; either between two guys discussing a girl, or from one guy addressing a girl. He also stated that he did not think that a girl appreciated the term, finding it derogatory. He cited the example of saying "Hiya, Tomato" to a Berkeley girl upon his return from Squaw Valley, and was harshly kicked in the shins and was rebuffed with, "Don't you ever call me that again!"[20]

Although "enlightened" about the *use* of the epithet, his consent to the iconicity of the tomato has remained untouched: "David admits he does not know the meaning of the term or its origination, but seems to think that it must refer to a girl's and a tomato's mutual qualities of being plump and squeezable."

Recognition of the corporeality of the tomato abound in children's ketchup-as-blood lore (its use as a substitute for gore in movie scenes is common knowledge) and in folklore in which the juice is called blood: "No matter which way you slice the tomatoe [sic], the blood always comes out."[21] The seeds of the tomato play an interesting part in this—they are commonly avoided, perhaps as if they were body bits not to be chewed: "Do not eat the seeds of a tomato. It may make you sterile," one man warned.[22] Other folklore items report a grosser lore in the humor attributed to GI's in which stewed tomatoes were called "Monkey's afterbirth" in about the same mood as chipped beef on toast was called "shit on a shingle."[23] Both make revolting connections between a disdained dish and bodily productions not fit to eat, but note that "afterbirth" retains an implicit corporeality and female identification in addition.

Popular culture, perhaps especially, revels in the tomato/breast metaphor. One T-shirt for sale at the Woodland Festival featured two large red tomatoes side-by-side and a motto about their having been "HAND SELECTED FOR FIRMNESS"; a busty woman in a T-shirt in the mock *Bumpee Gardening Catalog* flaunts the legend across her chest: "I grew these with BUMPEE seeds," with the capitalized "Bumpee" just at nipple-level.[24] In some of these breast/tomato representations, a kind of second-generation iconicity may be manifest. That is, while tomatoes may be body-like in the sense that they are skins full of "meat" (think of the "Beefsteak" and "Big Boy" varieties) and "blood," real tomatoes are not much like breasts in shape or size. The globular tomatoes of posters and catalogs, however, have been released from three-dimensionality and so are freer to pass for breasts (which in two-dimensional popular and folk graphics of women often appear as circles with dots for nipples). Tomatoes have been set loose as symbols and become available for use regardless of natural size or shape.

There is another quite different sense in which tomatoes realize an iconic eloquence; i.e., as the quintessential embodiment of summer gardening success. In numerous seed catalog covers and gardening magazine illustrations, it is the tomato that most flaunts the promise of home gardening. It is plump, purely red, juicy beyond all reason, and finished, ready to eat right off the vine.

*Fig. 9.2. Hunt's two-tomato, "HAND SELECTED FOR FIRMNESS" T-shirt. Photograph by David Scofield Wilson.*

The flavor and juiciness of the homegrown tomato are legendary, and the two charges most often made against commercial tomatoes is that they lack taste and juice. Professors of Vegetable Crop departments debunk the "superstition" and conduct blind taste tests to prove that their tomatoes taste just as good, but their defense as much as the charge affirm the integrity of the tomato and its status within the hierarchy of home garden produce.

Surely the most outrageous tomato-as-icon product of American culture in recent years appears in the cult film, *The Attack of the Killer Tomatoes*, produced first at the University of California at Davis by several undergraduates and then reshot for theater release in 16mm color in San Diego. In the movie tomatoes become ravening monsters, eating up unsuspecting citizens and generally terrorizing the populace. This ludicrous mock-horror musical extravaganza may realize a kind of revenge on agribusiness, as I will argue later, but on the surface it is a goofy take-off of science fiction films in which the military and scientific establishments prove inept in their thrashing about in response to a monstrous attack. The tomatoes, which grow to huge sizes and smear people to death can be controlled only by the playing of a particular vapid teeny-bopper record, "Puberty Love," crooned in a sappy falsetto: "Puberty, Puberty love,/There's nothing like puberty love./It's so neat,/It's so cool,/Weekends and Holidays,/And after school. . . . /I've fallen into puberty love." If nothing else, this film confirms the sexual tenor of tomatoes, and it suggests that adolescent humans of ripe sexuality pose a monstrous threat to the social order and that the music that shrinks these animate tomatoes back to manageable size is the equivalent of the bathetic music that pacifies teenagers. If that interpretation makes too much of the rather slapdash symbolisms, almost any viewer would have to admit that the tomato has become humanoid in the film. One even wears earmuffs to block out the music.

## The Tomato As a Challenge to Bricoleurs, Bureaucrats, and Big Farmers

The wealth of sensuous images and sexual allusions makes it obvious that one of the things Americans have made of the tomato is a symbol of ourselves as we sense what we could be and may become. But the more matter-of-fact thing Americans have made of it is a big, juicy, red, and meaty garden vegetable or market marvel. Hybridizers have civilized the wild little *tomatl* into a legion of hybrids, several for every taste or use.

The tomato we turn to now is as much the work of *Homo faber* as of God. The people of central Mexico began the work before "the Conquest," developing cultivars not found among the wild plants of the Andes. Tomatoes reached southern Europe within decades and found acceptance there. They were "eaten in Italy with oil, salt and pepper" and named *pomo d'oro* and *mala aurea* ("golden apple") for their golden color, or *poma amoris* for their inferred attributes.[25] A gradual migration up the continent and across the channel and finally across the ocean to the gardens of Monticello and other early-nineteenth-century gardens brought them back to America. Whatever tinkering was done by gardeners during those three and a half centuries made only modest alterations. A century ago there were still only a dozen plus varieties listed in gardening books; e.g., Apple-tomato, Feejee, Fig-tomato, Giant tomato, grape tomato, Round yellow, Large yellow, Large red oval, Cherry tomato, Round Yellow, white, yellow pear-shaped, etc.[26] Shape and color and size seem to have been selected for by early horticulturists.

By the turn of the century, "patent" tomatoes—Henderson's "Crimson Cushion," Ferry's "Optimus," Salzer's "Crimson Robe," and even Salzer's "Ferris Wheel" tomato—swelled the ranks of varieties one might buy. Huge size, "beefsteak meatiness," and ease of planting and tending was the aim of these tinkerers. I suppose Luther Burbank is the best-known American botanical *bricoleur* of this ilk.

Burbank is a story in himself, but his facility with hybrids was also the "dream" of G. C. "Jack" Hanna, a Texas boy who came to UC Davis in 1926 as an undergraduate, intending to work with Burbank. Burbank died that year, making that impossible, but Hanna went on to become "the father of 'the square tomato'" developed in the early 1950s to be "compatible" with a mechanized harvester, also developed at Davis. If Burbank and the early tinkerers tamed the tomato, Hanna squared it.

Carey McWilliams had earlier characterized Central Valley agriculture as a "factory in the field"—the land was flat, lending itself to mechanization—indeed, the tractor had been invented in Stockton, California. The logic of Detroit applied to the sowing and reaping of grain in the Valley produced huge bonanza farms. Where machines could not do the work, human workers, hired ad hoc and moved about from crop to crop, took the place of machines. Down in the asparagus field of the delta, the spears were harvested first by "Chinese, then Japanese, then Hindus, . . . Turks, Filipinos . . . and finally *Mexicans*," according to Hanna. "We bring in others to do our work—we should be doing it ourselves," he believed; as he tells it.[27] The official explanation deposited in oral histories says that the "political" decision to terminate the bracero program put California agriculture in a bind and made a machine substitute for cheap field labor necessary. The success of Hanna (from the Department of Vegetable Crops) and Coby Lorenzen (from the Department of Agricultural Engineering) which resulted in the VF 145 tomato and the Blackwelder/UC harvester is celebrated at UC Davis, and taken by Hanna and others to have been an interdisciplinary first. Lorenzen supposed that "we were the first to bring together two different disciplines on a single project with a single goal."[28]

Others see the achievement in a different light: California Rural Legal Assistance took UC Davis to court on behalf of seventeen farm workers and the California Agrarian Project, a Davis-based public interest group, claiming that the harvester was detrimental to the quality of life in rural communities and so in violation of the Hatch Act; they also argued that it was an instance of a too chummy cooperation between experiment stations and the private sector. The case was recessed for a time; the judge fell ill. We will return to this case later, but I cite it here to show how big business, the university, farmers, farmworkers, canners, engineers, and activists all converge symbolically in American culture as well as actually in the field. At such an abstract level, it is a little difficult to spot the familiar and humble *poma amoris* of lore or that object of loving nurture by suburban, backyard gardeners.

I was attracted to the tomato at first by its teasing quality as a "text," but I came to the tomato-harvester research reluctantly, feeling that I already knew as much as I cared to about single-mindedness and the humorless, practical mechanization of agriculture. Thus biased I was surprised to find a wealth of very human anecdotes, of nutty stories, of slapdash bricolage there. These tinkerers seem to have had fun doing the work they did and gave little thought to the eventual social consequences of mechanization. Instead, they embarked on projects so far-fetched that Hanna, for instance, did not tell his department what he was up to for two years. A picture emerges from around the edges of the oral history of a kind of irrepressible energy and amusement at tinkering with givens to come up with new contraptions and compatible fruits. Melvin P. Zobel, the Yolo County Cooperative Extension representative, tells of watching "the machine go from all sorts of different Rube Goldberg things into the one that they prototyped."[29] And, indeed, the early machines borrowed from the potato picker and other harvesters and sorters—of onions, gladiolus, citrus. The machine cut the plants off, moved them up a conveyor so the dirt clods dropped off and the tomatoes fell from the vines, took the tomatoes along belts beside which "hands" rode, picking out bad and green fruit, clods, twigs, etc., and finally raised them with another belt up and out through the air and on down into big bins. In these they were trucked to the canneries, processed, and canned. There were hundreds of ways for things to go wrong, and they did. Robert Hartzell, a canner, tells of an early field demonstration when Tillie Lewis herself, of "TLF" (Tillie Lewis Foods), came out to see the wonderful machine in action: "the tomatoes should have rolled out, but they didn't. . . . The fruit flies flew up by droves. Instead of tomatoes rolling out, as you would expect—one at a time—they came out as a huge glob—all at one time—about a thousand pounds of tomatoes. It was a horrible-looking mess."[30] Lorenzen tells of another very sloppy match of machine, crop, grower, and canner. They had harvested the first crop and ended up with "just a bunch of cores and about eight inches of juice in the bottom of the bins." This muck they termed "catsup."[31]

"Of course I could never forget the first designs of the machine that was developed by Coby Lorenzen," Charles Rick, the present "Mr. Tomato" of UC Davis, said in an interview: "Some of the contraptions that were first tried out were, to say the least, highly amusing."[32] One time Lorenzen tried out a kind of spinning bin as a centrifugal separator. They would run these things slowly through the field, earnestly attending to business, but at the end of the day, just for the hell of it, run it back at top speed sending "tomatoes all over the place," according to Rick.

I take these hijinks at the end of the day to be a kind of good-humored revenge by these "projectors" (to borrow Jonathan Swift's denomination for such inventors in Book III of *Gulliver's Travels*) on the recalcitrant tomatoes' passive resistance to becoming integrated neatly into the agribusiness machine, from sowing to picking to canning to consumer. As we have seen, the tomato got its own back two decades later with the filming of *The Attack of the Killer Tomatoes*, "a musical-comedy-horror show."[33]

On Hanna's side, the problem was to "build a tomato" that wouldn't turn to catsup before it left the field.[34] The problem was that the canners needed good fleshy fruits, but garden tomatoes had thin skins and broke easily. Hanna went to the pear-shaped San Marzanos, which "handled much better than the round." They aligned themselves on the vibrating belts in such a way that when they fell off they lit on their sides and absorbed the fall better. Cross-breeding took in all sorts of available domestic varieties' shape, color, and size,

*Fig. 9.3. Flyer advertising a showing of the* Return of the Killer Tomatoes. *Photograph by David Scofield Wilson.*

but also took from wild Andean and Galapagos strains such exotic features as "stemlessness" and salt tolerance. He finally ended with a "half-long tomato," which shortly got dubbed "the square tomato"—and the name has stuck, even though new generations of UC and other varieties have superseded that old VF 145.

Genetic tinkering takes time, takes keeping meticulous records, and takes going into the field continually to track what is happening. Hanna tells of going into the field to "tag" fruit at the "breaker stage" by reaching in very carefully and painting the date on fruits with an artist's brush. That way he could monitor the rate of fruits coming into ripeness. The idea was to get fruit that would ripen all at once and "store well on the vine."[35]

But the key question is whether the tomato will burst or not. In his own commonsense replication of evolution's survival-of-the-fittest drama, Hanna took a bushel of fruit and, one by one, dropped each on a bench from about eighteen inches and discarded the ones that splattered and saved for seed the ones that did not. The simplicity of such a sorting links Hanna to such vernacular inventors as Edison and Burbank, backlot bricoleurs of a sort seldom celebrated in the brochures or the catalogues published by the university. Evidence that Hanna's neat, no-nonsense approach touched some mythic chord is the way the story has grown at UC Davis. We hear that "they" went out in the parking lot and threw tomatoes up in the air and saved the ones that didn't burst when they hit the hardtop. Though this legend exaggerates what Hanna did, it is true to the toughness that came finally to characterize the canning tomato; one may drive down the highway at fifty-five miles per hour behind tomato trucks and watch a tomato fall out, drop ten feet to the pavement, and bounce along till it finally rolls onto the shoulder unharmed. Such toughness as that invites exaggeration. Even within the "Veg Crops" Department, the monstrous toughness of the tomatoes provokes humor—and probably a kind of bonding between workers. One professor has a magazine ad for a "ripe" piece of land near Mesa, Arizona, "developed" by Eaton International Corporation, which shows a red ripe tomato in the dirt about to be bulldozed by a huge Caterpillar. Tacked to the posted ad is a handwritten comment: "Stress Physiology gives you the next generation of machine harvestable TOMATO(E)S."

The more I learn about the tone and rhythms of the bricolage these tinkers enacted, the less I can blame them in any reasonable way for "the New Agricultural Systems that Evolved" and the social or environmental dislocations that eventuated. And the less I can imagine how the department of the investigators themselves might effectively have precensored or pre-edited inventiveness of this sort. Bricolage is a mode of creativity that fixes on proximate, practical, commonsense kinds of goals—a limited sort of vision that then liberates a kind of untamed, and often humorous, inventiveness. If Los Angeles had required an Environmental Impact Report from Simon Roddia before he started to build, we never would have had what we now celebrate as the Watts Towers. I do not mean to dismiss the concerns of those distressed by what mechanization seems to have contributed to social dislocation in California—I will take that up later—but I do want to appreciate the mode of inventiveness it seems to me that these first-generation geneticists and engineers and machinists manifested. It is a folk form generally, if not necessarily. And it enacts an aesthetic quite commonly disdained in academic circles and discounted in arts and sciences establishments. It is a kind of homemade art or science, a coping, day-by-day, making-do inventiveness raised (in this case) to a level of mechanical and botanical canniness and wed to the larger mechanization-of-America movement.[36] And it represents, I believe, a kind of inventiveness in danger of being lost just when its alternative pertinence is becoming urgent for facilitating low-tech farming and housing, heating, and transportation.

Regularizing and institutionalizing the methodical development of ever-improved machinery and cultivars calls upon a different mode of creativity, a kind of second-generation talent. Whereas Hanna and Lorenzen saw each other daily, talked about problems, got to where they could anticipate each other's thoughts, as in many face-to-face, high-context situations, once the tomato system takes off, it gets too big for intuitive quality perception and homemade tests. Hanna says about tomato color: "We used to have color sampling—a completely human decision. Color is now scored objectively by an Agtron."[37]

In the California Administrative Code Pertaining to Canning Tomatoes, the Agtron E5-M reading must read 39 or under for tomatoes to pass inspection. Or for tomatoes grown south and east of San Gorgonio Pass, 40 and under. In this sort of scoring, a sample of tomatoes is extracted from a load, liquified in a Waring Blender, and poured onto a pan, where its color is metered. No more "human decisions"—except, of course, the decision to abide by the Agtron E5-M.

In the first generation of harvesters, unripe tomatoes were spotted by people riding the rigs who picked them out and threw them off. The newer harvesters, such as those featured at country fairs and at the Woodland Tomato Festival, now "read" tomato color photoelectrically as the tomatoes come up the belt and punch unripe ones back into the field with a rank of little hydraulic plungers. Whereas a dozen workers rode the old harvesters in the past, now that electric eyes make most of the judgments, a half-dozen, or fewer, may "man" the machine.

The eight-page "Extracts" from the "Code" detail numerous definitions and standards, all "objective," as bureaucratic ones tend to be, so as to speak clearly to the least-inspired reader about what is acceptable and not.[38] The code defines color, worm damage, mold, and the percentages of each allowed in a load before it becomes non-tomato. Percentages make digital cuts. Over 2 percent of worm damage and the load is rejected as a whole. An excess of 8 percent mold tosses out another load. The code also develops a whole special glossary of terms, as well as taxonomy of pollution: "M.O.T." stands for "Material Other Than Tomatoes."[39]

Notwithstanding the provisions of Section 1332, each canning tomato processor may receive and process a maximum of twenty loads, not more that twenty-seven tons per load, of canning tomatoes that "exceed the comminuted raw color tolerance" to be used to manufacture "tomato products containing other ingredients, such as spaghetti with meat sauce, chili with beans, ravioli."[40] Any rancher wanting such a dispensation must notify the state in writing more than seventy-two hours prior to delivery. There is no evidence of humor in these regulations; no evidence of surprise in the world they describe. Uniformity of material and quality control overall is what is sought. Some tomato varieties go into sauce, as a rule, others into purée, but beyond that the identity of the tomato gets overridden. And, indeed, one of the things that happens is that tomatoes get made into sauce and put into twenty-gallon drums, or even into huge semi-trailer-size flexible tubes called "shoaly bags" and shipped east for "re-manufacture."[41] The code mediates the commerce between grower and cannery, establishing a language that gets embedded in inspection procedures and written into the countless contracts between growers and buyers, year after year. If the original mechanization was responsive at some minimal level to the nature of tomatoes, this commerce swamps entirely the natural tomato and translates everything (including 2 percent of worm damage and 3 percent M.O.T.) into an undifferentiated commodity.

Meanwhile, back in the field, farmers like Hiro Nishikawa teeter along a track between industry-set deadlines and quotas, on the one hand, and natural conditions, on the other. There may be an optimum time to harvest a crop, but with acres and acres to go, one must start before the crop is quite ready in one field and go beyond prime time in the last in order to average out the difference and do the best, for instance, against the weather, which threatens to come in early and turn the field to goo, or, for another example, against breakdowns of expensive machinery.[42]

And there are people pests to deal with, too; some see acres of tomatoes and suppose that nobody will miss a few. David Nishikawa says that does not bother him—though it does some. What he does hate is the people who drive out onto the tomato fields behind the local XXX-rated Drive-In Theater to watch films free and leave broken beer bottles behind. There is a nice if accidental symmetry about this squatting in fields of commodified "love apples" to watch actors make mass-mediated "love" on the silver screen.

But for all this Yolo County color, Nishikawa keeps his eye more on the tomatoes grown in Israel and Spain and feels the force of their competition, and the related cost of union labor at home (his is the only unionized field in Yolo County). Tomatoes are money; in a good year, lots of money. But David Nishikawa also claims that the vine-ripened "square tomatoes" taste better than those grown for produce and sold in the stores, which often have been picked green by machine and then colored up by exposure to ethylene gas. He carries his salt shaker with him in the field and eats tomatoes he picks, he says.

I had an image of The Big Farmer when I started that got, not discarded, but enlarged by my contact with the Nishikawas. The elder Nishikawa is a Nisei whose undergraduate life at UC Davis was interrupted by World War II and his interment, after which he came back and made a new start. Now his son, a math major from UC Davis, helps run the operation. Their lives have been molded by the machinery and hybrids and by the "New Agricultural System," just as have the lives of farmworkers and the livelihood of canners.

What of the suit against the university and the role the university ought to take in 1) overseeing what its faculty makes up, or in 2) addressing the environmental and social impact of research? In September of 1989 the California State Supreme Court upheld an earlier May 1989 Appellate Court decision in the university's favor on the grounds that to do otherwise would interfere with academic freedom. The Appellate Court had overturned an earlier 1987 finding that the university should be required to show that Hatch Act money was being used to benefit small and family farmers. In winning the suit the university sidestepped the social-impact issues. Tomatoes will continue to turn to purée and farmers into factory hands or managers as before.

It may be that that is the way the world is, that ad hoc evolution and make-shift melioration is the best we can hope for. But it is not the best we can imagine. Perhaps it is because I have been reading Gregory Bateson again and Thoreau, that I sense a niftier question behind all this muddle than anyone has asked yet.[43]

I would like to propose both that the asking of Batesonian questions is precisely 1) the sort of thing "a serious university should concern itself with," as he once said in a different context,[44] and 2) the sort of thing people in interdisciplinary studies may by training and practice be best-equipped to do. Bateson's most imaginative contributions to cetology, psychology, anthropology, psychiatry, epistemology, and aesthetics derive from his persistent asking of tough questions across disciplinary lines. Such questions puzzled and irked his fellow regents of the University of California. Countless students and colleagues, however, report being jolted into new levels of perception and interpretation by his questioning and assertions.

Bateson asked psychiatric residents back in the 1950s to think about sacrament and entropy, and how they were related. That is the level of connecting thought that the world needs if it is to address some of these tangled research and impact questions, and a quality of questioning for which the courts and regents and working scientists and technicians are ill-prepared to imagine or attempt. It violates the very categories that seem to give meaning to this department or to that discipline. While I have not found what feels like a deeply centered Batesonian question yet, I would ask, for starters—and do ask my students—to ponder the relationship between research and respect. Need research disdain nature? Need respect for plants or people as they are and have evolved amount to leaving them entirely alone? Bateson's work with the Balinese, with porpoises, with alcoholics and schizophrenics leads me to believe that a new epistemology such as he sniffed out ahead of himself as he explored these human systems merits a more serious (and playful) pursuit of new ways of thinking and feeling than those the academy usually takes to be worthy of attention.

More to the point perhaps, I would ask, as I know Bateson would, what is the difference between "impact" and "information" as an element in epistemology? "Impact" as an idea lies at the center of the case against UC Davis, and at the heart of the Environmental Impact Report legislation and bureaucracy. Impacts imply a kind of physics of victims in which agents force reactions. Information—or in Bateson's terms, "news of a difference"[45]—moves subjects in a quite different way, requiring them to perceive and to care about some subtlety available to their minds and senses. To bring this down to cases, I would ask, what is the difference between 1) tomatoes toughened to stand a machine, and 2) a machine made gentler so as to respect the tomatoes it meets? Or machines and institutions sensitized so that they could tell the difference and know how to care about the people they encounter?

The question is some form of "how do we care about the tomato?" Or if that sounds too precious, "how do we care about and care for the world, even as we work it, depend upon it, need to eat it and walk over it?" The cybernetics of respect and caring would seem to be quite different from the physics of mechanization and impacts, different in a way that makes a difference—a matter a "serious university should concern itself with."

What began as *tomatl* and became "love apple" and garden icon and then the focus of agribusiness inventiveness and popular culture extravagance may also be received as an occasion for epistemological and ethical alternation. Information does not ride on the might of messages or size of symbols but on the sense made of them by those in a position to perceive and to care. Subtle distinctions count in cybernetic systems, where even the absence of a sign may be a difference that means something to the whole. Just as some plant species mark subtle biochemical deficiencies in a natural setting and canaries are used to witness the quality of air in a coal mine, other organisms, like the tomato, may test our perspicacity and our eco-cultural imagination. Inasmuch as tomatoes own an iconic power, what we as a civilization make of tomatoes, we make of ourselves.

## Notes

1. John McDowell, "Growin' in the Wind," *National Gardening* (Oct. 1986): 5.
2. Virgil "VIP" Partch, *Crazy Cartoons* (Greenwich, Conn.: Fawcett, 1956).

3. Folklore Archives, Kroeber Hall, Univ. of California, Berkeley.

4. "The Gift Outright" (1942), *American Poetry*, ed. G. W. Allen, W. B. Rideout, and J. K. Robinson (New York: Harper and Row, 1965), 684–85.

5. On the ambiguity of rattlesnakes, their danger and "warning" rattle, see my "Rattlesnake," in *American Wildlife in Symbol and Story*, ed. Angus Kress Gillespie and Jay Mechling (Knoxville: Univ. of Tennessee Press, 1987); similarly, poison-ivy, so called, invokes beneficent nature with "ivy" and yokes it to poison; it has been called the "plant that bites."

6. Charles B. Heiser, *Nightshades: The Paradoxical Plants* (San Francisco: W. H. Freeman and Company, 1969), 54.

7. Charles Rick, "Tomato," in *Evolution of Plant Crops*, ed. N. W. Simmonds (New York: Longman, 1976), 269.

8. See *The Battle of the Books*, in *Gulliver's Travels and Other Writings*, ed. Louis A. Landa (Boston: Houghton Mifflin, 1960); Matthew Arnold, *Culture and Anarchy* (New Haven, Conn.: Yale Univ. Press, 1994).

9. Peter Berger and Thomas Luckmann, *The Social Construction of Reality* (Garden City, N.J.: Doubleday Anchor, 1968), 116–28.

10. Liberty Hyde Bailey, *How Plants Get Their Names* (1933; reprint, New York: Dover, 1963).

11. See his Charles Rick's lead essay in *Scientific American* 239 (2) (Aug. 1978): 76–87.

12. Ibid., 76.

13. For an informative work on the trade, see Alfred W. Crosby Jr., *The Columbian Exchange, Biological and Cultural Consequences of 1492* (Westport, Conn.: Greenwood Press, 1972).

14. Rick, *Scientific American*, 77.

15. *Co-op News* (July–Aug. 1984): 8.

16. *Sacramento Bee*, July 26, 1986.

17. *Sacramento Bee*, Aug. 9, 1986.

18. Robert Plant Armstrong, *The Powers of Presence, Consciousness, Myth, and Affecting Presence* (Philadelphia: Univ. of Pennsylvania Press, 1981), 28.

19. Damon Runyon, *A Dictionary of the Underworld* (London: Routledge and Kegan Paul, 1961).

20. Folklore Archives, Kroeber Hall, Univ. of California, Berkeley.

21. Archives, American Studies, Univ. of California at Davis; collected in 1983 and claimed to be translated from the Italian.

22. Archives, American Studies, Univ. of California at Davis.

23. Ibid.

24. *Bumpee Gardening Catalog* (Signet, 1983), 46.

25. Rick, *Scientific American*, 76.

26. Fearing Burr Jr., *The Field and Garden Vegetables of America* (Boston: Crosby and Nichols, 1893).

27. Interview with G. C. Hanna, Apr. 20, 1984, by the author.
28. A. I. Dickman, "Interviews with Persons Involved in the Development of the Mechanical Tomato Harvester, The Compatible Processing Tomato and the New Agricultural Systems that Evolved," 1978; Oral History, Shields Library, UC–Davis; Lorenzen's ignorance of a tradition of inter-disciplinary studies in the academy speaks eloquently of the chasm between research in the agricultural sciences and scholarship in the humanities and social sciences. But it also speaks well of the self-generated daring and imagination of Lorenzen and Hanna.
29. Ibid.
30. Ibid.
31. Ibid.
32. Interview with Charles Rick, 1983, by the author.
33. The characterization of the film on a promotional poster.
34. Lorenzen, in Dickman, "Interviews with Persons."
35. Interview by the author, Apr. 20, 1984.
36. For an extended and data-jammed thesis on such mechanization, see Sigfried Giedion, *Mechanization Takes Command: A Contribution to Anonymous History* (New York: Oxford Univ. Press, 1948).
37. Interview by author, Apr. 20, 1984.
38. "Extracts from California Administrative Code Pertaining to Canning Tomatoes," 1983.
39. Ibid., Section 1332.4, p. 2.
40. Ibid.
41. Interview with Hiro Nishikawa by author, Yolo County, California, 1983.
42. Ibid.
43. Gregory Bateson, *Mind and Nature: A Necessary Unity* (New York: Dutton, 1979).
44. I.e., his letter to University of California co-Regent Vilma Martinez, June 24, 1979, in regard to the university's management of the Lawrence Livermore Nuclear Laboratories, which does nuclear arms research.
45. Bateson, *Mind and Nature*, 68.

# Patricia A. Turner

In mid-August 1990, on an extraordinarily humid afternoon, I sat with my then eighty-five-year-old father on the porch of his somewhat dilapidated eastern Long Island horseback-riding stables. My three-year-old son, Daniel, was with us, as was a long-time friend of the family in her late sixties, Betty, and a fourteen-year-old "employee," Annie, who saddled horses, conducted trail rides, mucked out stalls, and performed any equestrian-related task that could be bartered for free time horseback riding. Our ethnic backgrounds are significant. My dad and I were African American, my son's father was of European descent, our friend Betty was a World War II French war bride, and Annie's father was Middle Eastern, and her mother was a first-generation immigrant of German and French ancestry.

Muttering something semi-profane about getting his chainsaw back from Moses, my dad drove off in his pickup. A week earlier, Hurricane Bob had uprooted trees throughout our area, and Moses, an eighty-plus-year-old "homeboy" of my dad's, had come to borrow his chainsaw for his cleanup efforts. Apparently since they were children, Moses had had a tendency to procrastinate about returning borrowed items. When Dad returned, he took not only the chainsaw but also a large green watermelon out of the back of his pickup truck. He dropped the watermelon into my lap and asked me to cut some slices. Moses's watermelon was juicy, cool, and wonderful. Five formerly cranky people were suddenly in a good mood. I can't remember what we talked about, but it was one of those special afternoons where every joke worked, where all of the spaces between us—age, gender, class, ethnic background were meaningless—the fresh watermelon from Moses's garden collapsed our differences—that afternoon.

The residue of that afternoon remained with me in other ways as well. For the next week, the bulk of Moses's watermelon dominated my father's small refrigerator. It seemed like whatever I needed was behind that watermelon. When I needed syrup for my son's pancakes, it was behind the watermelon; a medicine Dad took was behind the watermelon. To make matters worse, none of us wanted to eat any more watermelon. No moment was as perfect as the one that sultry afternoon. Neither Dad, Betty, Dan, Annie, nor any of the other Old Hickory Farm regulars wanted any watermelon, and after what seemed an interminable period of time, Dad gave me permission to feed the watermelon to the pigs.

Before tossing it into the pen I went to my in-laws' house to check their collection of over one hundred cookbooks to see if I could unearth anything creative that could be made with watermelon. I discovered that the world's most inventive culinary minds have not devised much in the way of watermelon recipes. You can pickle watermelon rind; incorporate it into fruit salad or fruit cup; you can inject it with vodka; you can eat it plain; you can salt it; but, beyond these options, watermelon does not lend itself to culinary experimentation.

Which, perhaps, makes all the more curious the symbolic ramifications of watermelon discernible in mass culture and folklore. It seems as though the lack of real culinary versatility in watermelon is compensated for by the infinite artistic and literary possibilities inspired by the fruit. In American popular culture, watermelon as a food and as a symbol is encoded in a wide range of ways, largely depending upon whether or not its image is being shaped to reinforce a seasonal (summer versus winter), regional (particularly North versus South), temporal (particularly nostalgic versus futuristic), or ethnic (particularly here white as opposed to African American) message. There is some overlap, and sometimes aspects of "watermelon-ness" transcend these categories. An exploration of watermelon iconography, folklore, and foodways sheds light on our understanding of the social construction of regional and racial identities.

I relied on a wide and somewhat unorthodox array of sources for this chapter. In addition to looking for the standard literary and historical references to watermelons, I also perused countless home and decorating magazines and books. I examined watermelon artifacts as they were displayed in department, craft, and antique stores. For two years, I watched as people ate watermelon and questioned them about their watermelon-consumption habits.

Watermelon *(Colocynthis citrullus* or *C. lanatus* formerly known as *Citrillus vulgaris)* is a member of the gourd family native to central Africa.

As a name for it exists in Sanskrit, it was probably introduced into India in early prehistoric times.[1] For several centuries, watermelon has been available throughout most of the world.

Nonetheless, watermelon's popularity is the highest in the United States. Cultivation of the annual plant was attempted in Massachusetts in 1629, and the fruit was apparently grown in present-day Florida by indigenous peoples before 1664. Successful watermelon crops require a long, warm growing season. Because it can be easily shipped from warmer parts of the country, watermelon can be purchased at modest prices throughout the United States in spring and summer.

## Regional Vines

Although advances in agricultural techniques have resulted in watermelon cultivation throughout the United States, the South retains a strong investment in watermelon production and dissemination. And just as southern watermelon farmers maintain a tenacious hold on the United States' watermelon market, Dixie is also the region more symbolically entrenched in the watermelon. Mark Twain's nineteenth-century novel *Pudd'nhead Wilson* contains a lengthy ode to the watermelon: "The true southern watermelon is a boon apart, and not to be mentioned with commoner things. It is chief of this world's luxuries, king by the grace of God over all the fruits of the earth. When one has tasted it he knows what the angels eat. It was not a southern watermelon that Eve took; we know it because she repented."[2] By drawing an analogy between the watermelon and the apple, Twain is acknowledging the strong symbolic components of both fruits.

The association of watermelon with the South and with "the good old days" continues to be strong. Watermelon pictures are common on southern postcards and calendars. Many southern communities—Luling, Texas; Hampton County, South Carolina; Chiefland, Chipland, Lakeland, and Monticello, Florida; Grand Bay, Alabama; Raleigh, North Carolina; Mize and Water Valley, Mississippi—boast annual watermelon festivals, watermelon seed-spitting contests, and watermelon-eating contests. The National Watermelon Association's annual convention is held in Moreven, Georgia.[3] Hope, Arkansas, birthplace of William Jefferson Clinton, the fortieth president of the United States, considers itself to be the nation's watermelon capital.

Ninety years after Mark Twain's salute to watermelon in *Pudd'nhead Wilson*, Arkansas novelist Bill Terry titled his book on the exploits of a young southern white man *The Watermelon Kid*. The novel's hero, A. J. Poole, earns this nickname as a result of his praiseworthy performance in an annual watermelon-eating contest. Poole doesn't really win the contest; it ends in a tie with the former year's winner. However, members of the contest audience, disappointed by the lack of an undisputed winner, make bets on which of the two victors will have to go to the bathroom first. Poole manages to outlast his opponent. The crowd is so impressed by the power of his bladder that they hang the watermelon kid title on him. Throughout most of the novel, the popular Poole is depicted as a young good-old-boy with a heart of gold. Set mostly in the 1950s, the novel offers only a cursory view of race relations, and it is told from a white point of view. The word "nigger" is used freely, and the narrator makes comments such as "The next morning A. J. checked in with Alvin Bates at the restaurant and told him to look after things for a couple of days. Alvin was the cook. He was black but smart."[4] In spite of a few scrapes with the law and some financial woes, the watermelon kid leads a fairly charmed existence. The author clearly expects his readers to link watermelon with an unencumbered way of life. The watermelon kid has no genuine responsibilities and is free to roam the roads and bars of the South. The last page of the novel tells the reader that Poole and his friends eventually settled down. Poole gets married, effectively ending his reign as the watermelon kid, and the reader is told that most people now call him Mr. Poole. The unabashedly southern novel perpetuates a strong association between watermelon and white regional folk culture.

Although watermelon is commonly thought of as a southern foodstuff, its appeal also extends to the North and to the West. In northern California, the symbol for the Davis Farmer's Market is the watermelon. This is a curious selection for several reasons. Although watermelon is grown in California, it is not grown in any appreciable marketable quantities in Yolo County, home of the farmer's market. According to the Cooperative Extension of the University of California, California annually produces ten thousand to twelve thousand acres of watermelon. The Imperial and Palo Verde Valleys, along with Kern County, are the most significant watermelon-producing regions. Half of the watermelon produced in California is marketed within the state.[5] The other half of California's watermelon crop is marketed in the Pacific Northwest, the mountain states, and western Canada. Some of the early crop is marketed in the Midwest, but, again, according to the Cooperative Extension, California does not compete well with southern watermelon-producing states for most of the U.S. market. Other crops are very much associated with Yolo County, home of the University of California at Davis and its world-class school of agriculture; one would think that in a community full of crop experts, the farmer's market organizers would have opted for a more regionally correct symbol. For Davis residents, like so many other Americans, the attraction of watermelon is apparently stronger than a desire for agricultural accuracy.

## Seasonal Celebrations

In Davis and throughout the United States, serving and eating watermelon often occurs in conjunction with spring and summer recreational activities and, in particular, with the three prominent long holiday weekends (Memorial Day, the Fourth of July, and Labor Day) that bridge spring to fall. There are several plausible reasons for its popularity during these warm-weather holidays. For one thing, watermelon constitutes a healthy choice. Even before Americans became concerned with cholesterol counts and fat contents, consumers knew that watermelon represented a fresh, sweet food substance lacking any nasty nutritional taboos. Convenience, however, is the most frequently offered reason for the omnipresence of watermelon at summer gatherings. After all, watermelons are big and relatively inexpensive. A host or hostess can feed large numbers of guests with one watermelon. Indeed, watermelon's low price/high yield resulted in its being nicknamed "depression ham." Because the fruit does not lend itself to culinary extravagance, it is simple to serve. A sharp knife is all one needs to tackle a watermelon. Nutritious, inexpensive, and easy-to-serve, watermelon is then truly ideal fare for summer holiday menus.

These attributes are reinforced in the print media and seasonal goods that merchants use to signal the coming of summer. Like full-color pictures of white wicker rocking chairs, geraniums and azaleas in window boxes, and jubilant children playing in the spray of a water hydrant or on the shore of a sandy beach, a photo of a cut watermelon communicates to consumers that it is time to purchase the accouterments of summer. Magazine covers and newspaper food pages designed for summer months frequently feature numerous pictures of watermelons.

Merchandisers of products associated with spring and summer have also utilized the power this image has on the public imagination. One can obtain beach umbrellas, windsocks, and directors' chairs inscribed with watermelon patterns. Outdoor paper plates, napkins, cups, tablecloths, and similar disposable items are available for purchase. Bathing suits and summer frocks for little girls also are rendered with the image of watermelons. Hats, socks, and even shoes have been made with watermelon likenesses imposed upon them. In these and a myriad of other ways, watermelon images are used to sell summer and the carefree good life supposedly intrinsic to it.

Watermelon artifacts do not disappear entirely from the pages of magazines and store shelves during the colder months. Indeed, watermelons are particularly plentiful during December, when they are commonly figured as Christmas tree ornaments. Throughout the year, however, watermelons, like geese, ducks, fluffy kittens, blue spongeware pitchers, and quilts, are often used to accessorize rooms and spaces intended to evoke warm, nostalgic sentiments. Mark Twain's reference to the forbidden fruit is once again relevant. Second only to the apple (often with the shape of one bite removed), watermelon is the favored food of decorators who specialize in country style. Apple and watermelon icons are often used to convey a sense of homeyness to domestic spaces.

Wooden, fabric, plastic, paper, and ceramic watermelon artifacts belong to the staple of icons often categorized as "Americana." As noted above, watermelon is often deemed an essential foodstuff for celebrations of Memorial Day,

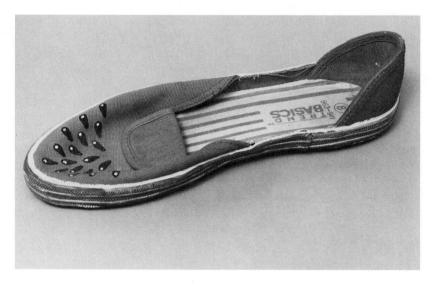

*Fig. 10.1. Red watermelon slipper with black seeds, c. 1990. From the collection of Patricia Turner.*

the Fourth of July, and Labor Day. These inherently American holidays are also noteworthy for the omnipresence of assorted configurations of the stars and the stripes during the parades and celebrations that accompany them. During the course of my conversations with informants about their water-melon-eating habits, several indicated that they felt compelled to purchase the fruit for their summer holiday meals even though much of it was left over. For many, watermelon and the summer holiday meals are as connected as cranberry sauce and Thanksgiving. One white female informant recalled her father's stalwart posture as he sliced and served the traditional Fourth of July watermelon as comparable to the one he assumed over the family's Thanksgiving turkey.

## Ethnic Seeds

Like most other products with a pronounced "southern" association, the meaning attributed to watermelon assumes different dimensions depending upon whether it is featured with whites or blacks. African American actress Butterfly McQueen, best known for her portrayal of the high-strung, inept slave Prissy in *Gone With the Wind* (1939), recalled several arguments she had with the producers of the film over derogatory characteristics and actions expected of her character. Although she reluctantly acquiesced to their demands for high-pitched screams, she was always proud that she steadfastly refused to eat watermelon on camera. McQueen's adamant refusal no doubt stemmed from a long-standing stereotype associating watermelon eating with unkempt and slovenly African Americans.

The image that prompted McQueen's firm stand dates back at least to the minstrel productions of early-nineteenth-century America. In these popular stage shows, white actors artificially darkened their faces and dressed up as slaves. Northern audiences embraced the precursor to slap-stick comedy and the somewhat exotic rhythmic music contained in these shows. Of course, the grim and sordid realities of actual southern slave life were not addressed in the lively minstrel shows. Instead, a highly romanticized picture of benevolent, patriarchal masters struggling to control the mirth and music of their childlike, lazy, self-indulgent, uncivilized charges emerged on urban and rural stages throughout America and in Europe. The uncivilized component of the picture was conveyed in a number of ways, including showing the slaves eating with their hands, thereby suggesting that they resembled animals more than human beings.

Before long, this coupling of blacks and watermelons extended to the artifacts of mass-produced American popular culture. On picture postcards, statuettes, sheet music, advertising icons, kitchenwares, and similar mass-produced American material objects, the smiling face of a benevolent-looking black man, woman, or child is frequently rendered in close proximity with a whole or cut watermelon. Elsewhere, I have argued that such objects belong to a category of memorabilia that can best be described as contemptible collectibles.[6] Like the minstrel shows that spawned them, the charm of contemptible collectibles resides in the depiction of carefree, happy-go-lucky blacks indulging in whatever craving they have. Like fried chicken and corn on the cob, watermelon belongs to that class of foodstuffs that suggests that blacks, eating with their hands, are less civilized than whites. Images of the watermelon when juxtaposed with blacks contribute to the all-too-familiar image of a savage/careless people who take a hands-on approach to pleasure.

In the late 1970s and through the 1980s, icons containing images of blacks and watermelons were frequently featured in the pages of home-decorating magazines, frequently those devoted to the increasingly popular country decor. These pictures implied that the modern woman could have the best of the old days along with all of the conveniences designed for modern households. She could have colorful, vintage artifacts along with a convection oven and a waterbed. Stores specializing in these nostalgia artifacts also highlighted such items in their displays. Kitchen shelves contained condiment shakers shaped like a black man holding a watermelon. Dining-room tables were adorned with tablecloths featuring black women handing large slices of watermelon to children. Bed coverings were enhanced by black fabric dolls holding watermelon in their hands.

The wide-open mouth and the fingers wrapped around it identify the black eaters as members of a savage, subhuman/animal-like order. When the

Fig. 10.2. Vintage sheet music depicting a couple seated on a huge watermelon slice, c. 1920. From the collection of Patricia Turner.

watermelon's size is exaggerated, and the watermelon is featured in a group setting, it conveys the mistaken notion that black parents always had enough to feed their families.

Several twentieth-century examples illustrate the tenacity of the watermelon/ black combination. In the film *Cotton Comes to Harlem*, most audiences laugh uproariously when the chase, being waged by African American officers Grave Digger Jones and Coffin Ed, is stopped when their police car smashes into a truckload of watermelons. In an episode of *All in the Family*, bigot Archie Bunker expresses his indignation over neighborhood integration by saying, "Let's see how wonderful they [liberals] think it is when the watermelon rinds start coming through the windows!"

One southern-born African American male informant recalled an incident from his childhood. As his mother selected various fruits and vegetables from a roadside stand, he repeatedly lobbied her to buy a watermelon. She refused, and he continued to plead. Finally, the stand's white proprietor said, "Aw, come on lady, buy little Sambo a watermelon."

For this informant and many other African American ones, public watermelon consumption poses a paradox. On the one hand, most informants say they genuinely like watermelon and enjoy eating it. On the other hand, the derogatory stereotypes linking blacks with watermelon often haunt them. Size here conveys a subtle message about African American foodways. As we know all too well from the documents of slavery as well as studies of African American diet in the late nineteenth and throughout the twentieth century, blacks have very often had limited access to a healthy diet. But the watermelon's largeness, along with the obvious gusto with which the black eater pursues it, suggests that blacks had access to food. One of the differences between the way watermelon is depicted in "white" culture stems from a tendency to place the fruit in an environment, indoor or outdoor, lacking any humans actually touching or eating it.

Many African American informants posited etiquette guidelines for watermelon consumption. Some refused to ever eat watermelon without some sort of utensil. Others said that they would use their hands to eat watermelon out-of-doors, but would insist on a utensil for indoor eating. One southern-born middle-aged female informant stated that she is unable to eat watermelon while in the company of whites. When she is with blacks, she rarely passes on it, but she could not bring herself to eat it with whites present.

## Red, Green, and Black

In *American Country Details,* author and interior decorator Mary Emmerling includes a provocative color photograph in her chapter on beds.[7] A large four-poster bed dominates the small room. An antique coverlet serves as a bed-spread, and a bright Texas Star motif quilt is draped over the lower part of

Fig. 10.3. Black folk doll holding a huge slice of watermelon over her head, recent reproduction, c. 1990. From the collection of Patricia Turner.

the bed. A Native American blanket is tacked to a wall, and the room contains several icons fashioned out of American flags. A mirror encased in wood painted to resemble the thirteen-star flag hangs over the center of the bed. An angel dressed in flag clothing and holding an American flag is also on the wall. A flag-frocked Uncle Sam statue rests on one nightstand. The other contains several black folk dolls dressed in tattered clothes. Situated amidst this display is a large watermelon slice, probably made out of wood.

This photo is reminiscent of the decorating magazines referred to earlier. These magazines went through a particularly strong nostalgia mode in the mid- to late 1980s, and pages such as these were not uncommon. Eventually some of the more astute readers complained about the rather obvious insensitivity of these portrayals, and most of these magazines now only rarely incorporate a mammy cookie jar or a Jolly Nigger savings bank. But watermelons are omnipresent, and I think it could be argued that the association between blacks and watermelon is so strong that the watermelon functions as a symbolic equivalent for black folks in these pictures.

## Symbolism

Given the relative uselessness of watermelon from a culinary perspective, how can we explain the watermelon's symbolic potency? People with whom I spoke at the Davis Farmer's Market always referred to the colors of watermelon as the qualities that contribute the most to its appeal. As the photographs suggest, the color(s) of watermelon lend themselves to a wide range of artistic purposes. The meat of the watermelon is imagined from pale pinks to deep red. The seeds are black or green. The rind is also depicted as white. Talented magazine editors and graphic artists can do a lot with these color combinations. These contrasting colors do evoke spring and summer.

Again, the watermelon's size is also suggestive. Probably the biggest single fruit marketed in the spring and summer, the appearance of the noble big fruits of the produce market counters, along with signs such as "watermelon 29 cents per pound," like the signs pitching the first strawberries or corn of the season, tell the shopper that the days are getting longer and that bathing suit season is upon us, ready or not. Simplicity is often the message inherent in the offerings of spring and summer—because watermelon requires no preparation, it is an appropriate symbol for the warmer seasons.

But watermelon images convey messages about other appetites as well. Poet Katie Donovan's poem, "watermelon man," was inspired by a painting entitled "El Comedor de Sandias" by Rufina Tamayo. The painting features a dark-complected, smiling black man with a broad, toothy smile. A disproportionately large slice of red watermelon with black seeds is situated in front of him. The speaker in the twenty-six-line poem elaborates on sexual fantasies inspired by the painting. "Your curved melonslice grin/is pink as your namesake," she begins, and then confesses, "you curve the ends of my black and white day . . . into a sticky pink smile." She imagines that his "big brown pink nailed hand . . . touches my lonely skin" and admits that "I'm beginning to feel pink/with grins slicing all over me." Finally, "I'm a seed, a fruit, a luscious thing," she declares. The teeth in the black man's smile and the seeds in the watermelon physically arouse the speaker in the poem.[8]

Many aspects of the watermelon do lend the fruit to a psychoanalytic interpretation. Its phallic properties include its shape and the fact that it is smooth and hard on the outside, but soft and moist and seedy on the inside. Watermelons can be cultivated in a variety of shapes, but oblong ones are those most frequently rendered in popular culture. Among other things, this analysis may explain the popularity of the many games and contests that involve eating prodigious quantities of watermelon or projectile seed spitting. Jay Mechling has argued that psychoanalytic analysis is useful for deriving the meaning of the watermelon-eating stage of the game Poison as it is played by Boy Scouts.[9] We have seen in Terry's *The Watermelon Kid* that the winners of these contests are local heroes. Just as young men are often able to gain the adulation of their peers by spreading their semen far and wide, so too are they able to garner envy by spewing the watermelon seeds far and wide. The seeds bear fruit. Female fertility is also evoked by the watermelon. Many female informants who had been pregnant recalled comments and thoughts about the discomfort associated with carrying around a watermelon. The difficulty of the birthing process is often compared to moving a watermelon through a narrow passageway.

The watermelon as a sexually potent symbol also gains credence from the life of President and Mrs. Clinton. Seeking to satisfy the American public's curiosity about the first meeting of the candidate and his wife, Clinton repeated the following story in several interviews. While they were both at Yale, she was aware of a good-looking law student and had caught him eyeing her from afar on several occasions. She kept her distance until one day she overheard him in a corridor boasting, "And not only that, we grow the biggest watermelons in the world there." After hearing that particular brag, Rodham paid more attention to the self-confident young man from Hope, Arkansas, and soon approached him in the library by saying, "If we are going to keep looking at each other, we ought to know each other's names. I'm Hillary Rodham."

If we accept that the widespread popularity of the watermelon in part derives from sexual associations, it is worth revisiting those texts that connect watermelons with African Americans. By considering its phallic attributes in conjunction with its frequent juxtaposition with blacks and the well-known folk belief about African American sexual dexterity and supposed superiority, we can explain the propensity to position blacks and watermelons together. Melvin van Peebles's 1970 movie entitled *Watermelon Man* chronicled the adventures of a white man who inexplicably woke up black one morning. Although his newly developed melanin disgusted his white wife, it increased his attractiveness to a white female co-worker, who, having had no interest in him as a white man, chased him to bed when he appeared as a black one.

In terms of physical weight and mass, watermelons are the largest of the fruits analyzed in this volume and they may exhibit one of the widest ranges of symbolic associations. The fruit's size, color, shape, and consistency coalesce in ways that prompt several patterns. Figured with beachballs, tennis rackets, and the like, the watermelon represents the recreational aspects of summer. Juxtaposed with butter crocks and patchwork quilts, it evokes nostalgia for a romanticized past. The unpleasant dimensions of that era are foregrounded when the watermelon is situated in proximity to blacks, thereby triggering tenacious negative stereotypes. As we have seen, the stars and stripes frequently hover within range of the mighty fruit. Given the American predisposition toward anything and everything big, we may find that the watermelon will emerge as the quintessential symbolic fruit for the nation.

## Notes

1. B. Brouk, *Plants Consumed by Man* (Academic Press: London, 1975), 203.
2. Mark Twain, *Pudd'nhead Wilson* (New York: Penguin Books, 1986), 152.
3. Charles Reagan Wilson, "Watermelon," in *Dictionary of Southern Folk Culture* (Chapel Hill: Univ. of North Carolina Press, 1989), 1142–43.
4. Bill Terry, *The Watermelon Kid* (Baton Rouge: Louisiana State Univ. Press, 1984), 14.
5. "Watermelon Production," leaflet #2672, Cooperative Extension of University of California, Division of Agriculture and Natural Resources, 1.
6. Patricia A. Turner, *Ceramic Uncles and Celluloid Mammies: Black Images and Their Influence on Culture* (New York: Anchor Books, 1994), 11.
7. Mary Emmerling, *American Country Details* (New York: Clarkson Potter, 1994), 38.
8. Katie Donovan, *Watermelon Man* (Newcastle Upon Tyne: Bloodaxe Books, 1993), 32.
9. Jay Mechling, "Sacred and Profane Play in the Boy Scouts of America," in *Play and Culture*, ed. Helen B. Schwartzman (West Point, N.Y.: Leisure Press, 1980), 210.

# Contributors

ANGUS KRESS GILLESPIE is associate professor of American Studies at Rutgers University. With an undergraduate degree in American Studies from Yale University and his graduate degrees in American Civilization from the University of Pennsylvania, Gillespie has done extensive fieldwork in the New Jersey pinelands. With Jay Mechling, he co-edited the 1987 collection of essays on American totem animals, *American Wildlife in Symbol and Story.* He is presently finishing a book on the World Trade Center.

VIRGINIA S. JENKINS has her doctorate in American Studies from The George Washington University and writes and teaches in the Washington, D.C., area, most recently at the University of Maryland at College Park. She is the author of *The Lawn: A History of an American Obsession,* which won the Ray and Pat Browne Award for the best book on popular culture in 1994. She is presently finishing a book on the impact of the importation of bananas on American culture and is exploring media coverage of the Spanish Influenza epidemic in the United States in 1918.

JAY MECHLING is professor of American Studies at the University of California, Davis. With graduate degrees in American Civilization from the University of Pennsylvania, he publishes widely in American Studies, folklore, rhetorical criticism, and popular culture studies. He co-edited *American Wildlife in Symbol and Story* with Angus Gillespie.

THERESA MELÉNDEZ is associate professor of English and director of Chicano/Latino Studies at Michigan State University. She teaches Chicano literature, Mexican folklore, medieval literature, and oral traditions. To the edited volume *American Wildlife in Symbol and Story,* she contributed a chapter on the Coyote.

Boria Sax holds a degree in German and intellectual history from the State University of New York at Buffalo and currently teaches at Mercy College in White Plains, New York. His many books and articles include *The Frog King, The Parliament of Animals,* and *The Serpent and the Swan.* He is founder and president of Nature in Legend and Story (NILAS), an organization devoted to animals and plants in literature and the arts.

C. W. Sullivan III is a professor of English at East Carolina University and a member of the Welsh Academy. He is the author of *Welsh Celtic Myth in Modern Fantasy* (1989) and the editor of *The Mabinogi: A Book of Essays* (1996), several other volumes of essays, and the *Children's Folklore Review.* He is the immediate past president of the International Association for the Fantastic in the Arts, and his articles on mythology, folklore, fantasy, and science fiction have appeared in a variety of anthologies and journals.

Tad Tuleja, who holds a master's degree in American Studies from the University of Sussex and a Ph.D. in anthropology from the University of Texas at Austin, has taught at Baylor University and the University of Massachusetts at Amherst. His extensive writings on folklore and popular culture include a chapter on the turkey for *American Wildlife in Symbol and Story, The New York Public Library Book of Popular Americana* (1994), and an edited anthology of essays on North American traditions entitled *Usable Pasts* (1997).

Patricia A. Turner is professor of African-American and African Studies at the University of California, Davis. She is the author of *I Heard It Through The Grapevine: Rumor in African-American Culture* and *Ceramic Uncles and Celluloid Mammies: Black Images and Their Influence on Culture.*

David Scofield Wilson is a senior lecturer emeritus of American Studies at the University of California, Davis. He earned his graduate degrees in American Studies at the University of Minnesota. The author of *In the Presence of Nature* (1978), Wilson teaches courses on nature and culture in America. He is presently at work with his wife, Sarah Newton, on the literature, graphics, and ideas behind the so-called nature-study movement of the late nineteenth and early twentieth century in America.

# Index

*Rooted in America* was designed and typeset on a Macintosh computer system using PageMaker software. The text is set in Aldus Roman, and the display fonts are Kollman and Brush Script. The book was designed by Todd Duren, composed by Kimberly Scarbrough, and manufactured by Thomson-Shore, Inc. The recycled paper used in this book is designed for an effective life of at least three hundred years.